军事访谈中刻意评价的语用研究

A Pragmatic Study of Deliberate Evaluation in Military Interviews

龚双萍　著

中国出版集团
世界图书出版公司
广州·上海·西安·北京

图书在版编目（CIP）数据

军事访谈中刻意评价的语用研究 / 龚双萍著. — 广州：世界图书出版广东有限公司，2012.8
ISBN 978-7-5100-5052-7

Ⅰ. ①军… Ⅱ. ①龚… Ⅲ. ①军事－新闻采访－语用学－研究 Ⅳ. ① G212.1 ② H1

中国版本图书馆 CIP 数据核字（2012）第 189433 号

军事访谈中刻意评价的语用研究

责任编辑　黄　琼
出版发行　世界图书出版广东有限公司
地　　址　广州市新港西路大江冲 25 号
http:// www.gdst.com.cn
印　　刷　虎彩印艺股份有限公司
规　　格　880mm×1230mm　1/32
印　　张　8.25
字　　数　230 千
版　　次　2013 年 5 月第 2 版　2014年 4 月第 4 次印刷
ISBN　978-7-5100-5052-7/E · 0051
定　　价　31.00 元

序

本书是龚双萍在其博士论文的基础上修改完成的，是她三年多的研究成果。

本书是针对军事新闻访谈中刻意评价现象的语用研究，这有别于日常言语交际和日常话题的语言学研究。回顾国内外的相关文献，专门基于军事方面的题材、交际领域、交际模式等的语言学探究却很少见，主要原因之一是这方面的研究往往涉及敏感话题或非公开话题，语料获取有一定难度，因此相关研究具有很大的挑战性。可以说，龚双萍博士知难而上，选择军事访谈中的刻意评价作为研究对象，这样的精神无疑值得称道。

评价是当今语言学研究中的一个热点课题。自系统功能语言学的著名学者马丁(J. R. Martin)提出评价理论(appraisal theory)以来，该理论引起了我国外语界学者及读者的很大兴趣，其运用性研究取得了丰硕成果。除系统功能语言学以外，社会语言学、语料库语言学、心理语言学、语义学、语用学等领域对评价体系、评价言语行为及其影响因素等都有一定研究或涉及评价理论的具体运用，但这些研究多以书面语篇中的评价语言作为探究对象，较少涉及动态会话语境中的评价体系、评价言语行为等现象。仔细观察会话中的各类评价及其语境制约，我们会发现评价现象涉及说话人的立场、观点、态度、情感、价值体系等，并与其自我身份及参与者的他人身份、地位等语境因素密切相关，从语言选择的角度看，它们的使用往往具有策略性，体现出明显的语用特征。这种语言现象在军事访谈的机构性言谈互动(institutional interaction)中亦是如此。

龚双萍博士从语用学的角度将“刻意评价”视为一种交际策略，这是评价研究的一种新视角。她抓住军事访谈所具有的机构性话语特点，从刻意评价的表现形式到影响其使用的语境因素，再到刻意评价在军事访谈中的语用功能，都做了详细的描写、分析和理论阐释，努力揭示刻意评价这一语用策略使用背后所隐藏的语用机制。本研究在理论上跳出了系统功能语言学中评价理论的限制，在Jef Verschueren 提出的语言顺应论基础上形成了自己的分析框架，丰富了有关语言选择的顺应论研究，可以说是评价性语言现象研究的新成果。

当然，这本书只是龚双萍博士的一个阶段性研究成果，还存在一些值得改进的地方，有的问题还可继续深挖拓展。做学问往往就是这样，在点滴积累中发现问题，先期成果可进一步激发自己的研究兴趣，当自己前行到一个更高的地方回望时才能看得更全面，才会有新的体会并发现新的研究思路。作为导师，我很高兴看到龚双萍博士出版自己的第一本学术著作，更高兴看到我国外语界又多了一位有潜质的青年学者，希望她在今后的学术生涯中永葆军人气质，锐意进取，在语用学研究中愈行愈深，愈行愈高，取得有影响力的新成果，与其他学者一起推进中国语用学学科的蓬勃发展。

冉永平

2012 年4 月于广州

摘　要

本文的研究对象是军事访谈中被访者对评价的刻意性使用。这种语言现象我们视之为一种交际策略，并冠名“刻意评价”。

本研究采取定性研究的方法，试图回答以下四个问题：①军事访谈中的刻意评价有哪些类别？②哪些语境因素影响被访者对刻意评价的选择？③刻意评价如何实现各种交际功能？④被访者为什么要选用刻意评价作为一种交际策略？

本研究的理论框架以 Verschueren 的“语言顺应论”作为基础，辅以 Spencer-Oatey 的“和谐管理理论”以及 Bucholtz 和 Hall 的“身份与交际理论”，依此形成一个更全面更具有解释力的框架。

刻意评价是一种违背交际常规的交际策略。从军事访谈这一特定的机构性话语中所获取的语料进行观察，被访者所使用的刻意评价的刻意性体现在两个方面：①刻意背离主持人的提问；②刻意背离军事访谈的话轮分配系统。由此，我们将语料中的刻意评价分为五大类：①追加性刻意评价；②替代性刻意评价；③离题性刻意评价；④打断性刻意评价；⑤竞争性刻意评价。

刻意评价的顺应过程分为三类，即自我顺应、他人顺应和群体顺应。与自我顺应相关的语境因素主要有：被访者的自我面子、身份、权势；与他人顺应相关的语境因素主要有：他人面子、认知需求、情感；与群体顺应相关的语境因素主要有：群体面子、群体利益、国际关系、公众理解。

军事访谈中被访者使用刻意评价可以实现三个方面的交际功能，即人际趋向性功能、自我趋向性功能、群体趋向性功能。人际趋向性功能包括缓和人际关系、利他功能，以及缩短心理距离；自我趋向性功能包括保护自我和加强说服性；群体趋向性功能包括构建正面群体形象、实施反驳、澄清事实和引导观众行为。

评价与身份有着固有的联系。通过情感表达或价值判断，说话者不可避免地构建了自身的身份。在言语交际中，说话者倾向于构建自身的正面身份而非负面身份。在军事访谈这一特定机构性话语中，构建正面身份这一需要尤为突出。这也就是被访者采用刻意评价的理据。被访者的身份并非预先确定、一成不变，而是具有多个层面。在访谈中，随着会话的进行，会话者根据交际需求，凸显自己不同的身份。在交际进程中，被访者选用不同类型的刻意评价调节各种和谐取向来实现一系列功能，从而满足交际需求，并构建自身在军事访谈这一特定机构中的正面身份。

ABSTRACT

The present study aims to explore the interviewee's deliberate use of evaluations in military interviews, which is perceived as a communicative strategy and termed as 'deliberate evaluation'(DE).

Based on the data obtained from Chinese military interviews, this study attempts to answer the following questions with a qualitative methodology: ①what are the various types of deliberate evaluation employed by the interviewee in military interviews? ②what are the contextual correlates that influence the interviewee's choice of deliberate evaluation in military interviews? ③how does deliberate evaluation in military interviews realize diversified communicative functions? ④why does the interviewee choose deliberate evaluation as a communicative strategy?

The research questions are tackled within the theoretical framework which takes Verschueren's Linguistic Adaptation Theory as the theoretical backbone, supplemented by Spencer-Oatey's Theory of Rapport Management and Bucholtz & Hall's Theory of Identity and Interaction, so as to make the analytical framework more comprehensive.

Deliberate evaluation is a communicative strategy which deviates from the norm of the interaction. In the specific context of military interviews, the deliberateness of deliberate evaluation is manifested in two ways: ①deliberate deviation from the interviewer's question; ②deliberate deviation from the turn-allocation system in military interviews. Based on the various forms of deviation, five groups of deliberate evaluation are identified, namely additive DE, substitutive DE, digressive DE, interruptive DE and competitive DE.

The adaptation process of deliberate evaluation is divided into self-oriented adaptation, other-oriented adaptation and group-oriented adaptation. The self-oriented adaptation gratifies the language user's communicative needs. The contextual correlates concerned with this process are self-face, identity and power. The other-oriented adaptation satisfies the addressees' communicative needs, and the related contextual factors are other-face, cognitive needs and emotions. Lastly, the group-oriented adaptation meets the communicative needs of the group which the interviewee identifies with. The pertinent contextual correlates are group-face, group interests, international relationship and public understanding. It is these contextual factors that impel the interviewee to opt for DE as a communicative strategy in the ongoing interaction.

The functions of deliberate evaluation in military interviews are three-field, namely interpersonal-oriented functions, self-oriented functions and group-oriented functions. The interpersonal-oriented functions include mitigating interpersonal conflicts, altruistic functions and decreasing psychological distance. The self-oriented functions comprise protecting the self and reinforcing persuasion. The group-oriented functions consist of constructing positive group images, implementing refutation, clarifying the truth and manipulating the audience.

People's evaluation is intrinsically related to their identity. By expressing his feelings and values, one construct who he is. In human communication, people have a propensity to show their positive attributes establishing positive images to others instead of negative ones. That is to say, people tend to construct positive identities in public. It is the motivates that the interviewee employs manner of deliberate evaluation in military interviews. In the dynamic process of interaction, the interviewee's identities are open to constant negotiation rather than predefined. Triggered by his communicative needs, the interviewee may deliberately foreground a certain identity, and deliberate evaluation is a linguistic device that can index it. By using different types of deliberate evaluation, the interviewee manipulates various rapport orientations and thereby realizes an array of functions. As a result, the interviewee satisfies his communicative needs and constructs a positive identity.

CONTENTS

FIGURES

Chapter 1 Introduction

1.1 The object of the study

Evaluation is a ubiquitous language phenomenon in human communication, both in written texts and in verbal interactions. Vološinov (1973) pronounces that no utterance can be put together without value judgement, and it is evaluation that determines referential meaning. Richards (1964) conceptualizes two functions of language, one is scientific, the other emotive. Hayakawa (1972) identifies three modes of information exchange—report, inference and judgment. More recently, Hurvitz and Schlesinger (2009) claim that evaluations lie at the heart of every discussion. Thus, it is not surprising that there is a notable upsurge of interest in the study of evaluation in recent years.

Military interviews in Chinese TV programs, an area never touched upon by scholars before, are characterized by the activities of questioning and answering. Questioning in this context primarily aims to elicit an answer and request information and/or opinions from interviewees. It is without doubt that interviewees overwhelmingly give information and express opinions in response to interviewers' questions, and evaluation is thus a frequent speech act. Consider the following example:

Example (1)

Situation: The interviewee, Luo Yuan is a major general from Chinese Academy of Military Science; Xu Sanduo is the protagonist in the best-selling TV series in China in 2007 entitled 'Soldiers, Charge'. In the story, Xu Sanduo grew out of an ugly stupid clumsy rural boy into a No.1 soldier through his persistence.

主持人: 罗部长觉得许三多是个什么样的兵?
嘉　宾: 他的个性 = 很 ^ 突出啊，我可以说他是 <MRC> 比较憨厚，比较执著, 比较善良 </MRC>。可能大家最看重的是他比较憨厚的一面, 这个给大家印象 ^ 很深。

《防务新观察: 未来士兵拿什么突击》[1]

In this conversation, when asked to give opinion on Xu Sanduo, the protagonist in the hottest TV series entitled 'Soldiers, Charge' in 2007 in China, the interviewee evaluates Xu Sanduo as simple, honest, and perseverant. By giving the assessment, the interviewee aligns with the interviewer's question and fulfills the institutional task.

However, a close examination of the evaluations given by the interviewee reveals that not all of them are elicited by the interviewer. Let us enumerate the excerpts below:

Example(2)

Situation: On September 3, 2007, the US claims that it is the Chinese People's Liberation Army who hacked into the Pentagon network.

主持人: 难在哪儿呢? ^ 怎么就找不出是谁干的呢?
嘉　宾: 一个是像我们刚才讨论的, (TSK) 他借助第三方进行攻击, 偷你的车坐你的车去做案, 这是一种办法。

[1]The symbols in this coversation here represents special functions which are illustrated in the appendix in detail.

(TSK) 还有呢，就是利用网络上的一些后门。现在黑客软件非常的普及，很多小孩在家里没事捉摸捉摸，他下载那个程序以后就能够上去以后搞黑客，然后大家集中向你那扔一炸弹，堵塞你的流量，让你的宽带慢慢变窄，变窄以后让你死掉，但是那个很快就恢复了，造不成很大的影响。现在呢，黑客已经进入了非常专业化的程序了，专门的黑客程序进入你的银行账户，(TSK) 要盗取你的金钱。另外呢，也有一些进入^ 军队的一些网络系统中窃取一些军事机密。美国还成立了 “网络战” 这样的专门部队，使用^ 网络作为一种专门的武器去进攻对方。...(GLOTTAL) 啊，这个呢 <MRC> 美国做得最好 </MRC>。 ((点头))

《防务新观察：谁触动了五角大楼的网络神经》

Example(3)

Situation: In a press conference, Li Zhaoxin, the ex-foreign minister, released the military budget of China for 2010.

主持人：罗将军，从发布会上透露的信息来看，中国的军费预算确实要比去年有所增长，涨幅是7%。但是(TSK) 从这几年情况来看，这个涨幅是有所回落的，涨幅正逐渐地往下降。 我记得以前有很多国外的媒体采访您，问您(TSK) 为什么中国的军费要涨，您的回答是<@ “为什么不？” @>，您的观点是什么？

嘉　宾：我就感到^ 非常奇怪，每次我们在 “两会” 的时候一公布我们的国防费，一些国家就开始说三道四。<A> 我就觉得奇怪了</A>，世界上军费^ 最多的国家你怎么不去问它？卖军火^ 最多的国家怎么不去问它？在国外军事基地^ 最多的国家怎么不去问它？介入军事冲突^ 最多的国家怎么不去问它？中国稍微增加一点军费，有些国家就对我们说三道四。从这一次我们的军费增长来看，我们这次军费李肇星公布的是5 321.15 亿元人民币，我给它按汇率折算了一下，也就是<MRC>783 亿美元</MRC>。美国是多少？美国2012 年全年的国防预算是<MRC>7 080 亿美元</MRC>。

《今日关注：中国军费增长，合理适度透明》

In example (2), the interviewer asks why it is impossible to find out the specific source of hacking on the global internet, the interviewee first answers the question, but then gradually shifts the topic and intentionally evaluates that America is the country which does best in attacking other countries by using the internet as a weapon.In example (3), the interviewer requests the interviewee to offer his opinion on the military budget of China for 2010. However, the interviewee does not focus his evaluation on the requested topic, but shows his surprise toward both the negative comments on the Chinese military expenditure spread by other countries and the over curiosity held by some foreign media.

Another deliberate evaluative maneuver is deployed in the following case where the interviewee digresses from the ongoing topic to employ evaluation as a means of supporting his viewpoint displayed in the current turn.

Example(4)

Situation: The topic under discussion is which party would win the presidential election in Israel.

主持人：那岂不是^ 正好和我们刚才记者的分析应该是吻合的吗？怎么您不同意？

嘉　宾：他说^ 吻合是对的。他说所谓的^“微弱”优势，我个人是这样看，利库德集团确实这次可能会赢得第一大党的= 这个位置。我个人看到以色列最新的民意调查，我认为是^ 非常准的。以色列历届，根据他的经验，选前的民意调查一般是正负3%，基本上不会出错。根据现在最新的民意测验呢.. 利库德集团可能是25 到27 个席位，第二大党利夫尼领导的前进党是23 到25 个席位。(H) 第三大党可能是利伯曼领导的我们的家园以色列，这是个移民党，(H) 可能是18 到19 个席位。第四大党可能是工党，工党大概14 席左右，(H) 那么是这么样的。接下来是沙斯党，可能10 个席位，再接下来是梅雷茨6 个席位，这样的。((省略))

《今日关注：鹰派，鸽派，加沙战火后的以色列大选》

When the interviewer asks whether the interviewee's point of view on Israel's election is consistent with the analysis given by the journalist, the interviewee offers his confirmation and presents his view that the Likud party may win the upper hand by a narrow edge and become the leading party, which is justified by the recent Israel poll. In order to support his view, the interviewee digresses from the ongoing topic to the accurate assessment of Israel poll.

The following example illustrates another way of deliberately using an evaluation.

Example(5)

Situation: The increasing threat posed by piracy off the Somali coast has caused concerns in many countries. Russia announced that it would join international efforts to combat piracy. However, America seems to be rather conservative.

主持人：现在我们^ 确实听到两种声音。那么主战派当然是以俄罗斯为代表，美国呢相对来说好像是.. 比较保守。(GLOTTAL) 为什么对于海盗这样一个小对手美国这次显得如此的犹豫不决?

嘉 宾1：世界上16 个咽喉要道那就属于一个。那是从太平洋进入地中海的(TSK) 一个要道，连接亚洲和欧洲的一个通道，那个地方是一个石油要道，那是美国^ 必须要控制的，而且美国在那个地方部署有他的海军陆战队，就在索马里挨着的。^ 这样的话呢美国的第五舰队那是他的巡逻海域。但是这一次非常奇怪，美国就不挑头。不挑头的主要原因呢就是美国感觉黑鹰坠落就是1993 年恢复希望行动他吃了败仗，他不愿意第二次挑头；再一个呢就是这两场战争让他闹得够呛，伊拉克和阿富汗；(H) 另外现在政权交接的时候，他不愿意再惹出另外一个新的事来。也没扣他的船， [说实在的...

嘉 宾2： [关键是事不关己，高高挂起，现在要是^ 扣他几个美国人，看他[打不打

嘉 宾1： [但是作为海上警察，国际警察，他应该抓这个事。结果这次他失职了，啊，(TSK)有点。((看嘉宾2))

《防务新观察：海盗猖獗，打不打，怎么打？》

In this example, when the first interviewee is offering his answer to the interviewer's question as to why America is so passive in fighting the Somalia pirates, the second interviewee intervenes into his ongoing turn and evaluates the behavior of America as 'shi bu guan ji, gao gao gua qi' (let things drift if they do not affect one personally). This evaluation aligns with the first interviewee's point of view on America.

As can be observed from the aforementioned examples, the evaluation in example (1) is a routine one which is requested by the interviewer, while in examples (2), (3), (4) and (5), the evaluations are deployed by the speaker strategically in order to achieve certain communicative goals. Our interest in evaluation in the present study is geared to the latter one which is motivated, and we will entitle these evaluations as deliberate evaluations.

Since the 1970s, studies on evaluation have emanated from such different fields as sociolinguistics, functional linguistics, discourse analysis etc. Though a large bulk of studies have focused on the evaluation in text, there is a trend to understand it in terms of its functions in the contexts within which it occurs (Englebretson, 2007). As a pervasive language phenomenon in military interviews, the deliberate use of evaluation merits an exploration from a pragmatic perspective in the present study.

1.2 The rationale of the present research

We choose deliberate evaluation in military interviews as the object of the present research based on the following considerations:

Firstly, military interviews in China have been neglected by scholars for a long time. As a sub-genre of news interviews, military interviews are quite different from talk shows, debates or other TV interviews. The interviewer in this program is a professional journalist who is well trained, and the interviewees are certified experts in the military field, such as professors in the University of National Defense, Commanders in a certain military branch etc. The audience usually does not get involved in the interaction. The topics of the discussion are matters related to recent military events, both domestic and international. Compared with other TV interviews, military interviews in China are unique because of the special identities of the interviewees and because military is always a sensitive topic in China. Military issues in China are not so popularly discussed or even debated on TV or in other mass media, which is quite distinct from the case in western countries. However, we are attracted by its uniqueness and make up our mind to probe into the language phenomenon in it.

Secondly, evaluation is pervasive in interactional communication and in many cases, it is used strategically and it is pragmatically oriented. The strategic employment of evaluation, which is entitled as 'deliberate evaluation' in the present dissertation, has seldom been researched into in the past studies. DE in military interviews is a frequent language strategy employed by the interviewees, so we are curious about how the interviewees in this context adopt it to achieve different communicative goals and we also wonder what the forces are that drive the interviewees to choose deliberate evaluation as a communicative strategy.

Thirdly, there are a large number of studies on evaluation in recent years, but by and large these studies are confined to the evaluations in text, and the researches are mostly based on the approach of discourse analysis, the majority of which adopt the appraisal theory as the overarching theoretical framework. Though there is a tendency to study evaluation in real world interaction (Du Bois, 2007; Rauniomaa, 2007; Scheibman, 2007), the studies are description instead of explanatory. Hence, the achievements of the past studies offer us a descriptive picture of the language devices of evaluation, but fail to explain the strategic use of evaluation in interaction. Traditional pragmatic theories such as speech act theory, Grice's cooperative principle can not offer a satisfactory explanatory framework for the deliberate use of evaluation. One of the research goals of the present study is thus to construct a unified theoretical framework to account for the dynamics of the deliberate employment of evaluation in military interviews from a pragmatic perspective.

Last but not least, the study of deliberate evaluation in military interviews may be of practical importance in that it would fill the gap of military interview research in China, and can offer us a chance to dig into the language phenomena in this context, which has never been researched into before. Besides, the study can also supply a chance for the interviewees to see different strategies and language devices to realize evaluation intentionally in an institutional context to fulfill their communicative purposes, thus enable them to use evaluation effectively. In addition, a thorough investigation into the deliberate evaluation employed by the interviewees may facilitate our understanding of the evaluative language in military interviews, and would help the audience to catch the genuine intention hidden behind the language phenomena.

On the basis of the above major considerations and in terms of the various pioneering efforts made on the study of evaluation which will be surveyed in Chapter 2, the present study will offer a dynamic and thorough exploration of the motivated use of evaluation in military interviews from a pragmatic perspective.

1.3 Problems existing in the past studies

Evaluation has been widely studied in various sub-disciplines of linguistics, such as sociolinguistics, systemic-functional linguistics, corpus linguistics, discourse analysis and pragmatics, etc. However, a critical observer of the preponderance of the existing work on evaluation may still find dozens of problems unsolved.

Firstly, though a wealth of studies have been conducted on evaluation, the range of evaluation studied is quite limited. Most of the past studies on evaluation concentrate on the evaluations in written text, and take appraisal theory as a starting point for investigating. The language phenomenon of evaluation in verbal communication, though pervasive both in our daily life and in news interviews, has hardly received any attention in the past years.

Secondly, the few studies on evaluation (assessment) done by the pragmatists or interactional linguists are quite limited in its linguistic realization and the range of its topics. Most of the previous studies mainly focus on one sentence pattern in English (Goodwin & Goodwin, 1987, 1992; Pomerantz, 1984) or Finnish (Rauniomaa, 2007), namely [third-person pronoun] + [copula] + [adverbial intensifier] + [assessment term]. And two studies (Geer, 2004; Geer,Mizera, & Tryggvason, 2002) focus on the use of comments on socio-moral behavior during dinner time in Estonian, Finnish and Swedish families. As to the pragmatic functions of evaluation, these studies view evaluation as means to show agreement or disagreement, as ways to organize the ongoing talk, or as methods to direct children's social behavior. No clear definition has been provided in these pragmatic studies. Therefore, a lot of questions remain to be tackled further.

Thirdly, the study of strategic use of evaluation in verbal communication to approach communicative goals in an institutional setting such as military interview is not touched in the literature. We are then curious about how interviewees employ various types of deliberate evaluation to meet various communicative needs. It would also be quite interesting to find out the forces and the hidden mechanism of deliberate evaluation.

Lastly, evaluation involves a characterization of both the object of evaluation, and the person who is making the evaluation, thus raises the issue of identity. Identity is no doubt a major contextual factor of the act of evaluation, and constructing identity is one of the functions of evaluation. However, the existing studies just have mentioned the importance of the speaker's identity in the act of evaluation (Eggins & Slade, 1997; Linde, 1997; Martin & White, 2005), but never dig deeply into the dynamic construction of the speaker's identity on the level of evaluation and the impact of the speaker's identity on his strategic use of evaluation.

It can then be concluded that the present study on evaluation is far from being complete. Evaluation is undoubtedly omnipresent in conversation, and the study of the deliberate evaluation is in urgent demand, for the reason that this long-neglected language phenomenon clearly has pragmatic effect and it plays an active role in identity construction. Consequently, the present study will focus on the intention-driven strategic use of evaluation in verbal communication.

1.4 Objectives of the current research

Drawing on the previous researches, and enlightened by the view that pragmatics should be conceived as the study of the mechanism and motivations behind the linguistic choices and of the effects they have and are intended to have (Verschueren, 1987:14), the present study aims to present a systematic and coherent account of the mechanism underlying the use of deliberate evaluation in military interviews, as well as the pragmatic effects it may achieve or be intended to achieve. We formulate the practical-sounding research questions which are amenable to answer as follows:

1) What are the various types of deliberate evaluation employed by the interviewee in military interviews?

   When the interviewee decides to take up deliberate evaluation as a communicative strategy, he or she must decide how to deliberately utilize it. We intend to scrutinize the various ways adopted by the interviewee to deliberately realize evaluation.

2) What are the contextual correlates that influence the interviewee's choice of deliberate evaluation in military interviews?
The property of adaptability of language enables the interviewee to make negotiable linguistic choices from a diversified range of deliberate evaluations so as to approach his communicative goals. The endeavor made here is to delve into the complexity of contextual factors that various types of deliberate evaluation interadapt with in military interviews.

3) How does deliberate evaluation in military interviews realize various communicative functions?
DE is goal-driven and it is employed by the interviewee to realize a range of pragmatic functions so as to satisfy his communicative needs in military interviews. Here we plan to explore the rich functions of deliberate evaluation in military interviews.

4) Why does the interviewee choose deliberate evaluation as a communicative strategy?
Deliberate evaluation in the present study is a kind of motivated language use. Our central task here is to reveal the production mechanism of deliberate evaluation.

1.5 Data of the research

The target data in the present study is confined to the military interviews in China. As a new program in Chinese mass communications, military interviews have their unique features and norms, which will be dealt with in the following section.

1.5.1 Features and norms of military interviews

1.5.1.1 Institutional roles and their respective tasks in military interviews

Military interview, just as other subgenres of interviews, is an institutional talk. Agar defines 'institution' as 'a socially legitimated expertise together with those persons authorized to implement it'.[2] According to this definition, institutions produce binary and asymmetrical roles: the 'expert' (or 'institutional representative') who is invested with institutional authority and the 'non-expert'(usually the client), who must conform to the institutional norms. As far as military interviews are concerned, the institutional roles involve an interviewer who is the institutional representative, two or more interviewees who should conform to the institutional norms of the interview, and the audience who is the target of the program. Unlike other context-specific institutional talks, such as the talk between doctor-patient, teacher-student, judges-criminal, in which there is one-sided imposition of power from one dominant party upon a subordinate second party, military interviews are the forums in which both the interviewer and the interviewee are powerful. However, both of them are constrained

---

[2] Argar, M. Institutional discourse. *Text, 5*(3). 1985. 164.

by speaking rights tied to their respective institutional roles. And the audience, who may or may not be present at the program, is not actually involved in the asymmetrical power relation in the verbal communication.

The interviewer in this context restricts herself (or himself) to asking questions. The interviewer's questions set up particular agendas, both topic agenda and action agenda, for the interviewee's responses and incorporate preferences. A well-trained interviewer will always be conscious of her neutral stance and she does not state her own opinion, at least overtly. If she really wants to give an opinion, she does this in a strategic way without doing damage to her neutral stance. What's more, she avoids any kind of evaluative comment, even in the form of minimal response token — her task is to elicit opinions and information from the interviewec on behalf of the audience (Benwell & Stokoe, 2006:91), control the progress of the program and the interactional management of the interview, allocate turns to the interviewees, etc. In a word, the interviewer acts as the facilitator of a certain military interview. When the interviewer's power endowed by this specific institution is challenged by the interviewee's use of language, deliberateness may occur.

In contrast, the interviewees are obliged by the norms of the interview to answer the interviewer's questions. They can not ask questions (to the interviewer or other interviewees), nor make unsolicited comments on previous remarks, initiate changes of topic, or divert the discussion into criticisms against the interviewer. Furthermore, when there are two or more interviewees, it is the interviewer's questions that determine which interviewee is selected to speak next and whether, and when, other interviewees will be permitted to address the question under discussion

(Clayman & Heritage, 2002:98-99). The linguistic choices of the interviewee which deviate from these norms may be deemed as intentional and strategic.

As to the audience of the military interviews, they act rather passively. They do not participate in the discussion for most of the time, but still exert impact on the interaction in the program. It is the audience who are the ultimate target of the verbal communication in the military interviews. Therefore, their cognitive state, emotions, etc. would significantly affect what and how the interviewer questions, as well as influence the content of the interviewee's answer and the way he organizes his comments.

Both the interviewer and the interviewee share the common tasks of smoothly developing the program, educating the audience, and jointly promoting the authority and the reputation of military interviews. As a consequence, they ought to cooperate with each other, and be concerned with the other's communicative needs on the whole. Nonetheless, there still exists some divergence. For example, they may diverge from each other on the focus of a certain issue. What's more, sometimes what the interviewer queries may be inappropriate, or not to the point, and the interviewee, who is an expert in the field, has the authority to negotiate with the host, trying to correct the possible improper attitudes, adjusting the agenda that has been set, etc. All these make the interviewee's deviation from the norm possible, and may result in deliberate evaluation.

1.5.1.2 Topic sensitivity of military interviews

The topics in the military interviews are always recent newsworthy military events, and are obviously distinct from those of other TV interviews. The new development in China's military technologies and military power is one of the typical topics of the interviews of this type, such as the technological improvement of weapons and equipments, the development of various military branches, etc. Another type of topic is about regional military clashes, such as the war between Israel and Palestine, the conflicts between Russia and Georgia. The topic of International or domestic political disputes is also frequently discussed, such as Iran and Korea's nuke issue, the groundless accusation against China by foreign countries, America's global military strategies, and the sabotage hatched by the separatists, etc. These topics are sensitive for the reason that the interviewee's comments unavoidably concerns political stances, national dignity, and relations between various interest groups. The sensitivity of the topics in military interviews requires the interviewee's strategic use of language when evaluations are put forth.

1.5.1.3 Institution-specific goals of military interviews

The next feature of military interviews is that it is driven by institution-specific goals. Military interviews consist of distinctive, definitive and identifiable institutional goals, amounting to a unique 'fingerprint' for this particular context. The major goals of military interviews are listed as follows: first, it aims to show the audience the remarkable military development in China, enhance the sense of national pride, and maintain a positive military image. Second, when there is an ulterior attack from other countries which would damage the international positive identity of China, military interviews are forums for the interviewer and the interviewees to co-work to rebut the unjustified accusations, and avoid potential misunderstandings. Third, military interviews also target at the mass audience, with the intention to enrich their military knowledge, enhance their national defense awareness, and foster their patriotism.

The abovementioned features and norms form the basis of a military interview. The participants always employ devices to display a specific alignment with the institution. Through the whole program, the participants are quite aware of their incumbents of the institutional roles and act accordingly, while keeping the institutional goals in mind. Nonetheless, these organizational conventions may be displayed in the breaching due to the sensitivity of the topics or the current communicative goals. The interviewer might take a position on her own behalf, and the interviewees might intervene in the ongoing talk, attack the interviewer, or attack question prefaces, etc. The phenomenon of breaching can be analytically useful, since it tells us that 'rules that we initially hypothesize from empirical regularities in the participants' actions are in fact rules that participants recognize that they should follow as a moral obligation' [3]. The violation of the basic ground rules in news interviews can be attributed to some underlying motivations which are embodied as some special language phenomena. DE, as one of such language phenomena(Yang, 2006), thus merits academic investigation.

1.5.2 Data collection and transcription conventions

The data in the present study are gathered from the military interviews in CCTV — Defense Review Week in CCTV 7 (中央电视台第7频道,《防务新观察》), Focus Today in CCTV 4 (中央电视台第4频道,《今日关注》) and People in the News in CCTV4 (中央电视台第4频道,《新闻会客厅》). According to Clayman and Heritage (2002), the prototypical news interview involves a distinctive constellation of participants, subject matter, and

[3] Heritage, J. Conversation analysis and institutional talk. In K. F. Fitch and R. E. Sanders (Eds.), *Handbook of language and social interaction,* Mahwah, NJ: Lawrence Ehlbaum, 2005, p.117.

interactional form. The interviewer is known as a professional journalist rather than a partisan advocate or well-known entertainer. The interviewees have some connection to recent events, either as primary actors, or as certified experts. The audience plays no active role in the interaction. The discussion normally focuses on matters related to recent events, is highly formal in characters, and is managed primarily through questions and answers. The military interviews in the present research meet all of the aforementioned requirements of a typical news interview. The hostesses/hosts of the interviews are professional journalists. For example, one of the interviewers, Fang Jin has been trained in Beijing Broadcasting University and was awarded her Bachelor degree in Broadcasting. What's more, she has been a visiting scholar to Harvard University and has had an experience in academic exchange with Fox News Channel, a famous news channel in America. As for the interviewees in the interviews, they are primary actors or experts in the military events, such as generals, commanders, professors in military universities, celebrated editors of military magazines, etc. In most cases, there is no studio audience, while on some occasions, even though there is audience present, they do not play an active role in the program. The subjects of the interviews are confined to military news. It is organized as a question-answer turn-taking system.

The data on which the present study is based was obtained from 90 military interviews which were downloaded from the internet at http://military.cntv.cn, http://news.cntv.cn, or http://space.tv.cctv.com. The play time for the interviews is 45 hours. These conversations were closely examined for tokens of deliberate evaluation. The isolated cases and relevant parts of the interviews in which they occurred were then transcribed by us. The excerpts which serve as examples in the present dissertation are exclusively taken from these transcriptions.

There are in current use various transcription systems, such as Du Bois et al.'s Discouse Transcription (1993), Ehilich's Heuristic Interpretative Auditory Transcription (1993), MacWhinney's Codes for the Human Analysis of Transcripts (1991), etc. Across these systems, there is general agreement as to what is to be transcribed, but little agreement as to how to do so (O' Connell & Kowal, 2009:245). The transcribing of the present study was done following the conventions devised by Du Bois, for the reason that the signs for notation in this system are more accessible to discourse research, more economical, and more keyboard-friendly. Using such conventions, we managed to capture such important interactional details as transitional continuity, speech overlap and voice quality in our transcriptions. However, as the interviewees' turns tend to be rather long, the intonation units are separated only by signs of notation, instead of being presented in separate lines. In addition, since the symbols used to represent transitional continuity are drawn from those employed in written punctuation (Du Bois et al., 1993:53), the final of an intonation unit is indicated by the period of the punctuation system of Chinese. The transcription conventions of this dissertation are given in the Appendix.

1.6 Notes on methodology and terminology

As far as methodology is concerned, the present study is characterized by the employment of qualitative analysis of the data. Being theory-driven, our ultimate goal is to set up an explanatory model from the data and for the data. The whole process of the investigation is speculative and introspective. Before proposing a model, we pin down a working definition (which is presented in Chapter 3) of deliberate evaluation which guides the effort-consuming search for data. We base our conceptual framework on Verschueren's (1999) Linguistic Adaptation Theory. Other theories are also appealed to in the development of the dissertation, notably Spencer-Oatey's Theory of Rapport Management (2008), Bucholtz and Hall's Theory of Identity and Interaction (2005), and Grice's Theory of Conversational Implicature (1975). The conceptual framework acts as the basis for the ensuing inductive data analysis. The careful scrutiny of the data will offer an illustration of various types of deliberate evaluation, contextual factors, pragmatic functions, and the hidden mechanism of deliberate evaluation in military interviews.

Terminologically, the terms with special senses in this dissertation need to be clarified before we move to the next chapter. As our research targets at the verbal interactions in military interviews, the interviewer and the interviewee are two indispensable parities. For the variety of language use, we will refer to interviewer also as hostess, and the interviewees either as experts or their professional titles. When pronominalization is necessary, 'she' is used for the interviewer, and 'he' is used for the interviewee, which follows the terminological convention originated from Sperber and Wilson (1986, 1995) and Verschueren (1999).

The words 'answer', 'reply' and 'response' are endowed with different meanings in the present study. 'Answer' is utilized when the interviewee proffers the information as requested by the interviewer. Both 'reply' and 'response' are deployed when the information provided by the interviewee fails to meet the interviewer's expectation.

The lexicons 'deliberately' and 'intentionally' are used interchangeably; and the terms 'evaluation', 'assessment', 'appraisal' and 'comment' in the present dissertation are employed with identical meaning.

Finally, for the sake of convenience, the clumsy phrase 'deliberate evaluation' is abbreviated into 'DE' hereafter.

1.7 The outline of the dissertation

The present dissertation consists of seven chapters.

Chapter 1 is the introductory chapter. It deals with the objective and the rationale of the current research, the problems in the previous studies, the features and norms of military interviews, and the notes on methodology and terminology.

Chapter 2 provides a review of the related literatures and points out their achievements and limitations.

In Chapter 3, we present the working definition of DE in military interviews and try to set up a coherent conceptual framework of the current study. Spencer-Oatey's Theory of Rapport Management, and Bucholtz and Hall's Theory of Identity and Interaction are integrated into Verschueren's Linguistic Adaptation Theory to offer an interpretive theoretical framework to explain DE in military interviews.

Chapter 4 explores the various types of DE employed by the interviewee in military interviews.

Chapter 5 scrutinizes the contextual factors that the linguistic choices of DE interadapt with in military interviews.

Chapter 6 delves into the multifarious functions realized by DE in military interviews, as well as the hidden mechanism underlying the use of DE.

Chapter 7 summarizes the major findings of the research, points out its implications and limitations, and makes suggestions for future study.

Chapter 2 Literature Review

2.1 Introduction

The elapsed few decades have seen a notable upsurge of interest in the study of evaluation in various academic disciplines and a wide range of approaches to evaluation have been proposed. As a point of departure of the present study, the relevant studies in the field of sociolinguistics, discourse analysis, corpus linguistics, systematic functional linguistics, and pragmatics will be reviewed in this chapter. Terminological issue arises as the heterogeneous range of research reveals that evaluation is by no means a monolithic concept. Therefore, though the major part of this chapter is dedicated to the review of the pertinent literature, the terminological issue will be dealt with first to decide which term will be adopted in the present research. Following a brief review of the related studies on evaluation, the achievements and limitations of previous efforts will be presented to direct the unified and systematic account of DE in military interviews.

2.2 Terminological issues

Due to the different objectives of the researches and the diversified academic background of the researchers, there are a variety of terms used to explore this language phenomenon.

Both sociologists and discourse analysts adopt the term evaluation in their investigation though the definition varies a bit according to the respective goals of their researches. The term evaluation in Labov's work (1972) refers to the point of the narrative story which constitutes an essential element of the narration, whereas for Linde (1997) the term evaluation covers any instance of a speaker demonstrating the social meaning or value of a person, thing, event or relationship. In the field of discourse analysis, some scholars (e.g. Bybee and Fleischman, 1995) employ evaluation to relate to speaker/writer's view of something as desirable or undesirable, while others (e.g. Thompson and Hunston, 2000) use evaluation as a superordinate term for the expression of the speaker or writer's attitude or stance towards, viewpoint on, or feelings about both entities or propositions.

Corpus linguists use both the term stance (e.g. Biber et al., 1999; Conrad and Biber, 2000) and evaluation (e.g. Bednarek, 2006). Systematic functional linguists (e.g. Martin and White, 2005), aiming to expand the account of attitudinal meaning given by Halliday (1994), adopt the term appraisal and establish three sub-categories: affect, judgement and appreciation. However, sometimes, in the illustration and explanation of their theory, functional linguists use the term appraisal and evaluation interchangeably (e.g. Eggins and Slade, 1997).

Being a less cultivated territory in pragmatics, the language phenomenon of evaluation does not have a consistent heading in the works of pragmaticians. The correspondent language phenomenon is probed under different labels out of different considerations. Assessment is the term employed in the study carried out by Pomerantz (1984), Goodwin and Goodwin (1987), and Rauniomaa (2007). Pomerantz (1984:58) considers 'assessments' as products of participation in social activities which are occasioned conversational events with sequential constraints. Goodwin and Goodwin (1987) attach the term assessment to different analytical levels, such assessment segments, assessment signals and assessment actions, all of which convey the speaker's opinion toward the object being assessed. Comment is another frequently adopted term by pragmaticians, for instance, in the researches done by De Deer et al. (2002, 2004) and the works of Heisler et al. (2003). In another investigation, Scheibman (2007) refers to evaluation as a common type of linguistic subjectivity and the expression of attitude. Still others term the related phenomenon as evaluative stancetaking (Shoaps, 2007) or evaluative statement (Searle, 1969).

As can be seen from the aforementioned publications, though there is no uniform technical term to capture the provision of the expression of the speaker's point of view, the term evaluation has obviously won the upper hand by being the only term that is employed across discipline borderlines. Following this trend, and also for the ease of illustration and consistency, the present dissertation will take the term evaluation. Furthermore, the focus of the present investigation, viz. the strategic use of evaluation with the aim of achieving certain communicative goals in institutional talks such as talks in military interviews, has never been probed into in previous researches. We will therefore introduce the term DE to cover such language phenomenon throughout the dissertation.

2.3 Approaches to evaluation

The investigation on DE is inspired by the existing studies on evaluation. It is then inevitable for us to review the literature of evaluation. Five pertinent approaches, namely the sociolinguistic approach, the discourse analytical approach, the corpus linguistic approach, the functional linguistic approach and the pragmatic approach will be reviewed in the following section, with the endeavor to find implications for the present study.

2.3.1 The sociolinguistic approach

2.3.1.1 Labov's narrative model

In the course of their study of the black English vernacular language, Labov and his co-workers developed a sociolinguistic model of narrative that outlines the formal structural properties of oral stories of personal experience in relation to the social functions of narrative. They put forth a fully developed narrative structure (Labov & Waletzky, 1967; Labov, 1972; Labov & Fanshel, 1977) which is composed of six parts: ①abstract; ② orientation;③complicating action; ④evaluation; ⑤result or resolution; ⑥coda. The abstract makes a general proposition that the narrative will exemplify and encapsulates the point of the story. In orientation, the narrator identifies the time, place, persons, and their activity or the situation. The complicating action addresses the main narrative sequence of events, which commonly encompasses a problem, dilemma or change, adding a sense of interest to the story. The result or resolution depicts the outcome or solution. The coda signals the ending of the story. It has the property of bridging the gap between the moment of time at the end of the narrative proper and the present and brings the narrator and the listener back to the point at which they entered the narrative (Labov, 1972:365). The Evaluation is considered by Labov to be the heart of the narrative, which makes the narrated events reportable, repeatable, and relevant. Labov defines evaluation as 'the means used by the narrator to indicate the point of the narrative, its raison d'etre: why it was told, and what the narrator is getting at'[4](ibid.:366).

[4] Labov, W. *Language in the inner city: Studies in the black English vernacular*. Philadelphia: University of Pennsylvania Press, 1972, p.366.

Labov classifies evaluation into several types, namely external evaluation, embedding of evaluation, evaluation action and evaluation by suspension of the action. External evaluation is the evaluation given by the narrator directly to the listener, telling the listener what the point is. It is a universal trait of middle-class narrators. Embedding of evaluation has various degrees: quote the sentiment as something occurring at the right moment of the narrating, quote oneself as addressing someone else, and introduce a third person who evaluates the antagonist's action for the narrator. Evaluation action is a further step in dramatizing the evaluation of a narrative which tells what people did rather than what they said. Evaluation by suspension of action is for the narrator to stop the action to call the listener's attention to that part of the narrative and indicate to the listener that it has some connection with the evaluative point, the purpose of which is to achieve a greater force of the resolution.

Labov (1972), Peterson and McCabe (1983) give a comprehensive list of evaluation devices which depart from the basic narrative syntax. These evaluative elements in narrative are categorized into four major headings: intensifiers, comparators, correlatives and explications. Each of these four headings can be carried out in many ways. Intensifiers are realized by gestures, expressive phonology, quantifiers, repetition and ritual utterances. Comparators are listed as negatives, futures, modals, quasimodals questions, imperatives, or-clauses, superlatives and comparatives. Correlatives include progressives, appended particles, double appositives, and attributives. Explicatives are explanations of why or how an event happens. They are done in separate clauses which are appended to the main narrative clause or to an explicit evaluative clause and are introduced by conjunctions such as while, though, since, or because etc. Narrators can realize evaluation phonologically, lexically, and syntactically. Phonologically, a narrator may use heightened stress, vowel lengthening, marked changes in volume, speech rate and pitch, or whispers, song, rhyme, and non-linguistic noises. Lexically, tellers may choose words from a different register, change degree of formality, or use profanities and words with rich connotations. Syntactically, any marked change in complexity or use of tense may signal evaluation. These categorizations help us to recognize the enormous range of evaluative possibilities.

Labov's model has been widely utilized in a number of different fields, such as in literary analysis (Carter & Simpson, 1982; Maclean, 1988; Pratt, 1977); in education (Taylor, 1986; Wilkinson, 1986; Hicks, 1990), in developmental psycholinguistics (Kernan 1977; Peterson & McCabe, 1983; Bamberg & Damrad-Frye, 1991), and in mass communications (van Dijk, 1988a, 1988b).

2.3.1.2 Linde's evaluation as social practice

Charlotte Linde has studied the relation of linguistic structure and social practice in a variety of real-world settings, including life stories, aviation accidents, police helicopter flights, the process of the design of computer technologies, and the New York real estate industry. She considers evaluation as a major component of the linguistic structure of discourse, and an important part of social interaction which has serious consequences for real-world decisions. Evaluation in her works is defined as follows:

> *We may include as evaluation any instance of a speaker indicating the social meaning or value of a person, thing, event or relationship — 'I like it', 'I don't like it', 'She's*

smart', 'It's terrible the way they treat you in hospitals', 'All used car salesman can't be trusted', 'Blast this machine, anyway', 'I'm so stupid at computers', 'I wish I had a more powerful computer'. Evaluation may thus be viewed as an important part of the moral dimension of language, providing indications of the social order which the speaker reproduces by assuming.[5]

In order to understand evaluation as social practice, Linde distinguishes three levels of evaluation: incidental level evaluation, constituent level evaluation and topic level evaluation. Incidental level evaluations are small evaluations made in passing. They work at the sentence level or lower and usually do not receive a response from their recipient. For example:

(1) That's excellent, that just worked dandily.
(2) (Page 39) shows you how to add them. But it' not working for me.
(3) Well, this is the second time. I'm adding New Entry now. Hopefully.

(ibid.:154)

Constituent level evaluation appears as structural components of a discourse unit, the scope of which may include the entire discourse unit. A response to the constituent level evaluations must be negotiated and agreed on by the parties before the discourse unit can be completed.

---

[5] Linde, C. Evaluation as linguistic structure and social practice. In B. L. Gunnarsson, P. Linell and B. Nordberg (Eds). *The construction of professional discourse*, Harlow: Longman. 1997. p.152.

Topic level evaluations, featured by the discourse form of argument, refer to cases in which the purpose of the discourse is to arrive at an evaluation. They represent actual negotiations concentrated on value and the appropriate actions to take.

According to Linde, evaluation as a social practice is the co-construction and the negotiation among the participants in a conversation. The negotiation of evaluation may have immediate and long-term consequences. One major function of evaluation is to serve as an end marker for a discourse unit, a section of activity, thus it can be efficiently used in agenda management (Linde 1993, 1997). Evaluation can also act as gap filler when people work together on the telephone (Linde, 1997).

Considering evaluation as a part of social practice, we may observe at least three levels at which evaluation has an effect: first, speakers must agree on the evaluation of a discourse before they can proceed with that discourse; secondly, speakers must agree on an action to allow the activity to proceed; thirdly, speakers must agree about the value of an artifact to proceed with appropriate group action about adopting, rejecting or modifying that artifact.

The importance of the identity of the evaluator is also mentioned by Linde (1993). She asks what kind of self is created by evaluation — that is, what qualities of the self are supported by language, leaving out the aspects of the self that are created and maintained nonlinguistically (Linde, 1993:99). She contends that by saying what one likes or dislikes, one says who he/she is.

In a word, Linde's study on evaluation directs people's attention to an important fact about evaluation: evaluation embodies the social determination of the meaning of one's self, one's action, and one's environment. However, Linde's discussion on the practice of evaluation is restricted only to American English.

It is without doubt that the investigation on evaluation as a social practice in other languages would definitely bring benefits both for linguistics and for the understanding of the range of variation of a social practice.

2.3.2 The discourse analytical approach

With the publication of Evaluation in text: Authorial stance and the construction of discourse co-edited by Hunston and Thompson in 2000 and the convening of the international conference on evaluation and text type sponsored by the University of Augshurg in 2005, studies of evaluation in text has quickened its step (胡壮麟, 2009).

Thompson and Hunston (2000) assemble the previous sporadic researches in this field into one comprehensive canon. They adopt evaluation as a superordinate term which covers both propositional opinions and attitudes toward entities. Therefore, they define evaluation as the expression of the speaker or writer's attitude or stance towards, viewpoint on, or feelings about the entities or propositions that he or she is talking about. That attitude may relate to certainty or obligation or desirability or any of a number of other sets of values (Thompson & Hunston, 2000:5).

What's more, Thompson and Hunston identify three important functions performed by evaluation: expressing opinion, maintaining relations and organizing the discourse. Expressing opinion is the most eye-catching function of evaluation which express the speaker's or writer's opinion about something, and in doing so, reflect the value system of that person and their community; maintaining relations includes three main areas — manipulation, hedging and politeness, with the aim to construct and maintain relations between the speaker or writer and hearer or reader. These two functions have been dealt with adequately by functional linguists, such as Halliday (1994), White (1998), and Martin and White (2005), which will be reviewed in the next section. The third function, organizing the discourse, is first spotted by Labov (1972) when he researches the stories told by adolescent African Americans (see the previous subsection). Sinclair (1988) makes the point that evaluation provides a clue to the organization of the discourse both in texts and discourses and establishes a tri-partite model of discourse, which can be summarized as ①posit (proposing, imposing, opposing), ②react (reacting to posit), ③determine (determining the previous posit-reaction pair). The last stage represents an evaluation which marks that a point has been made and that the reader's acceptance of that point is assumed. Sinclair contends that 'following this kind of structure is a well-formed basis of in texts'. This organizing function of evaluation in discourse is also made explicit in the investigation done by Francis (1986, 1994), Hoey (1983, 2001) and Tirkkonen-Condit (1989).

Hyland (1998, 2000, 2004, 2005) examines evaluation in academic discourse with an emphasis on the interaction between the writer and his readers. One of his considerations is that evaluation is always carried out in relation to some standard. Personal judgements are only convincing, or even meaningful, when they contribute to and connect with a communal ideology or value system concerning what is taken to be normal, interesting, relevant, novel, useful, good, bad and so on (Hyland 2005:175). The writer-reader interactions are motivated by the fact that readers can always refute and can thus play an active and constitutive role in how writers construct their arguments. Evaluation is therefore decisive to academic writing as effective argument represents writers' careful considerations of their colleagues as they situate themselves and their work to reflect and shape a valued disciplinary ethos. These interactions are managed by writers in two main ways: stance and engagement. Stance is an attitudinal dimension which expresses a textual 'voice'. It encompasses features which refer to the ways writers present themselves and convey their judgements, opinions, and commitments. Engagement is an alignment dimension by which writers connect to their readers with respect to the position advanced in the text, and include the readers as discourse participants. Stance and engagement are two sides of the same coin and both contribute to the interpersonal dimension of discourse. The major resources of academic interaction are presented in the following diagram:

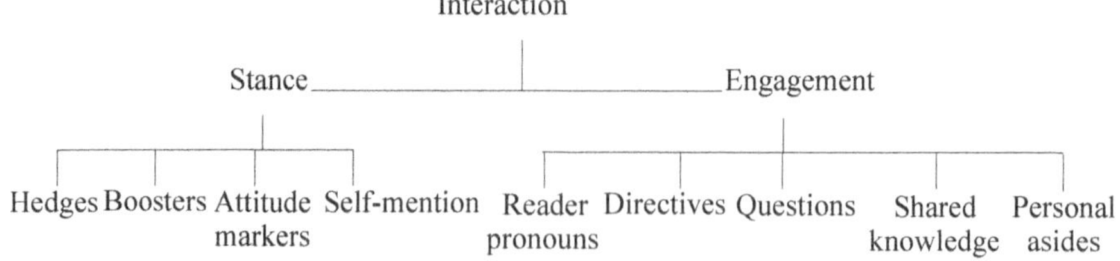

Figure 2-1 Key resources of academic interaction (Hyland, 2005)

Numerous other discourse analysts have made effort on the study of evaluation in discourse. Fairclough (2003) examines the evaluative meaning of political texts, with Tony Blair's public speech in the context of new capitalism as the target data. Lombardo (2004) surveys the evaluative meaning of that-clause and reporting verbs in TV news discourse. And Webber (2004) investigates the evaluation of negation in research articles.

2.3.3 The corpus linguistic approach

Hunston (2007:27-28) argues that corpus methods make a

useful contribution to the investigation of evaluation in discourse studies for two reasons: firstly, corpora give us the opportunity to quantify and make it particularly easy to quantify forms; secondly, corpora allow us to observe multiple uses of a word or phrase in context. Hunston (ibid:46) suggests that qualitative work using corpora can show typicality of use and in doing so can enable us to identify previously unknown stance markers— particularly markers of evaluative stance. These markers are typically phrases rather than individual words.

One of the best-known corpus studies of evaluation is carried out by Biber et al.(1999), and Conrad and Biber (2000) furthered the study. They favor the term 'stance' in their study which they define as '[speakers and writers]'s personal feelings, attitudes, value judgements, or assessments'[6]. They examine the structure, meanings, and register distribution of the major grammatical devices used to mark stance. There are five categories of major grammatical devices used to express stance:

(1) stance adverbials, namely single adverbs and adverb phrases, hedges, prepositional phrases, adverbial clause and comment clauses
(2) stance complement clauses which are controlled by a verb, an adjective, or a noun
(3) modal or semi-modals
(4) stance noun + prepositional phrase
(5) premodifying stance adverb

The major semantic distinctions conveyed by stance markers

[6] Biber, D., Johansson, S., Leech, G., Conrad, S. & Finegan, E. *Longman grammar of spoken and written English.* Harlow: Longman. 1999. p.966.

are categorized into epistemic stance (e.g. typically), attitudinal stance (e.g. fortunately) and style of speaking stance (e.g. to tell you the truth).

With the above mentioned variables, Bible et al. proceed to compare four broad registers: conversation, fiction, news, and academic prose. A number of conclusions are drawn from the corpus findings. As for major stance devices across the registers, they find that: ① generally speaking, stance markers are widespread in all four registers. Stance markers are particularly more common in conversation than in the written registers. Meanwhile, stance markers are unexpectedly frequent in written registers; ②modal and verb/adjective/noun complement constructions are the most common grammatical categories of stance marker. Modals are by far most frequent in conversation, and complement constructions are more common in fiction and news than in the other registers, but they are also common in conversation; ③overall, adverbial stance markers, which are most common in conversation, are significantly less frequent than the other grammatical categories. The corpus findings for stance adverbials are: ①single adverbs are the most common category in the four registers; ②prepositional phrases are far more common in academic prose than in other registers; ③adverbial clauses are more frequent in conversations; ④comment clauses only moderately appear in conversation. Finally, the corpus findings of stance complement constructions across registers reveal that:①stance complement constructions appear to nearly the same extent in conversation, fiction and news, while they are less frequent in academic prose; ②the specific grammatical devices preferred in conversation and academic prose are nearly opposites; ③fiction and conversation have similar preferred stance complement clause types, while news is similar to academic prose in this respect.

The corpus linguistic approach can also be found in the works of Francis (1998) who draws data from COBUILD 'bank of English' and finds that the adjectives that occur at the first slot in the pattern 'it is (very)...that...' are all evaluative; Lemke (1998) develops semantic dimensions of evaluative orientation based on a corpus of newspaper texts; Englebretson (2007) observes the frequency of the occurrence of stance in two corpora: the Santa Barbara Corpus of Spoken American English (SBCSAE) and the British National Corpus, World Edition (BNC). Du Bois (2002, 2004), Rauniomaa (2007) and Keisanen (2007) also employ the corpus approach in their research.

What should not be neglected is that there is a trend to combine discourse analysis on evaluation with corpus analysis in recent years. A prominent amalgamation of corpus analysis and discourse analysis is done by Bednarek (2006) in her research on evaluation in media discourse. The study is based on a corpus of 100 news stories taken from ten British national newspapers: five broadsheets and five tabloids. Bednarek proposes a parameter-based framework to analyze her data. She identifies the sets of values as evaluative parameters, assuming that speakers can evaluate aspects of the world as follows:

(1) good or bad (the parameter of emotivity)
(2) important or unimportant (the parameter of importance)
(3) expected or unexpected (the parameter of expectedness)
(4) comprehensible or incomprehensible (the parameter of comprehensibility)
(5) (not) possible or (not) necessary (the parameter of possibility/necessity)

(6) Genuine or fake (the parameter of reliability)

Moreover, she presumes that speakers can evaluate propositions as more or less reliable (reliability: low/median/high), and that they can make evaluative comments on the language that is used (the parameter of style), on other social actor's mental states (the parameter of mental state) and on the source of their knowledge (the parameter of evidentiality). This framework is then applied to study the difference between tabloids and broadsheets.

2.3.4 The functional linguistic approach

A group of functional linguists in Sydney, including Martin, White, Feez and Iedema, began their investigation on evaluation in the early 1990's under the heading of 'appraisal'. Predicated on the general framework of systemic functional linguistics (hereafter SFL), these scholars aim to develop a more comprehensive framework for analyzing evaluation in discourse. In their seminal book *The language of evaluation: appraisal in English* which was published in 2005, Martin and White state that:

> *[Appraisal] is concerned with the interpersonal in language, with the subjectivity presence of writers/speakers in texts as they adopt stances toward both the material they present and those with whom they communicate. It is concerned with how writers/speakers approve and disprove, enthuse and abhor, applaud and criticize, and with how they position their readers/listeners to do likewise. It is concerned with the construction by texts of communities of shared feelings and values, and with the linguistic mechanisms for the sharing of emotions, tastes and normative assessments, It is concerned with how writers/speakers construe for*

themselves particular authorial identities or personae, with how they align or disalign themselves with actual or potential respondents, and with how they construct for their texts an intended or ideal audience.[7]

It can be discerned from the above statement that for functional linguists, the range of research covers several traditional notions: ①affect — the means by which writers/speakers positively or negatively evaluate the entities, happenings and states of affairs; ②modality and evidentiality — issues of speaker/writer certainty, commitment and knowledge; ③intensification and vague language — ways in which speakers/writers increase or decrease the force of their assertions and how they sharpen or blur the semantic categorizations with which they operate.

As discourse semantic theorists, the Sydney scholars divide the attitudinal meaning into three types: affect, judgement and appreciation. Affect construes emotion, with the canonical grammatical form I feel (very) 'x'...; judgement construes attitudes about character, designed to sanction or prescribe behavior, with the distinguishing grammatical frame It was 'x' for person/of person to do that...; appreciation construes attitudes about texts, performances and natural phenomena, and fits into frames as I consider it 'x'... (Martin, 2003; Martin & White, 2005).

Engagement and graduation are the other two components of the appraisal theory. Engagement is concerned with the interpersonal nature of evaluation. It considers the evaluative resources of providing the writer/speaker's point of view, adopting intersubjective positions and negotiating alignment/disalignment

[7] Martin, J. R & White, P. R. R. *The language of evaluation: Appraisal in English.* New York: Palgrave Macmillan. 2005. p.1.

with the addressee in the dialogic context. Utterances can be categorized into two groups, viz. monoglossic (where the source of an opinion is simply the writer/speaker) and heteroglossic (where the source of an opinion is other than the writer/speaker). Heteroglossic can be dialogically expansive and dialogically contractive in their intersubjective functionality. Expansiveness is realized by modality, evidentiality, and attribution. While the resources of dialogic contraction are disclaim (deny or counter) and proclaim (concur, pronounce and endorse).

Graduation has to do with adjusting the degree of an evaluation. The semantics of graduation is the defining property of all attitudinal meanings and it is also a feature of the engagement system. It operates along two axes—the grading of intensity or amount, and the grading of prototypicality or preciseness. The former adjusts the degree of evaluation and is called force, with the realization as intensification, comparative and superlative morphology, repletion, and various graphological and phonological features. The latter adjusts the strength of the value of the evaluative meaning and is entitled focus. It indicates the evaluative investment of the writer/speaker's attitude in value positioning.

The most comprehensive account of the theory can be found by Martin and Rose (2003, 2007), Macken-Horarik and Martin (2003), and Martin and White (2005). We can also obtain a detailed introduction to the theory and its application on the website, www.grammtics.com/appraisal.

A wealth of works on evaluation has been inspired by the appraisal theory in mainland China. This can be witnessed by the numerous articles published in recent years and the First International Conference on Appraisal System held in China in 2005. I would like to just name the prominent researchers here.

Wang (王振华, 2001) introduces the appraisal theory, presenting its background knowledge, the framework and its operation. Wang (王振华, 2004) applies the sub-system of attitude to the analysis of both Chinese hard news and English hard news. The linguistic device of judgement is found to be employed more than that of affection and appreciation in the data. Wang and Ma (王振华、马玉蕾, 2007) tackles three questions: ①how appraisal theory gains its charm and where its charm lied; ②what questions and dilemmas it brings to us learners; ③how to get out of the dilemmas. Li (李战子, 2004) summarizes the application of appraisal theory in analyzing commercial, historical and autobiographical discourse in English and explores several aspects: the interpersonal nature of attitudes, contextual factors in distinguishing the appraisal categories, the division of interpersonal and ideational meaning, and the relationship between appraisal and genres. She also gives comments on cross-language evaluation and its application in English teaching in China. Liu and Han (刘世铸、韩金龙, 2004) discuss appraisal system and its manifestation in English news discourses and propose a new way of reading news texts, i.e. evaluative reading, which they deem will benefit the foreign language teaching in reading. Zhang and Liu (张德禄、刘世铸, 2006) briefly compares Halliday's systemic functional linguistics with Martin's appraisal theory. The results show that Halliday's approach is multi-leveled, but it is limited by formal categorization, while the appraisal theory offers the social semiotic aspects a more comprehensive and systematic coverage though it still needs to perfect the relevant formal categorization that realizes the appraisal system.

2.3.5 The pragmatic approach

Compared with other approaches to the study of evaluation,

the pragmatic approach lags far behind. Pragmatists prefer the terms 'assessment', 'comment', 'evaluative statement', 'evaluative stance', or 'evaluation'.

Austin (1962) baptizes complete speech acts as 'illocutionary acts', and 'comment' is one of the English verbs that denote illocutionary act. Searle (1969) briefly distinguishes between descriptive statements (e.g. my car goes eighty miles an hour) and evaluative statements (e.g. my car is a good car) by pointing out that for the descriptive statements the question of truth or falsity is objectively decidable, for the reason that to know the meaning of the descriptive expression is to know under what objectively ascertainable conditions the statements which contain them are true or false. In contrast, the situation for evaluative statements is dissimilar in that to know the meaning of the evaluative expressions is not by itself adequate for knowing under what conditions the statements containing them are true or false, as the meaning of the evaluative expressions is such that the statements are incapable of objective or factual truth or falsity at all. The origin of the difference lies in that evaluative statements perform a completely different job from descriptive statements. '[The job of evaluative statements] is not to describe any features of the world but to express the speaker's emotions, to express his attitudes, to praise or condemn, to laud or insult, to commend, to recommend, to advise, to command, and so forth' [8]. However, the two can also be related as the following model shows:

Evaluative major premise:
e.g. one ought to keep all one's promises;

---

[8] Searle, J. R. *Speech acts: An essay in the philosophy of language*. Cambridge: Cambridge University Press. 1969. p.183.

Descriptive minor premise:
e.g. Jones promised to do X;
Therefore, evaluative conclusion:
Therefore, Jones ought to do X.

Goodwin and Goodwin (1987) address the interactive organization of assessments. As the word 'assessment' can be used to refer to a range of events that exist on analytically distinct levels of organization, they distinguish between assessment segment, assessment signal and assessment action. Assessment segment refers to a structural unit that occurs at a specific place in the stream of speech, for example the adjective 'beautiful'; assessment signal is the speech signal used to embody assessment, such as intonation; assessment can also designate a particular type of speech act. Goodwin & Goodwin point out several issues relevant to the analysis of assessment as a speech act: ①Different from other speech acts which are embodied in complete sentence or turns, assessment is a speech act that can occur in the midst of an utterance; ②A crucial feature of assessment actions is that they involve an actor taking up a position toward the phenomenon being assessed; ③Affect displays are pervasive in the production of assessment, and are central to their organization; ④Individual assessment actions can be organized as an interactive activity which includes multiple participants. Goodwin & Goodwin's investigation on assessment reveals that assessment is a central resource available to the participants for organizing the perception and interpretation of what is being talked about, providing them with the ability to not simply display alignment to ongoing talk, but establish and negotiate that alignment through a systematic process of interaction while the talk being aligned to is still in progress.

Moreover, assessments are achieved through the collaborate action of multiple participants, and provide an elementary example of social organization within the boundaries of the turn. In addition, they constitute a key locus for the display and achievement of congruent understanding and provide an example of how affect and the expression of emotion are organized as interactive phenomenon.

De Geer et al. (2002) focus their study on the use of comments on socio-moral behavior during dinner time in Estonian, Finnish and Swedish families. Comment in their research is the linguistic tool used in the process of pragmatic socialization. Parents give comments in order to point out either lack of observance to a norm, as in the case of turn-taking rules, and politeness phrases, or they may be used as an explicit directive to encourage proper behavior. The analysis stresses the comments' focus, form and outcome. Focus can be non-linguistic (table manners, moral and ethics, prudential norms or other behavior) or linguistic (turn regulation, maxim violations or metalinguistic comments). They were further divided into moral rules and social-conventional rules. Form refers to sentence type, time and directness. The syntactic form of a comment can be declarative, interrogative, imperative or ellipses; the comments can focus on both the immediate situation (the mealtime), on previous or future occasions, as well as on more general situations; they may be directed both towards people present at the table and towards those who are not, which can be seen as a most indirect way of setting, stressing and transferring norms of behavior. Therefore, comments can explicitly or implicitly aim to influence a conversation partner to speak or behave in a certain way. There are four different reactions to comments: agreement, negotiation, resistance and ignoring. The results show that Swedes use considerably more comments on ethical and moral questions, whereas all other groups are more concerned with table manners. It is obviously the case that different social norms were emphasized in the Estonian, Finnish, and Swedish families.

De Geer (2004) focuses the study on comments in Swedish families, and she finds that parents' comments are mainly aimed at children, whereas children are more likely to comment on each other's behavior than on their parents' and their comments are often aimed at people not present at the table. Furthermore, comments directed toward people present at the table mainly concern social-conventional rules, while comments on other's behavior more often relate to moral rules. Moreover, comments aimed at people present at table are more indirect than comments aimed at people who are not present. Finally, the responses to comments are affected by contextual factors. Comments whose focus are moral rules and which are directed at someone not present at the table are more likely to meet agreement, whereas comments directed at someone who is present at the table will more often be negotiated, encounter resistance, or be ignored.

Heisler et al. (2003) analyze the relationship between evaluative metadiscursive comments and face-work in conversational interaction. Evaluative metadiscursive comments play an essential role in face-work in conversation inasmuch as the qualification of what has been said or is about to be said exert impact on the interlocutor by modifying the image that he might construct of the speaker. By contemplating would-be negative reactions that can be put forth by the hearers with respect to the content of a particular utterance, the speaker exhibits awareness to the potential shocking of his talk, and as such reduces the threat that this talk may represent for the participants' faces. In addition, when speakers themselves introduce the plausible negative evaluation of some item of their own talk, they ward off the negative evaluation from the hearers. Heisler et al. identify three specific features of these comments that have particular relevance to a speaker's self-presentation in conversation interaction, namely the type of qualifier at the center of the comment, the type of threat to the speaker's face represented by the target utterance, and the location of the comment in the speaker's discourse.

Scheibman (2007) examines evaluations with general subject (e.g. they, you, one, those guys, etc). She contends that generalizations in evaluation have the function to strengthen the speaker's stance. Additionally, evaluations with general subject participate in intersubjective activities at an interpersonal level (e.g. politeness, demonstration of solidarity) and more globally in the maintenance of cultural norms. The subjectivity of evaluations is tied to their intersubjectivity use in several ways through generalization. The evaluations with they subjects convey speakers' evaluative stances as they function to create ingroup solidarity by othering outsiders. The general subject you can broaden the speaker's stance in an appeal to the belief of the addressee. These analyses support the idea that in English conversations, an individual's expression of stance by means of generalizations has interactive consequences. Evaluation in this way contributes to the construction and reproduction of cultural belief systems and shows the reinforcement of the links between expression of individual stance and social attitudes in conversational interactions.

Liu (刘戈, 1998, 1999, 2000) investigates evaluation in Russian from a pragmatic perspective. Liu (刘戈, 1998) considers lexicons an important way to express evaluative meaning. He divides the adjectives in Russian into three groups, viz. adjectives of general evaluation, adjectives of specific evaluation and adjectives of description. His research shows that even adjectives of description can obtain evaluative meaning in some context, for example, when the object of evaluation is related to the living circumstance of human beings. Liu (刘戈1999) categorizes evaluation in conversation into the expressive speech acts, and discusses its illocutionary force. What's more, hc deems that the success of the intentionality of evaluation is closely connected with politeness principle. Another research done by Liu (刘戈2000) deals with evaluation in conversation. He identifies three patterns of adjacency pair in conversation containing evaluation: question-evaluation, evaluation$_1$-evaluation$_2$, (surprised) evaluation$_1$-(surprised) evaluation$_2$. The negotiation principle is an important principle for the use of evaluation in conversation.

2.4 Achievements and limitations in the past researches

In retrospect, the aforementioned efforts on the study of evaluation establish the foundation and the departure point for the present study. It is on these achievements and limitations in the past researches that the author of the present dissertation depends to get the sparkle of inspiration and find the point of breakthrough.

The sociolinguistic approach tells us that evaluation embodies the social determination of the meaning of one's self, one's action and one's environment; the discourse analytical approach offers us a superordinate definition of evaluation, and identifies some important functions; the corpus linguistic approach identifies some major grammatical devices, the major semantic categorization of evaluation, and also compares the grammatical devices across registers; the functional linguistic investigations have contributed to a more detailed categorization of the semantics of evaluation, the major syntactic patterns, and above all establishes a discourse semantic theory to account for evaluation in discourse, emphasizing how writers/speakers establish an interpersonal relationship with their readers/hearers. The pragmatic studies on evaluation have pointed out some limited pragmatic functions performed by evaluation in verbal communication.

Notwithstanding all these contributions, there still exist some limitations. First, the majority of the data come from written text, and the interactional nature of evaluation is underexplored. Second, evaluation in face-to-face interaction can be manipulated to achieve a large array of pragmatic functions, so as to meet the speaker's communicative needs. But 'how do language users utilize evaluation strategically? What are the rich pragmatic functions realized by the deliberate employment of evaluation in verbal communication'? The existing literature can't provide a satisfying answer to these questions. Thirdly, the previous studies mainly focus on revealing the linguistic devices or grammatical patterns of realizing evaluation, but never tackle the contextual factors that affect the expression of evaluation. Therefore, the question of 'what are the contextual correlates that influence the use of evaluation' is never explored. Fourthly, the past studies do not delve into the hidden mechanism of the employment of evaluations, not to mention the mechanism of the use of DEs. Hence the question 'why do language users use evaluation strategically' is left unanswered. Lastly, though appraisal theory is a theory of evaluative language, it can not offer a satisfactory interpretation of the use of DE in face-to-face interaction, for it is a discourse semantic theory. An alternative theory must be set up to explain DE in verbal communication.

The present research respects all the contributions made by the previous studies as a fruitful starting point, but aspires to go beyond and seeks for a coherent and unified account of DE in military interviews.

2.5 Summary

The major concern of the current chapter is to provide a review of the related literatures on evaluation, so that we can get the inspiration for the study of DE in military interviews. Evaluation has been studied in diversified approaches from multifarious perspectives. Due to different research objectives, scholars employ various headings to cover the language phenomenon. Therefore, in the beginning of the chapter, we address the terminological issues and select the term to be used in the present study. The major part of the chapter is dedicated to the literature review which is categorized into five approaches, namely the sociolinguistic approach, the discourse analytic approach, the corpus approach, the functional linguistic approach and the pragmatic approach. We further point out the achievements and the limitations existing in the past researches, which we consider as the springboard for the ensuing research.

Chapter 3
A Description of the Conceptual Framework

3.1 Introduction

In order to overcome the limitations in the previous researches pointed out in Chapter 2, and properly answer the research questions outlined in Chapter 1, we need to identify our research object, and establish an overall descriptive and explanatory framework as the springboard for the understanding of DE in military interviews. Therefore, the purpose of the present chapter is twofold. First, the working definition of DE is provided and the distinguishing properties are pointed out. The distinction between DE and two other similar notions are also clarified. Second, a detailed description of the related theories is presented as the basis for the ensuing conceptual framework, which paves the way for the further investigation of the study.

3.2 The working definition of DE

As can be seen from the literature review in Chapter 2, evaluation can be actually utilized to refer to a range of events that exist on analytically distinct levels of organization. Discourse analysts and functional linguists mainly focus on the semantics of the words or phrases which express evaluative meanings. Some scholars put emphasis on nonsegmental phenomenon such as intonation (Wennerstrom, 2001), gaze and gestures (Haddington, 2006), which can display evaluation. Pragmaticians deem evaluation as a speech act which can either be embodied by complete sentences or occur in the midst of an utterance. The present study investigates the interviewee's deliberate use of evaluation in military interviews from a pragmatic perspective. It connects evaluative meanings with actual contexts and enables the interviewee to interact successfully in the actual social encounter. The working definition of DE in this study is presented as below:

> *DE is a communicative strategy whereby the speaker goes out of the way to intentionally express his/her subjective value judgement toward the person or matter being addressed, with the purpose of achieving certain communicative goal(s).*

The working definition highlights several properties of DE: ① subjectivity; ② value-ladenness; ③ intentionality; ④ optionality. Each of these properties is further discussed below. For the convenience of exposition, we will use the following excerpt for demonstrative purposes:

Example(6)

Situation: The trade route through the Gulf of Aden has long been suffering from the pirate plague. According to the relevant UN Security Council resolutions and with the approval of the Somali transitional government, China begins to send destroyers and supply ships to the Gulf of Aden off Somalia at the end of 2008, offering protection for Chinese civilian vessels and crews, including those from Hong Kong, Macao and Taiwan, and foreign vessels on request as well. The first interviewee, Senior Captain Chen, who is the general manager of the department of Security and Surveillance in China Ocean Shipping Company, has the experience of fighting against the Somalia pirates. The second interviewee, General Zhang, is an expert in military equipment and he frequently participates in military interviews.

主持人: 陈船长，这次 ^中远公司听到我们军队派出军舰去亚丁湾，是 ^什么样的一种感受呢?

嘉宾 1: <MRC>这次我们听到我们海军要出去，在这个水域为我们商船队护航的这个信息以后呢 </MRC>，我 ^本来也是一个 '船员，所以我从心底里感觉得到船员的一种感觉，就是 ^最简单的一个，就是 '高兴、'放心，心里就 ^定了。

嘉宾 2: <A>我是 1998年离开海军到国防大学工作的 </A>。十年以后，那么我是前不久又到了南海舰队，到了南海舰队登上了舰艇以后，我是感慨万千呀。好多老华侨离开祖国四五十年了，一看，呀，中国的舰艇 ^那么大啊，还有 ^那么大的舰艇。<u>我是刚离开 ^十年啊，我是 ^一直研究武器装备的，我回去以后都特别吃惊啊。我就这么告诉你，我不说多强 ..这次出去的舰艇，比美国的驱逐舰 ^一点点都不落后，在很多方面比美国都要 ^强。如果说和俄罗斯的舰艇相比，比俄罗斯舰艇要先进 ^十年以上。</u>

((观众热烈掌声))

《防务新观察：抗击海盗真实全过程》

3.2.1 Subjectivity

Language subjectivity is a general phenomenon that refers to the expression of self and the speaker's point of view in discourse (Finegan, 1995:1). DE is a common type of subjectivity with a focus. To put it in another way, while subjectivity of utterance is broadly termed as the locutionary agent's (the speaker's or writer's, the utterer's) expression of self in the act of utterance (Lyons, 1994), DE indicates the evaluator's self-expression that is restricted in a narrow purview — self-expression about the 'person or matter' addressed in the utterances that the evaluator is currently producing. It results from the speaker's intentional breaching of the norms of verbal interaction in the institution where the interaction takes place.

When talking about subjectivity of language, we cannot neglect the other pole of objectivity. According to Lyons, the scholar who has long championed the recognition of subjectivity in language (Englebretson, 2007), subjectivity expresses the speaker's own beliefs and attitudes or their own will and authority, while objectivity reports the existence of the state of affairs, and 'can be described as having an unqualified I-say-so component but it-is-so component' (Lyons, 1977). This does not mean that there is a clear-cut distinction between the two concepts. As far as evaluation is concerned, it is considered to form a continuum from more objective to more subjective (Martin & White, 2003). The kind of 'objectivity' appears to involve a range of factors, basically as little attitude, graduation and heteroglossia as possible. This kind of evaluation may be thought of as a kind of faceless stance. While at the other end of the spectrum, the more subjective evaluation is featured by a full range of attitudinal, graduating and engaging resources.

DE, as the speaker's deliberate expression of attitude, takes up the more subjective pole of the continuum of evaluation. When the speaker proffers an evaluation deliberately, he is not simply describing an event or presenting an objective statement of some events, he represents an event or state of affairs from a particular perspective, and at the same time fulfills the expressive, emotive, affective, or attitudinal function of language. Compared with more objective evaluations, the DEs provided by the interviewee in military interviews have the following subjective traits: ① DE reflects the speaker's subjective choice of how to present the evaluation according to the speaker's communicative needs; ② There is an imprint of self and an explicit expressing of the speaker's attitudes or stances in DE; ③ DE is full of attitudinal, graduating and engaging resources.

Let us demonstrate the subjectivity of DE in the above excerpt: the subjective dimension of DE in this excerpt is registered overtly through discrete linguistic elements, including the metapramatic awareness indicators 'wo jiu zheme gaosu ni' (Let me tell you in this way), and 'wo bushuo duoqiang' (I won't say how advanced it is) personal pronoun 'wo' (I), and the evaluative adjective 'chijing' (be surprised), 'qiang' (better) and 'xianjin' (advanced). The two metapragmatic awareness indicators clearly reflect the fact that the way of presenting the evaluation is the result of the interviewee's subjective choice to meet his communicative needs. The person pronoun I points directly to the speaking subject who takes the evaluative stance. 'zheci chuqu de jianting' (the Chinese escort ships which are sent to the gulf of Aden this time) specifies the object of the evaluation. The evaluative stance predicate indexes specific aspects of the speaker's point of view, positioning the speaker subjectively along the scale of evaluative value. What's more, the graduation marker 'yidiandian' (a little) and 'shinian yishang' (more than ten years), together with the engaging marker 'yao'(must) reinforce the subjectivity of the DE.

3.2.2 Value-ladenness

In conveying opinions, evaluations invariably reconstruct cultural norms and values. Just as Thompson and Hunston argues, 'Every act of evaluation expresses a communal value-system, and every act of evaluation goes towards building up that value-system.'[9]Linde (1997) asserts that evaluation is the speaker's indication of the value of a person, thing, event or relationship. As we have reviewed in Chapter 2, there are several different value parameters for evaluation, such as the parameter of good and bad, of certainty and uncertainty, of important or unimportant etc. Among these parameters, the good/bad is the most basic one and can be related to the others (Thompson & Hunston, 2000; Bednarek, 2006).

DE in military interviews, as a subtype of evaluation, embodies the values which are especially emphasized by the speaker in a specific context and which are placed on the value scale intentionally to achieve certain communicative goal(s).

Let us again examine the example. The evaluative predicates are 'buluohou' (not lag behind), 'qiang' (better), 'xianjin' (advanced). These values are considered as positive values in the Chinese value system. The speaker further adjusts the degree of evaluation deliberately with the intensification 'yidiandian' (a little) and 'shinian yishang' (more than ten years) and the comparison between Chinese vessels and American vessels, and between Chinese vessels and Russian vessels.

---

[9] Thompson, G. and Hunston, S. Evaluation: An introduction. In S. Hunston and G. Thompson (Eds.). *Evaluation in text: Authorial stance and the construction of discourse*. Oxford: Oxford University Press. 2000. p.6.

3.2.3 Intentionality

Communication involves speakers expressing their intentions, and hearers attributing intentions to those speakers. If the intentions attributed by the hearers are roughly the same as those expressed by the speaker, then communication is considered to have been successful (Haugh, 2008). 'Intentionality' is used with two interrelated meanings: one is concerned with purposiveness, involving means-ends reasoning in planning a desired outcome (Bratman, 1999); the other sense, which incorporates the first one, considers intentionality as a feature of the mind which can be directed at, be about, and represent thoughts, beliefs, desires, emotions and intentions and capable of attributing such mental states to others (Searle, 1983). DE, which is defined as a communicative strategy, is no doubt imprinted with the feature of intentionality.

The intentionality of DE presupposes its purposiveness and deliberateness. A particular DE is deliberately selected by the speaker from a range of options to apply to a specific occasion with the purpose to achieve certain communicative effects. Its employment involves the speaker's deliberate flouting of conversational maxims and his deliberate breaking away from the pre-allocated turn system in a specific communicative context. The intentionality of DE can be reconstructed by the addressee who would be able to infer likely goals that would have motivated the behavior. As a decisive deliberation, the interviewee's DE is situated in a special setting — military interviews, where exists the asymmetry of power, status or rights. The knowledge of this asymmetry plays a role in the reconstruction of the interviewee's intentionality and defines the meaning of this verbal act. Moreover, the participants' (including the interviewer, the interviewees, the studio audience or TV viewers) tacit knowledge of the existing norms of communicative behavior influence the way they apprehend an utterance. A marked choice[10] such as DE, then, is understood within the context of military interviews and can stand on its own, conveying both evaluative meaning and the interviewee's intention.

Furthermore, according to Malle, a distinguished psychologist working on intentionality, a behavior is judged intentional when the agent has at least five aspects in the mind: a desire for an outcome, a belief that action leads to that outcome, an intention to perform the action, the skill to perform the action, and an awareness of fulfilling the intention while performing the action (Malle, 2001). When using DE, the speaker has the desire to achieve some communicative goal, and he believes that the linguistic choice made is the optimal option at that moment to assist him in reaching the goal. Therefore, DE in military interviews, a marked linguistic choice which is utilized by the speaker with high degree of consciousness,is an intentional use of language.

For the sake of a better comprehension of this feature, an illustration via the excerpt is needed. In the excerpt, the interviewee takes the floor without being assigned the right by the host, and he covertly shifts the topical agenda set by the interviewer, for it is obvious that the content of his utterance shows no direct connection with the interviewer's question. As an experienced interviewee in news interviews, the speaker certainly knows that when there are two or more than two interviewers in a news interview, it is the

[10] It is contended that within any interaction there is often a single linguistic variety that participants recognize as the unmarked choice for that type of interaction as part of their innate communicative or cognitive competence. This competence has been termed the markedness metric or the markedness evaluator (Myers-Scotton & Ury, 1977).

interviewer who determines which interviewee will be permitted to address the topic. His positive evaluation of the Chinese escort ship is intentionally proffered with the communicative goal to set a positive image of the Chinese army. And this intentionality can be reconstructed by the listeners on the strength of their tacit knowledge of the existing conventions of communicative behavior in military interviews.

3.2.4 Optionality

Another distinguishing feature of DE is its optionality. Evaluations can be both a social index and a strategic device. In other words, the employment of evaluation may either be non-motivated in accordance with social norms, or be motivated with the speaker's intentions. In the case of non-motivated evaluation, the choicc is more often than not obligatory and automatic. Its employment can be considered to be the speaker's passive subjection to the requirements of norms in an institution and the choice of its appropriate linguistic form is the result of almost automatic observation of those socially agreed-upon rules. DE is the motivated use of evaluation with the speaker's intention to reach a current goal in the ongoing verbal communication. Compared with the non-motivated use of evaluation, DE is characterized as being optional. That is to say, the speaker has the freedom to choose to evaluate or not to evaluate according to his communicative needs. Contrary to non-motivated evaluations which inscribe the speaker's recognition of the norms in a specific context, DE is strategically used by the speaker to avoid interpersonal conflict, to maintain one's face, etc. What's more, such type of evaluations enables the speaker to select from a comparatively wider range of possibilities.

Now, let us turn to the excerpt. In the interview, the question raised by the interviewer is directed to the first interviewee, Senior Captain Chen, who has experienced the fighting with the Somalia pirates. The second interviewee, who is not assigned the task to answer the question, has the option of not giving comments. However, after Senior Captain Chen answered the question, the second interviewee takes the turn to appraise the Chinese escort ships. The evaluation here is obviously optional and is employed to satisfy the speaker's communicative needs.

3.3 Delimitation of DE

Having given a working definition of DE, it is time for us to make a clear delimitation of the concept by demarcating DE from such similar language phenomena as stancetaking and overinformativenss.

3.3.1 DE vs. stancetaking

One important concept that is closely related to DE is stancetaking. The similarity of the two consists in that they both refer to speaker's adoption of a certain attitude toward an object in the interactional conversation.

Definitions and conception of stance vary a lot in different studies. Englebreston (2007) provides a qualitative analysis of stance, trying to find out the diversified meanings of it in naturally-occurring speaking and writing. His analysis brings to light five key conceptual principles of stance: ①stancetaking takes place on three (often overlapping) levels—stance is physical action, stance is personal attitude/belief/evaluation, and stance is social morality; ②stance is public, and is perceivable, interpretable, and available for inspection by others; ③stance is interactional in nature; ④stance is indexical; ⑤stance is consequential, which means taking a stance would bring real consequence for the person or institutions involved.[11] This qualitative understanding of the meanings of stance opens a window into the academic concept of stance.

In a study of how stance can be accomplished interactionally through the use of linguistic resources or other practices, Wu (2004) defines stance as 'a speaker's indication of how he or she knows about, is commenting on, or is taking an affective or other position toward the person or matter being addressed.' We can draw three types of stances from this definition, namely epistemic stance, which addresses the knowledge state of the speaker, evaluative stance, which indicates the speaker's characterization of the object of stance as having some specific quality or value, and affective stance, which positions the speaker's emotional state toward the entity being addressed.

While Wu categorizes stances into separate groups, Du Bois (2002, 2004, 2007) presents a more unified way of understanding stance. Her approach seeks to interpret the diversity of stances not as distinct types of stance, but simply as a single unified act encompassing several triplet sets of dissimilar components and processes. Stance in interaction is then defined by Du Bois (2004) as 'a public act by a social actor, achieved dialogically through overt communicative means, of simultaneously evaluating objects, positioning subjects (self and others), and aligning with other subjects, with respect to any salient dimension of the sociocultural field.' The stance model can be represented in the form of a triangle as below.

---

[11]Englebretson, R. *Stancetaking in discourse: Subjectivity, evaluation, interaction*. Amsterdam/ Philadelphia: John Benjamins Publishing Company. 2007. pp. 6-7.

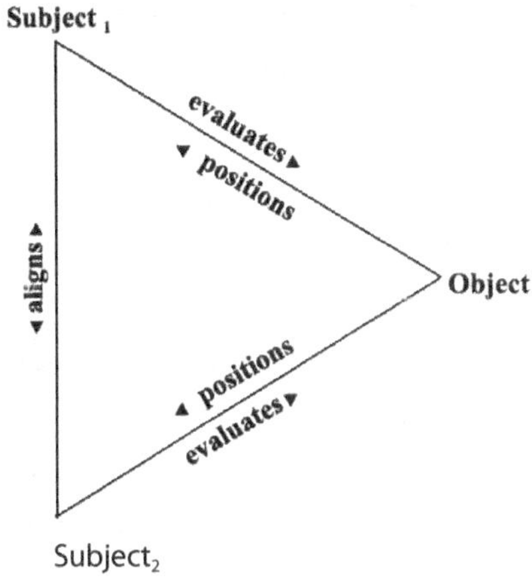

Figure 3-1 The stance triangle (Du Bois, 2004)

Based on the stance model developed by Du Bois, Haddington (2006, 2007) takes the term stancetaking as referring to 'a dynamic, dialogic, intersubjective, and collaborative social activity in which speakers actively construct stances by building on, modifying aligning and engaging with the stances of other speakers'. He further distinguishes two types of intersubjectivity of stancetaking, viz. forward intersubjectivity and backward intersubjectivity.

As can be clearly seen from the above studies on stancetaking, the act of stancetaking covers a wider range of language phenomenon than that of DE. Let's consider the following example:

Example(7)
Jennifer: Are we not attacking each other until we get rid of the striped guy?
Mary: <u>I don't know.</u>

(Du Bois, 2007: 156)

In this example, Mary's utterance shows her state of knowledge of the particular stance object — 'if we are not attacking each other until we get rid of the striped guy'. It is an epistemic stance that she is taking. This does not belong to DE, for the speaker does not point out any value or quality of the stance object.

DE unavoidably indexes the speaker's various positions toward a stance object in the conversation. It is concerned with the speaker's positive or negative feelings, positive or negative attitudes to people and the way they behave, or positive or negative view to things or performances. That is to say, it involves both affective stance and evaluative stance, while epistemic stance is not included. Therefore, the relationship between the two may be an inclusive one, which can be visualized in the following diagram:

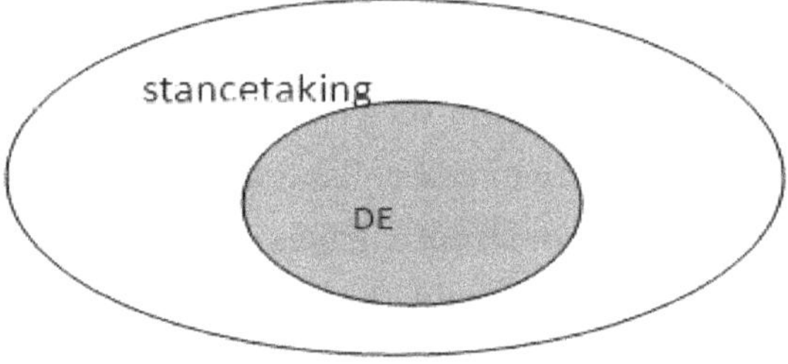

Figure 3-2 The relation between DE and stancetaking

3.3.2. DE vs. overinformativeness

Another concept which to some extent cuts across the area of DE is overinformativeness. The resemblance lies in that both of them are optional in the ongoing interaction.

Chen (2004) defines interactional overinformativeness as 'the act of providing propositional non-natural information apart from the supply of natural information in conversational exchange'. He identifies two related forms of the realization of overinformativeness: the initiator's interactional overinformativeness and the responder's interactional overinformativeness. An initiator is overinformative if he provides propositional non-natural information apart from the supply of the natural information literally necessary to the performance of a given speech act in an idealized context. As for the responder, he is interactionally overinformative if he provides propositional non-natural information apart from the supply of the natural information literally necessary to the satisfaction of the initiator' need conveyed by the natural information that his utterance contains or implies.

Overinformativeness has the property of optionality for the reason that the speaker has the freedom to choose between the provision of additional information and the presentation of only the required amount of information in an interactional context. This property is reminiscent of DE, when it is up to the speaker to decide whether to evaluate an object or not. Therefore, a piece of added opinion may also be a DE at the same time. Consider the following Example:

Example(8)

Situation: The interviewee is the superintendent of the research institute of Chinese military supplies

主持人：最后确定的这个颜色在您这个色板里面吗？

嘉　宾：这个色板是一个标准色板，但是我们在这个基础上进行了改进之后变成了松枝绿，也就是我们现在看到的陆军军服的松枝绿。<u>它 ^ 更能代表解放军的威武，大家认为这个颜色 ^ 非常稳，不跳跃，这样使我们的军服配上服饰之后是一幅画，^ 非常美。</u>

《新闻会客厅：将军解密三军换 07 式新装内情》

In this excerpt, the interviewer asks whether the color of the new uniforms for the soldiers serving in the army is in the color panel. The interviewee first provides the information required by the interviewer, but then moves on to add an evaluation on the color of the new uniforms. The added evaluation is optional rather than obligatory in the current situation. It can be identified both as overinformativeness and as DE.

Nevertheless, the two concepts are not identical but exhibit some divergence. For one thing, DE is subjective, while extra information may either be subjective or be objective. For another, DE is value-laden, while information surplus does not have this property. Hence, a piece of extra information does not need to be a case of DE. Here is an example.

Example(9)
A:Have you seen my guitar?
B:No. Mary was in your room this afternoon.
(Chen, 1999: 18)

In example (9), the additional information B provides in the underlined part can be considered as a case of overinformativeness. However, it is not a DE since it states an objective past fact rather than offer a subjective assessment.

In addition, overinformativeness is internally related with the dominant proposition to which it is attached. In terms of thematic content, it serves to complement rather than shift from what precedes it. However, DE may be illogically related to, or semantically irrelevant with the preceding information. So, a DE has the possibility of not being a piece of extra information.

From the above discussion, we can infer that DE overlaps with overinformativeness to some extent. The relation between the two can be represented as follows:

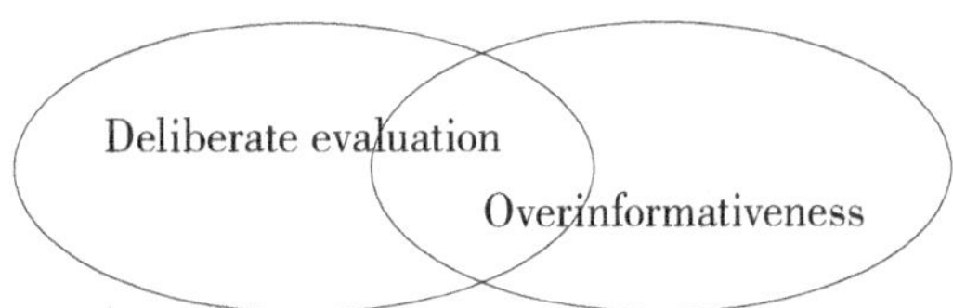

Figure 3-3 The relation between DE and overinformativeness

3.4 A sketch of the theoretical basis

Three theories act as the footstone of the present conceptual framework, namely the Linguistic Adaptation Theory proposed by Verschueren (1999), the Theory of Rapport Management put forth by Spencer-Oatey (2008), and the Theory of Identity and Interaction held by Bucholtz and Hall (2005). Among these, the linguistic adaptation theory offers the overarching explanatory framework for the present research, while the other two are incorporated into it to provide a more comprehensive interpretation of DE.

3.4.1 Verschueren's linguistic adaptation theory

The Linguistic Adaptation Theory is initiated, enriched and accomplished by Jef Verschueren, the secretary general of International Pragmatic Association (IPrA). It is not conceived and completed in one breath. The embryonic form of the theory appeared in the form of a working document entitled Pragmatics as A Theory of Linguistic Adaptation in 1987. Ever since, it underwent a series of modification and amendment on various aspects (Verschueren, 1995a, 1995b, 1998). In consequence, the publication of the book Understanding Pragmatics (1999) signals its maturity. The contribution of the theory lies in that it presents a brand-new coherent explanatory theory to the use of language, namely a general functional perspective. The kernel of this theory is illustrated in the following statements.

Distinct from the component view of traditional linguistic study, which divides linguistics into component disciplines such as phonetics, phonology, morphology, syntax and semantics, Verschueren holds the view that pragmatics, which at a most elementary level can be defined as the study of linguistic phenomena from the point of view of their usage properties and processes, is impossible to be identified with a specific unit of analysis. Therefore, it can be situated at any level of structure or may pertain to any type of form-meaning relationship (Verschueren, 1999:2). At the same time, Verschueren contends that pragmatics is concerned with the full complexity of linguistic behavior and functions effectively as the latch connecting the linguistic of language resources with the interdisciplinary field such as psycholinguistics, sociolinguistics etc. Inspired by this insight, Verschueren specifies pragmatics as a general cognitive, social, and cultural perspective on linguistic phenomena in relation to their usage in forms of behavior.(ibid:7)

One of the key notions of the linguistic adaptation theory is making choices. It is said that using language must consist of the continuous making of linguistic choices, consciously or unconsciously, for language-internal (i.e. structural) and/or language-external reasons. These choices can be situated at any level of linguistic form: phonetic/phonological, morphological, syntactic, lexical, and semantic. They may range over variety-internal options, or they may involve regionally socially or functionally distributed types of variation (ibid: 55-56). Choices are actually made at three overarching levels, viz. languages, codes and styles. Once natural language has been opted for, a particular language has to be chosen. And codes involve systematic sets of choices which are related to a specific geographic area, a social class, an assignment of functions, or a specific context of use. Style is reserved to the variability of formality and informality. Moreover, choices are also made among basic utterance-building ingredients which are to be found at different levels of structure. Additionally, a speaker may also choose strategies in order to achieve her communicative goals.

To further make sense of the notion of making choices, Verschueren introduces three hierarchically related key concepts, viz. variability, negotiability and adaptability. Variability is the property of language which defines the range of possibilities from which choices can be made; negotiability is the property of language responsible for the fact that choices are not made mechanically or according to strict rules or fixed form-function relationships, but rather on the basis of highly flexible principle and strategies; adaptability is the property of language which enables human beings to make negotiable linguistic choices from a variable range of possibilities in such a way as to approach points of satisfaction for communicative needs (ibid: 59-61). What should be kept in mind is that these three notions are interrelated properties of the overall object of investigation for linguistic pragmatics, the meaningful functioning of language.

Based on the notion of adaptability, four tasks or angles of investigation can be assigned to pragmatic descriptions and explanations, namely contextual correlates of adaptability, structural objects of adaptability, dynamics of adaptability, and salience of the adaptation process. These four tasks do not constitute separate topics of investigation, but are complementary and have different functional loads to carry within the overall framework of the pragmatic perspective. The relation among them is depicted by the following figure.[12]

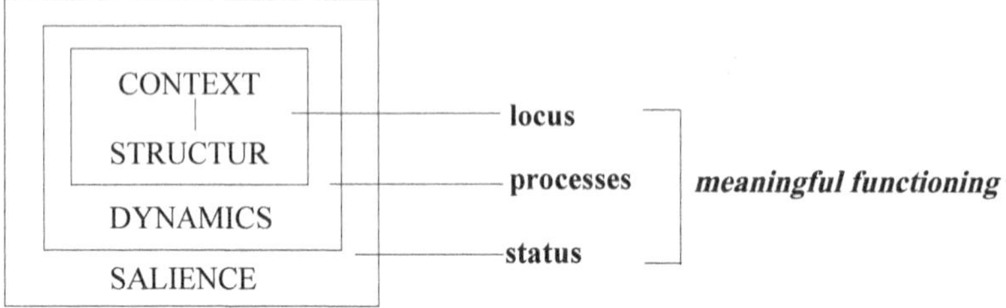

Figure 3-4 The structure of a pragmatic theory

Contextual correlates of adaptability consist of all the ingredients of the communicative context with which linguistic choices have to be interadaptable. Such correlates range from aspects of the physical surroundings to social relationships between speakers and hearers and aspects of the interlocutors' mental states. By including states of mind under the label of context, the theory eliminates the misleading implications of taking context as statically laid out there. Structural objects of adaptability include any layer or level of structure, from sound feature and phoneme to discourse and beyond, or to any type of inter-level relationship. It involves both structure and principles of structuring. The combination of contextual correlates and structural objects of adaptability describes the combination of linguistic and extra-linguistic co-ordinates in the communicative space of a speech event, and thus constitutes the locus of adaptation phenomena. The dynamics of adaptability is the actual processes of (inter) adaptation. All dynamic aspects of language use require processing in a medium of adaptability, i.e. a medium through which people

[12] Verschueren, J. *Understanding pragmatics*. London: Edward Arnold.1999. p.67.

can use language in a variable, negotiable and adaptable fashion. And salience is the general cover term used to designate the status of processes of meaning generation in relation to the medium of adaptability. Linguistic choices are made with different degrees of salience. Some operations are highly conscious, some are not conscious at all, with every shade in between. The idea revealed by the figure sketches out the adaptation process and its characteristics. The four tasks depicted above can be viewed as necessary ingredients of an adequate pragmatic perspective on any given linguistic phenomenon.

All in all, the linguistic adaptation theory helps us understand the motivations and mechanisms behind linguistic choices and capture the effects they have or intended to have in the context of their use. The pragmatic perspective it offers endeavors to answer the question 'what do people do when using language?' It thus provides us with an approach for the study of DE from a functional perspective and enlightens us as to the linguistic devices, the adaptability and the functions of DE.

3.4.2 Spencer-Oatey's theory of rapport management

Spencer-Oatey's theory of rapport management (2008), which develops from Brown and Levinson's politeness theory (1987), examines the way language is used to construct, maintain, neglect and/or threaten social relationships (Spencer-Oatey, 2008:12). Rapport refers to the relative harmony and smoothness of relations between people, and rapport management refers to the management of harmony-disharmony among people.

It is proposed that rapport management entails three main interconnected components: the management of face, the management of sociality rights and obligations, and the management of interactional goals. These three elements are visualized in Figure 3-5, reproduced from Spencer-Oatey[13].

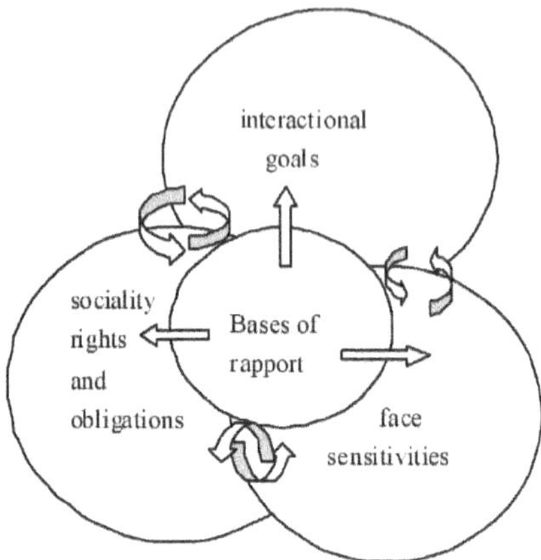

Figure 3-5 The bases of rapport

Face management involves the management of face sensitivities. Spencer-Oatey identifies three types of identity to which face is closely related, namely individual identity, group identity and relational identity. In all these three respects, people have a fundamental desire for others to evaluate them positively, and so they typically want others to acknowledge (explicitly or implicitly) their positive qualities and not to acknowledge their negative qualities. Face management is associated with the management of these affectively sensitive attributes. The management of social rights and obligations, on the other hand, encompasses the management of social expectancies, which is defined as fundamental social entitlements that a person effectively claims for him/herself in his/her interactions with others'. People

[13]Spencer-Oatey, H. *Culturally speaking: culture, communication and politeness theory.* Cornwall: MPG Books Ltd. 2008. p.14.

develop behavior expectations in relation to their perceived sociality rights and obligations, and the failure to fulfill these rights and obligations would affect interpersonal rapport. Bases of perceived sociality rights and obligations include contractual/legal requirements, explicit and implicit conceptualizations of roles and positions, and behavior expectations associated with the conventions, styles and protocols. The third element that contributes to judgements on rapport management is interactional goals. The specific goals of the communicators can significantly impact their perceptions of rapport for the reason that any failure to achieve them can cause frustration and annoyance.

There is a wide range of linguistic options that can be used to manage rapport. Till now, a very large portion of work on rapport management has its focus on the illocutionary domain. The speech act strategies include the selection of speech act components, the degree of directness-indirectness and the type and amount of upgraders/downgraders.

What is of paramount importance is that Spencer-Oatey mentions four general types of rapport orientations, viz. a rapport enhancement orientation, a rapport maintenance orientation, a rapport neglect orientation and a rapport challenge orientation. When the interlocutors hold a rapport enhancement orientation, they want enhancement of the harmony of relationship; when interlocutors hold a rapport maintenance orientation, their desire is to maintain or protect the current quality of relationship; when interlocutors hold a rapport neglect orientation, they lack concern for the quality of the relationship between the other speaker(s) and themselves, perhaps because of a focus on self; when interlocutors hold a rapport challenge orientation, they have a desire to challenge or impair the harmony of the relationship.

Though developed from Brown and Levinson's politeness theory, Spencer-Oatey's rapport management theory is more powerful and comprehensive for the explanation of DE. Firstly, in Brown and Levinson's politeness model, the central notion 'face' consists of two related aspects, namely positive face and negative face. Positive face represents a desire for approval, while negative face represents a desire for freedom or autonomy. However, this conceptualization of face is challenged by other linguists for ignoring on social perspective on face, and its overemphasis on the notion of individual freedom and autonomy, which make it less persuasive in explaining the language phenomena in eastern countries such as China and Japan (Matsumoto, 1988; Ide, 1989; Gu, 1990; Mao, 1994). In contrast, the notion 'face' in Spencer-Oatey theory is applied to a person as an individual and also to the group or community that the person belongs to and /or identifies with. What's more, the management of face sensitivity involves both quality face and identity face. By incorporating both the personal value and the social value into the notion of face, Spencer-Oatey makes her theory sounder than the classical politeness theory. Secondly, the politeness theory is now frequently criticized for its only focus on the negotiation of harmonious relationships between people. However, the rapport management theory takes four rapport orientations into consideration and is thus more inclusive.

To sum up, Spencer-Oatey's theory offers a concept of face and identity which deviates from that in Brown and Levinson's theory. Fortunately, this new perspective on face and identity fits well into the pragmatic explanation in the production process of DE. In addition, the rapport orientations in her theory include not only the negotiation of harmonious relations but also rapport neglect and rapport challenge. This more comprehensive view makes the theory gain advantage in explaining why the interviewee employs DE as a pragmatic strategy to alleviate the communicative problems he encounters in the interview. It can then be incorporated into the Linguistic Adaptation Theory to form a more convincing explanatory framework for the production of DE.

3.4.3 Bucholtz and Hall's Theory of Identity and Interaction

Based on the existing literature in various fields of identity study, Bucholtz and Hall propose a theory of identity and interaction in 2005, which is considered as the best current guideline for the study of identity construction (Locher, 2008). They suggest that the study of identity in interaction should take the following five principles into account: the emergence principle, the positionality principle, the indexicality principle, the relationality principle and the partialness principle.

a. The first principle is the emergence principle:

Identity is best viewed as the emergent product rather than the pre-existing source of linguistic and other semiotic practices and therefore as fundamentally a social and cultural phenomenon.[14]

This principle gives emphasis to the emergent and the relational aspect of identity construction. It enables us to view identity not simply as a psychological mechanism of self-classification that is reflected in people' s social behavior but rather as something that is constituted through social action, especially through language. By explicitly pointing out that identity is a product of interaction, the

[14]Bucholtz, M.& Hall, K. Identity and interaction: A sociocultural linguistic approach. *Discourse Studies*, 7 (4-5), 2005, p.558.

authors subvert essentialist preconception of linguistic ownership, and steer clear of imposing preexisting membership categories as the unique explanatory factors and highlight the social and cultural aspects of identity.

b. The positionality principle is defined as follows:

Identities encompass: ①macro-level demographic categories; ②local, ethnographically specific cultural positions; and ③ temporary and interactionally specific stances and participant roles. (ibid: 592)

This principle faces up to an extensively circulating view of identity, that it is just a collection of broad social categories. It is more effective in capturing the more nuanced and flexible kind of identity relations that arise in local context in interaction. Altogether, it highlights three points: ①it points out that even though being constructed relationally, identity is also the product of a combination of different dimensions including the previously mentioned influence of age, gender, and social class, etc.②the meaning of linguistic strategies for the members of a particular social practice uncovered by ethnographic work can not be discerned. ③the authors contend that at the most basic level, identity emerges in discourse through the temporary roles (e.g. evaluator, joke teller, or engaged listener) assumed by participants in an ongoing interaction. These participant roles, no less than larger sociological and ethnographic identity categories, contribute to identity construction.

c. The third principle is named the indexicality principle:

Identity relations emerge in interaction through several related indexical processes, including: ①overt mention of identity categories and labels; ②implicatures and presuppositions regarding one's own or others' identity position; ③displayed evaluative and epistemic orientations to ongoing talk, as well as interactional footings and participant roles; and ④the use of linguistic structures and systems that are ideologically associated with specific personas and groups. (ibid:594)

This principle, which is known as the indexicality principle, refers to the actual linguistic mechanisms the interactants use in identity construction. Though the most obvious and direct way to construct identities through talk is the explicit introduction of referential identity categories, the identity indexical process is said to occur at all levels of linguistic structure and use, such as implication, stance taking, assessment, style marking and code choice. By considering identity construction at multiple indexical levels, we can accumulate a much richer portrait of subjectivity and intersubjectivity.

d. Building on the emergent, positional and indexical aspects of identity and its production, the fourth principle stresses identity as a relational phenomenon:

Identities are intersubjectively constructed through several, often overlapping, complementary relations, including similarity/difference, genuineness/artifice, and authority/delegitimacy.(ibid:598)

In calling attention to relationality, the authors aim to underscore the point that identities are never autonomous or independent but always acquire social meaning in relation to other available identity positions and other social actors. In addition, the principle works on many different levels. The first relation is found between 'adequation' and 'distinction', which addresses the processes in which similarities with or differences from other perceived groups are constructed. The further pair of relations which are named authentication and denaturalization refer to the processes by which speakers make claims to realness and artifice respectively. Finally, the relation of authorization and illegitimation considers the structural and institutional aspect of identity formation. Authorization addresses the affirmation or imposition of an identity through structures of institutionalized power and ideology, while illegitimation addresses the dismission or ignorance of identities by using these same structures.

e. The final aspect of the identity framework—the partialness principle—states that:

> *Any given construction of identity may be in part deliberate and intentional, in part habitual and hence often less than fully conscious, in part an outcome of interactional negotiation and contestation, in part an outcome of others' perceptions and representations, and in part an effect of larger ideological processes and material structures that may become relevant to interaction. It is thereforc constantly shifting both as interaction unfolds and across discourse contexts.*
>
> *In this principle, the authors point out that identity construction can both be deliberate and habitual. In addition, they stress that since identity is relational, 'it will always be partial, produced through contextually situated and ideologically informed configurations of self and other'.*(ibid:605)

As can be seen from the above brief introduction, identity can be constituted through various indexical processes, in which evaluation is an important resource. In addition, participant's identities are open to constant negotiation in the dynamic process of interaction, rather than predefined. What's more, since 'identity is inherently relational' (ibid:605) it can be seen as the product of the speaker's rapport management (Locher, 2008). It is these insights that make it possible to combine Bucholtz and Hall' s theory of identity construction with the linguistic adaptation theory and the theory of rapport management to offer a better explanation to the production of DE in military interviews.

3.5 The conceptual framework of the present research

The current section elaborates on some key notions and intends to establish a comprehensive framework for the explanation of DE.

3.5.1 DE as a result of making choices

The fundamental postulation of the adaptation theory is that language use consists of the constant making of linguistic choices. Actually, as early as 1975, Giles and Powesland pointed out, 'Linguistic interaction can most fruitfully be viewed as a process of decision-making, in which speakers select from a range of possible expressions. The verbal repertoire then contains all the accepted ways of formulating messages. It provides the weapons of everyday communication. Speakers choose among this arsenal in accordance with the meanings they wish to convey'[15]. This idea is also supported by Sperber and Wilson who contend that, 'to achieve her communicative intention, the communicator has to choose one of a range of different stimuli which would all make her particular informative intention mutually manifest' [16]. DE, as a language phenomenon in real world interaction, is the result of the speaker's linguistic choice making.

In the process of language use, choices may show various degrees of consciousness. Some choices are virtually automatic, while others may be highly motivated. Haverkate (1983) makes

[15] Gile, H & Powesland, P. F. *Speech style and social evaluation*. New York: Academic Press. 1975. pp.114-115.

[16] Sperber, D & Wilson, D. *Relevance: Communication and cognition* (2nd ed.). Oxford: Blackwell Publishing. 1995. p.157.

a distinction between the strategies that are applied almost automatically, which is the case with speech acts that are performed as a form of routine behavior, and strategies that require careful planning by the speaker. Fisher and Adams (1994) suggest that when a person is engaged in an interpersonal situation in which he wants to persuade the other person or to control the other person's response, he will develop strategies with a high degree of awareness. DE in military interviews is a motivated speech act which purposefully exerts an impact on the other participants in the interview or the audience who is watching the program so as to manipulate their belief, attitude, response, etc. Therefore, it is an intentional or deliberate linguistic behavior which is chosen with high degree of consciousness.

As a communicative strategy, the variability of DE is also revealed by the various ways of DE manipulation. Haverkate (1983:640) identifies two types of strategies in linguistic interaction. One is global strategy which is determined by the over-all purpose of the interaction, for instance, different strategies to be involved in social talk, political debates and telling stories. The other is local strategy which depends on the concrete course and evolution of the interaction, as determined by the reactions of the interlocutors to each other's speech act. As a global strategy, DE in military interviews is the optimal choice made by the interviewee in a specific communicative context to achieve his communicative goal(s). However, the choice of a certain global strategy can not guarantee the success of the communicative behavior. To put the global strategy in effect, the speaker has to make choice on the context-sensitive local language options. The choice of local language options comes after the choice of the global strategy. According to the data at hand, we divide the DEs in military interviews into five groups, namely additive DE, substitutive DE, digressive DE, interruptive DE, and competitive DE. Each type is further categorized. These DE manipulations are guided by the interviewee's communicative goals and communicative intentions.

Summing up, DE, as a communicative strategy employed by the interviewee in military interviews, is a result of the interviewee's linguistic-choice making with a high degree of consciousness. Having studied within the framework of adaptation theory, we then encounter with the question, 'what are the contextual correlates that influence the interviewee's choice of DE in the process of language production in a specific context?' To answer this question, we now turn to the next section.

3.5.2 DE as a product of dynamic adaptation to contextual correlates

Accounting for the dynamics of adaptability, or studying the actual processes of inter(adaptation), taking into account the full power of variability and negotiability is the central task of specific pragmatic investigation. What pragmatics adds to the traditional linguistic study is the specifically dynamic perspective on the interadaptability of context and structure in actual language use (Verschueren, 1999:147).

In military interviews, the interviewee's choice of DE as a communicative strategy involves the dynamic linguistic adaptation to various contextual correlates. The concept 'context of situation' is formulated by Malinowski (1923), who contends that the utterance only has meaning when it is in the context of situation. Besides linguistic context, Malinowski advocates that context should also comprise larger socio-cultural framework within which discourse is embedded and the momentary situation in which an utterance is spoken. Postulated on Malinowski's view on context,

Verschueren (1999) explores into both the linguistic context and communicative context. Our research on DE puts emphasis on the momentary situation in which DE is utilized, that is to say, we mainly address the communicative context of DE.

In the figure of contextual correlates of adaptability depicted by Verschueren(ibid), utterer and interpreter are the focus points because the contextual aspects of the physical, social, and mental worlds do not usually start to play a role in language use until they have somehow been activated by the language user's cognitive processes. In principle, every aspect of context within the lines of vision can function as a correlate of adaptability. However, not all possible ingredients of a speech act are relevantly mobilized on every occasion. The participants in communication need to reduce the information in a context in terms of a few schematically organized processing in working memory (van Dijk, 2008). In military interviews, the interviewee's social world and mental world play a crucial role in the strategic use of DE, and we will gather the major contextual factors accordingly. This doesn't mean that we treat context as something that is stable and static and all the factors identified are relevant to the production of DE at all times. Instead, we hold the view that contexts are generated in language use and it is chosen rather than given. Since one fundamental idea is that language use is a dynamic process full of negotiation, the context is considered dynamic.

In the social world, most of the social factors that linguistic choices are interadaptable with are related to the properties of social setting or institutions. In the present research, the setting in which DE takes place is military interview. One of the distinguishing characteristics of the communication in this institution is that the interviewees are certified experts in military fields, ranging from professors in the University of National Defense, generals or researchers from Chinese Academy of Military science, chief editors of famous military magazines, to commanders of a certain military branch. Hence, the speaker's identity is the major contextual correlate that the interviewee should take into consideration when employing DE. In addition, since the topics under discussion are international or domestic military events which are newsworthy, the evaluations given by the interviewee on the persons, events or things associated with these topics are sometimes the view points given from the vantage point of the group where the interviewee comes from. Therefore, contextual factors such as group interest, public understanding etc. should also be examined.

Since verbal interaction is communication from mind to mind, we have no reason to neglect the mental world. According to Verschueren, the mental world includes elements such as the speaker's personality, emotion, belief, desires, motivations and intentions. What's more, it is said that any systematic attempt to take mental states into account will have to allow for a variety of interacting mental phenomena to move in and out of focus in a mental space that is perpetually in motion (Vershueren, 1999:88-90). Personal states of mind can be shown to develop through out an interaction. In the present study, the addressee's communicative needs and emotions such as indignation, admiration and national pride are the most essential correlates that DE in military interviews interadapts with in the mental world. Since these are ingredients of a speech event which are in constant flux, the process of the adaptation is a dynamic one.

Nevertheless, the adaption to the social world and the mental world can not be separated (吴亚欣, 2004) and the choice of DE is the outcome of the interaction between social and psychological factors. Hence, instead of simply categorizing the contextual correlates into those of social world and mental world, we need to find a more detailed and empirically warranted way to establish the kind of categories that make up the context in which DEs take place. Earlier studies on context categories reveal that speakers and interpreters are the focal point around which a specific context is built, and the contextual correlates, which impact and are impacted by linguistic choices have close link with the properties of speakers and interpreters (Firth, 1930; Hymes, 1972; Biber, 1988; Verschueren, 1999; van Dijk, 2008). As for the choice of DE in military interviews, apart from the speaker and the interpreters, the group with which the speaker is associated is another essential constituent of the context. Based on the above considerations, with the determination to present a systematic and lucid analysis, we divide the contextual correlates which interadapt with the linguistic choice of DE into three groups: self-oriented adaptation, other-oriented adaptation and group-oriented adaptation. As far as self-oriented adaptation is concerned, the contextual correlates such as the speaker's identity (e.g. professional identity, national identity), power (e.g. expertise-based power, experience-based power), and the speaker's face are considered to be the constraints that prominently motivate the employment of DE in military interviews. Contextual ingredients related to other-oriented adaptation are other-face, cognitive needs and emotions. Contextual variables linked to group-oriented adaptation involves group face, group interest, international relationship, and public understanding.

In a word, DE in military interviews is the result of the interviewee's dynamic adaptation with various contextual correlates. The study of a pragmatic phenomenon ought to focus straightforwardly on the functioning of language in actual contexts of use (Verschueren, 1999:10), and the study of DE from a pragmatic perspective is no exception. Therefore, the question arises that 'What are the pragmatic functions of DE in military interviews? What is the mechanism hidden behind the production of DE?'

3.5.3. DE as a strategy to achieve communicative functions

DE in military interviews, as was defined in the beginning of this chapter, is a communicative strategy employed by the interviewee to achieve certain communicative goal(s). Therefore, the reason why the interviewee chooses DE as a communicative strategy at the cost of flouting the conversational principle or infringing the turn-taking system of news interviews is that DE in a specific communicative context can realize the pragmatic functions that the interviewee craves for to meet his communicative need.

The present study of DE focuses straightforwardly on the functioning of language in actual context of use, since the analysis of language use cannot be independent of the analysis of the purposes and functions of language in human life (Schiffrin, 1994). The functional analyses of discourse, as pointed out by Schiffrin(ibid), have two directions. One is an etic direction which delimits the functions served by a system (such as language or communication) and match particular units (such as utterance or action) to those functions. The other is an emic one which begins with the observation of the language data, and then the inference from analysis of the data and its context what functions are being served. The functional analysis of DE in military interviews in the current research takes the second direction since the choice of DE in a communicative context is highly negotiable and thus doesn't presume static form-function relationships.

The interactional goal of the speaker's negotiable linguistic choices of DE from a range of various types by adapting to a range of contextual correlates is to realize the pragmatic functions that approach points of satisfaction for the speaker's communicative needs in a specific communicative context. Communicative needs are fractionized by (Chen, 1999) into several types, viz. essential needs, contextual needs, expressive needs, and phatic needs. However, the data in the current research are from military interviews, and belong to institutional talk, while Chen's research is targeted at the data in ordinary conversations. The specialty of military interviews therefore breeds different communicative needs. In this institutional talk, the interviewee uses evaluation intentionally so as to satisfy his own communicative needs, to maintain relationship with the addressees and to vindicate the interest of the group he identifies with. The communicative goals thus are directed at the interviewee himself, the addressees or the group. Accordingly, we identify three types of communicative needs, namely self-oriented communicative needs, other-oriented communicative needs and group-oriented communicative needs. The functions which satisfy self-oriented needs are dubbed as self-oriented functions. According to the data at hand, this categorization of functions includes protecting the self and reinforcing persuasiveness. The communicative functions which gratify the other-oriented communicative needs and thus exert impact on interpersonal relationship are labeled interpersonal-oriented functions. Three categories of sub-functions are differentiated, namely maintaining interpersonal relationship, altruistic functions, and decreasing psychological distance. Lastly, the group-oriented functions, which are in favor of the group which the interviewee belongs to and meet the group-oriented communicative needs, consist of constructing positive group images, implementing refutations, clarifying the truth, and manipulating the audience.

The pragmatic mechanism lying behind the production of DE in military interviews is the speaker's management of rapport so as to construct a positive self. The data collected till now unearth four kinds of rapport orientations, namely rapport neglect orientation, rapport maintenance orientation, rapport enhancement orientation, and rapport challenge orientation. When the evaluator is more concerned about his own communicative needs, he neglects the quality of relationship between the other participants and himself and thus holds a rapport neglect orientation. When the language user proffers DEs to attenuate the negative effect that his point of view may bring about, he is orienting to maintaining a harmonious interpersonal relationship with the utterance interpreters. When DE is motivated by offering benefit to the addressees or narrowing down the psychological gap between himself and the interlocutors, a rapport enhancement orientation is obtained. When DE is used as a tool to counter attack previous offence, a rapport challenge orientation occurs. A thread that runs through all of these rapport concerns is the issue of the evaluator's identity construction.

In a nutshell, DE is performed by the interviewee to adapt to his communicative needs which are satisfied by the various pragmatic functions realized by it. When realizing various pragmatic functions, the evaluator holds different rapport orientations so as to construct a positive self in the ongoing conversation. The functions of DE, as well as the hidden mechanism of the production of DE will be detailed in Chapter 6.

3.6 Summary

This chapter is dedicated to set up a coherent conceptual framework for the explanation of DE in military interviews. In order to clarify our research object, we first offer a working definition of DE and list its defining features, namely, subjectivity, value-ladenness, intentionality and optionality. We then demarcate DE with stancetaking and overinformativeness. In the last section of this chapter, we present a conceptual framework for the explanation of the production of DE. The conceptual framework is presented in the ensuing flowchart.

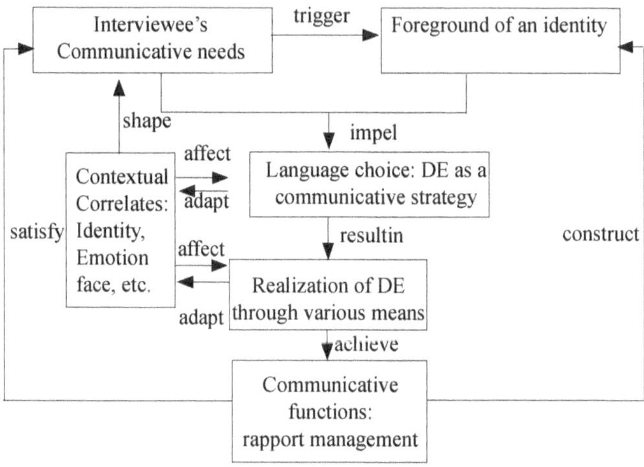

Figure 3-6 The conceptual framework for the explanation of DE

As indicated in the figure, the interviewee's communicative needs trigger the foreground of one of his identities, and the two jointly impel him to opt for DE as a pragmatic strategy. After such a choice is made, the interviewee's next step is to pick out a specific type of DE from a range of possibilities by adapting to the contextual correlates in a negotiable manner. When using DE, the interviewee manipulates various rapport orientations and thus realizes an array of functions. The realization of functions satisfies the interviewee's communicative needs and helps the interviewee to construct a positive identity in the specific institutional setting of military interviews.

Chapter 4
A Classification of DEs in Military Interviews

4.1 Introduction

The purpose of this chapter is to present the full range of DE types found in the data. According to Verschueren (1999), the making of linguistic choices occurs at various levels. This is certainly the case with the use of evaluation in verbal communication. Therefore, the variability of DE can be manifested in various facets. Structurally, it can be realized either explicitly by evaluative terms, statements with deontic modalities, statements with affective mental process verbs, or implicitly by value assumptions (Fairclough, 2003; Martin & White, 2005). Semantically, it can be divided into affection, judgement, and appreciation (Martin & White, 2005). It can also be used along the scale of intensity, ranging from attenuated evaluation, bare evaluation, to boosted evaluation.

Unlike the earlier studies on evaluation,which neglect the language user's intention in using evaluation, DE is considered in the present study as a communicative strategy which is deployed by the speaker intentionally to meet his communicative goal(s). As defined in Chapter 3, DE is featured by subjectivity, value-ladenness, intentionality, and optionality. What makes DE different from non-motivated evaluation is that it is an intentional violation of communicative norms. Therefore, its deliberateness is characterized by its incongruence with the ongoing talk, which might involve incoherence across speaker turns, recurring interruptions, semantic redundancy, sequential disruption, or illogicality (Fairclough, 1989; Thornborrow, 2002). A careful examination of the data at hand reveals two ways in which the deliberateness of evaluation is manifested: ① deliberate deviation from the interviewer's question; ② deliberate deviation from the turn-allocation system in military interviews. Based on various forms of deviation, the DEs are divided into five large groups, namely additive DE, substitutive DE, digressive DE, interruptive DE and competitive DE. Each group is further subcategorized. Paralinguistic channels such as intonation contours, gestures, gaze, etc., though important in conveying the speaker's evaluative attitude, as we have mentioned in Chapter 3, are beyond the scope of the present study because of the limited length of the dissertation.

4.2 Additive DE

Additive DE is the evaluation which is deliberately employed by the interviewee in addition to his required answer to the interviewer's question. The use of additive DE breaches the maxim of quantity in Grice's co-operative principle (1989) which says 'do not make your contribution more informative than is required'. It may also violate the maxim of relevance, if the topic of the additive DE deviates from the topic put forward by the interviewer. The additive DEs are often tacked on after the expected answer offered by the interviewee, though they may also appear in the beginning of the turn. Based on the relation of DE to the information requirement of the interviewer's question, the additive DEs in the data are further categorized into four groups.

4.2.1 Reparative DE

Reparative DE is used by the interviewee when his opinion does not conform to that of the addressees', or when he anticipates that his words may induce potential disagreement, objection or attack from the audience. Semantically, it is incongruent or contradictory with the aforementioned evaluation offered by the interviewer, or it is not consistent with the addressees' expectation. In specific contexts, reparative DE changes the addressee's existing or possible opinions, and reduces the negative effects that the interviewee's words may bring on the addressees. In other words, it repairs the inappropriateness or negative effect of a previous evaluation actually made or potentially derivable. The following example is a case of the former one, where the interviewee uses reparative DE to redress the interviewer's opinion on developing the technology of weapons.

Example(10)
Situation: The interviewee, Duo Yingxian, is the designer of the Chinese 5.8mm caliber assault rifle.

主持人：您是科学家，(GLOTTAL) 科学应该是造福人类，带来和平，(TSK) 更好地生活，而枪支表面上看它是一种暴力手段，@@@ 您在这几十年做这项工作的时候需要去平衡这之间的某种矛盾吗？

嘉　宾：……

主持人：像诺贝尔发明了炸弹，他 ^ 本来是想改善人们的生活，当他发现被用做武器的时候，他觉得跟他的初衷是 ^ 相悖的？

嘉　宾：是。<u>这个诺贝尔 = 诺贝尔的东西呢是我们生活里的潘多拉盒子一样，就是你看你 = 为善还是为恶，技术本</u>

身是双刃剑，它始终是这样的，任何技术都可以转化到军备上去，你要想杀人，手段多的是，(TSK) 这个东西跟我们的工作我觉得ˆ无关。

《新闻会客厅：95 枪族设计师解密新型武器》

The interviewer assumes that science should bring peace to human beings, however, guns and bombs are weapons which are used in wars or violent cases. This negative view on guns certainly threatens the positive identity of the interviewee, who is a professional weapon inventor. The interviewer asks the interviewee a Yes/No question whether it is contrary to Nobel's expectation when he finds that bombs are used as weapon. A simple 'yes' would have satisfied the interviewer's query, and the following utterance would be expected to provide a further explanation. However, the interviewee continues to evaluate technology indirectly after he answers with a 'yes'. And the extra evaluation, which tries to repair the interviewer's negative view on weapons, is semantically unmotivated by the interviewer's question and is illogically connected with his own current utterance. This reveals the deliberateness of the evaluation. Moreover, no explicit attitudinal lexemes are deployed in the evaluation, but technology is compared to Pandora's box and a double-edged sword. In this way, the interviewee provokes the reappraisal of technology in analogy with Pandora's box and a double-edged sword. The analogy of the technology of weapons with these two concrete things provokes the appraisal that technology can do both good and bad to human beings, but the inventors are not to be blamed. Therefore, by adopting the reparative DE, the interviewee redresses the interviewer's opinion which may pose damage to his public image, and prevents the audience from forming a negative impression of the researches in developing the technologies of weapons. In a word, from the discussion we can infer that the evaluation used in the example is a reparative DE.

Apart from rectifying existing opinions, reparative DE is also used when the interviewee foresees the possible negative impact that his words may exert on the addressees. Here is an example:

Example(11)

Situation: The interviewee is a professor from the University of National Defense. Xu Sanduo is the protagonist in the hot TV series entitled 'Soldiers, Charge'. In the story, Xu Sanduo grows out of an ugly stupid clumsy rural boy into a No.1 soldier through his persistence.

主持人: 你 <RH> 喜不喜欢 </RH> 许三多这个人?

嘉　宾: 许三多这个人, 从 @@, 如果说从 <@ 这个 @> 完整角度来说的话呢, 应该说是 ... 要我说, 不是 ^ 太喜欢他的这种 = 类型的人, <u>但是他的这个精神我还是很佩服的</u>。

《防务新观察: 未来士兵拿什么突击》

In this example, when the interviewer raises a question whether the interviewee likes Xu Sanduo, the interviewee favors a negative assessment. As we know, Xu Sanduo, the protagonist in the best-selling TV series entitled 'Soldiers, Charge' in China in 2007, is considered to be an excellent model of modern soldiers and is admired by the majority of audience throughout China. Therefore, when the interviewee gives the negative assessment on Xu Sanduo, he prefaces his assessment with laugh, pause, and also the repeated use of hesitation markers such as 'yinggai shuo shi' (It should be said that), 'yao wo shuo' (I should say) etc. This shows that the interviewee anticipates that his negative assessment on Xu Sanduo may arouse objections or disagreements in the audience. Under this situation, the interviewee resorts to a reparative DE after he offers a negative comment on Xu Sanduo. The reparative DE is introduced by a topic orientation marker 'danshi' (but), which signals the inconsistency between the DE and the preceding evaluation. What's more, the DE employed here is semantically irrelevant with what has been required by the interviewer. By adding the extra positive evaluation that 'danshi tade zhege jingshen wo haishi hen peifu de' (but anyway, I still admire his spirit), the interviewee intends to forestall the possible negative impact which his previous negative evaluation would have on the viewing audience.

4.2.2 Elaborative DE

Elaborative DEs are extra evaluations which are deliberately offered by the interviewee to elaborate either on a topic[17] irrelevant to what the interviewer has questioned, or on a topic which although is mentioned in the interviewer's question, is not at all the focus of it. The topic of the DEs of this type is elicited by and wholly dependent on the speaker's preceding utterances and the full interpretation of them depends on the specific context of the interaction. The following example illustrates the case when the interviewee does not only talk about one topic but intends to deliberately shift the topic of the conversation to evaluate on a new one.

[17]There is no acceptable formal definition for the concept of topic. Some borrow it from the strictly linguistic work of the Prague school (Keenan & Schifflein, 1976). Some view it as socially constructed (Dascal, 2003). For the purpose of the present analysis, we agree with Fraser (2009) that topic is what the discourse is currently about, what the participants recognize they are talking about from what has been contributed to this point.

Example (2)

Situation: On September 3, 2007, the US claims that it is the Chinese People's Liberation Army who hacked into the Pentagon net work.

主持人：难在哪儿呢？怎么就找不出是谁干的呢？

嘉　宾：一个是像我们刚才讨论的，(TSK) 他借助第三方进行攻击，偷你的车坐你的车去作案，这是一种办法。(TSK) 还有呢就是利用网络上的一些后门，现在黑客软件非常的普及，很多小孩在家里没事捉摸捉摸，他下载那个程序以后就能够上去以后搞黑客，然后大家集中向你那扔一炸弹，堵塞你的流量，让你的宽带慢慢变窄，变窄以后让你死掉，但是那个很快就恢复了，造不成很大的影响。现在呢，黑客已经进入了非常专业化的程序了，专门的黑客程序进入你的银行账户，(TSK) 要盗取你的金钱。另外呢，也有一些进入^军队的一些网络系统中窃取一些军事机密。美国还成立了网络战这样的专门部队，使用^网络作为一种专门的武器去进攻对方。... (GLOTTAL) 啊，这个呢 <MRC> 美国做得最好 </MRC>。 ((点头))

《防务新观察：谁动了五角大楼的网络神经》

In this excerpt, what the interviewer's question queries about is the difficulty in finding out the hacker. The interviewee first orients to the question, offering various methods that hackers may use to avoid being traced when attacking other computers. However, he gradually departs from the topic domain set by the interviewer's question, and moves beyond it to evaluate America, which is not mentioned at all by the interviewer. The use of the evaluation is semantically unmotivated, and is deviant from natural course of action, for he is expected to offer various means of hacking and put emphasis on the concealment of each means. What's more, the deliberate assessment on America here is illogically related to the ongoing utterances and its interpretation is contextually dependent. The seemingly positive evaluation on American specialized military network unit in fact conveys a negative implication here. The interpretation of the DE 'Ah,zhegene meiguo zuode zuihao'(ah, Ameircan does best in this aspect) involves an interaction between linguistic structure and non-linguistic information. 'ah' (ah) is an attention marker, which betrays the interviewee's deliberateness of the use of the ensuing evaluation and functions to draw the audience's attention to it. The deixis 'zhege' (this) is an anaphora which refers to 'shiyong wangluo zuowei yizhong zhuanmen wuqi qu gongji duifang' (using internet as a specialized weapon to attack other countries). The background information of this interaction is that On September 3, 2007, the US publically claimed that it was the Chinese People's Liberation Army who hacked into the Pentagon net work, which incurred international accusation of Chinese illegal hacking. The accusation is totally unfounded and groundless for the American government did not provide any evidence and did not ask for assistance from Chinese police. In this context, it can be inferred that what the interviewee means by the seemly positive DE is 'how ridiculous it is for America, who is quite good at using internet as a specialized weapon to attack other countries, to accuse China of hacking into its Pentagon network!' From the preceding analysis, it can be seen that an elaborative DE is adopted by the interviewee in the interaction.

Sometimes, in order to approach his communicative needs, the interviewee may evaluate a topic which is mentioned by the preceding turn, but not its topical focus after he has offered the required answer. Let's consider the following example:

Example(12)

Situation: An American military research institute released a report on the positions of American nuclear power in 2009. It is said that the American nuclear powered submarines are targeting at China, South Korea and Russia.

主持人: <H> 这份报告中, 特别点了三个国家的名字, 我想对于这些被点名的国家, 究竟该如何面对这样的一份报告?

嘉　宾: 我们现在说, 这份报告它还 ^ 不是一份官方的文件, 它仍然可以定义为一个民间的智囊机构, 对美国政府下一次在修改他的核政策的时候提供了一个咨询。<H> 那么在这种情况下, 我认为就是说你其他的回应不是就现在马上就 ^ 强硬地要做出。<u>但是他这个潜在的影响和后果他是很大的。因为我们知道呢, <H> 它本身这样一种 = 我认为 <MRC> 以美国为主, 而也以美国的视野</MRC>来评判全球的力量,有点指手画脚的感觉, 所以 ^ 我觉得它会对目前这个核武器的扩散会造成 ^ 一定的负面影响。</u>

《防务新观察: 美核报告威慑亚太》

In this example, the interviewer asks the interviewee how the listed countries, viz. China, South Korea and Russia, should react to such a report. The interviewee, a professor from the University of National Defense, explicitly expresses his position toward the question. That is to say, he fulfills what has been requested. However, he continues his turn by shifting the topic set by the interviewer to further elaborate on the report itself, which is signaled by the topic orientation marker[18] 'danshi' (but). The topic of the DE is mentioned by the interviewer. However it is not at all the focus of what she is questioning. The interviewee intentionally assesses the report as judging the global power from an American perspective, which implicates that the result of the report, which is exploited by America as the pretext to station nuclear powered submarines, is indiscreet and incredible. The assessment that the report will bring negative effect on the diffusion of nuclear weapon is to insinuate that America's station of powered submarines is actually a diffusion of nuclear weapon which threatens the security of other countries. What the American report claims does exert negative influence on China's image. Therefore, the interviewee intentionally makes use of what has been under discussion to satisfy his communicative need of counterattacking America.

4.2.3 Comparative DE

Comparability is one of the typical characteristic of evaluation (Thompson & Huston, 2000). By putting the evaluated against the background of another event or object, the evaluator highlights the value of the evaluated and thus upgrades the illocutionary force of the evaluation. Comparative DEs are often deliberately made in the disguise of another non-DE. They are semantically irrelevant to the interviewer's question. Sometimes, in order to cater to his communicative needs, the interviewee may deliberately introduce a new object of evaluation by comparison. This is what the interviewee, an expert and General from the University of National

[18]Topic orientation markers constitute a type of discourse management markers which signal a meta-comment on the structure of the emerging discourse. They display four uses in a discourse, namely return to a prior topic, continuation with the present topic, digression from the present topic, and an introduction to a new topic (Fraser, 2009).

Defense does in the following example:

Example(13)

Situation: The topic of the interview is the asymmetrical war between Israel and Gaza.

主持人: ^具体来说，成功在什么地方?

嘉　宾: 从军事角度上来讲呢，怎么评价以色列打的这场战争，<A> 咱们抛开人道主义危机不讲 </A>，以色列这场仗打的 = 和美国在伊拉克打的相比，那美国是以色列的学生。我体会到呢一个是战争发起时机，这个运用得 ^ 非常好，利用了以色列的大选，以色列大选之前 = 美国总统交接班阶段，然后又是安息日，你看战争发起时间非常好。第二个呢就是空袭选择的时间 ...

《防务新观察：透视非对称战争（上）》

When the interviewer asks in which aspect should we say Israel gains success in the war, the interviewee begins his turn as if he is going to give an assessment on Israel. However, he does not assess Israel directly but introduces America as the object of his evaluation, which is totally irrelevant to the interviewer's question. Generally speaking, when evaluating a war in the modern time, humanitarianism is one of the essential dimensions. Any war that neglects it would be strongly criticized by the international community. Strangely, the interviewee consciously abandons this dimension when he evaluates. Additionally, there is good reason to directly evaluate the war launched by Israel as successful, without bothering to compare it to America, which would definitely cost less cognitive effort for the addressees to interpret. Therefore, the DE employed here manifests irrelevance and illogicality.

Both characterize the underlined evaluation as deliberate. During the process of evaluating, the interviewee evaluates America as the student of Israel, which is intentionally disguised in the superficial evaluation to Israel. Though the word student is not clearly evaluative, it can not be understood as value-free or purely descriptive in the present context. According to Thompson and Hunston (2000), the word student can have either a positive connotation (associated, perhaps, with a reforming, courageous intelligentsia) or a negative one (associated with laziness, unkempt appearance, and heavy drinking habits) depending on the specific context in which it is used. As far as this conversation is concerned, student has a negative connotation of being inferior in combating capability and strategies. Therefore, by introducing America as the object of the evaluation by the use of comparison, the interviewee strategically shows his contempt for America and his condemnation toward the Iraq war.

4.2.4 Conclusive DE

Conclusive DEs are the evaluations intentionally added by the interviewee at the end of his turn. They function to put the previous evaluation in a more comprehensible light. When there are various claims advanced in the turn, the conclusive DE synthesizes the different ideas into a condensed and unified form; when there is only one idea put forward, the conclusive DE is a simple reiteration of the central point with the function to ensure the audience's understanding. The employment of conclusive DE reminds the audience of the interviewee's position on a certain topic and helps to solidify their recognition of the message. Conclusive DEs are usually given in a rather simple sentence structure but convey a clear and concise evaluative stance. Moreover, the DEs of this type usually convey a sense of completeness and finality by using transition phrases such 'zongzhi' (in summary), 'zheyang kanlai'(It can be concluded that), 'yinggai shuo/keyi shuo' (It should be said that), 'suoyi' (so), etc. When there are no explicit discourse markers signaling the finality, they can be identified by the feature of redundancy or its logical relation with the interviewee's hitherto speech. The following extract illustrates the use of a DE of this category.

Example(14)
Situation: A British and a French submarine, both of which nuclear-powered and carrying nuclear weapons, collided in the Atlantic Ocean on February 16, 2009. Both countries remain silent on the accident for a few days.

主持人：那您觉得不是这个原因？
嘉　宾：对。我觉得呢，这个可能是一方面的原因。还有一个呢，你比如说，英国和法国，在水下能够攻击他们这种潜艇的 ^ 只有俄罗斯，那么他的这个声学数据库里边的敌方的音响特征并不是对方的，而更多储存的是俄罗斯潜艇的这个噪音特征，^ 一旦发现了，它有时会自动报警提示你。(H) 俄罗斯这个潜艇有它的特点，因为它是双轴双桨，它听起来是比较有连续性的。(H) 而比如像这次的"前卫"或者"凯旋"或者美国的一些艇，它是单轴单桨，而且它是喷式的，就是它的声音肯定有另外一种特征。(H) 当然，我要防范你的时候，我肯定注意听你的声音，而我友方的声音我可能忽略过去，或者我的声呐兵没有认真值班,等等等等,这些都有可能。总之，<L> 他们现在公布的这种可能 </L>，说是因为超静音，是他们双方能承担责任 ^ 最小的一种可能。

《防务新观察：核艇相撞，北大西洋起波澜》

In this excerpt, the interviewer asks the interviewee whether he does not believe in the reason provided by the press which announced that it was the undetectablility of the two submarines due to their super-mute system that incurred the collision. The interviewee begins his turn with a confirmation and goes on to offer various possible whys and wherefores of the collision of the two submarines. At the end of his turn, the interviewee adds a conclusive DE which synthesizes the diversified guesses into one clear evaluative stance, viz. the reason of super-mute system announced by the governments of Britain and France can reduce their respective responsibilities to the minimum degree. The employment of the conclusive DE in this interaction helps the audience in catching the interviewee's clear stance toward the issue under discussion.

4.3 Substitutive DE

It is an incontestable norm in news interviews that the interviewee should provide proper information or opinions according to what the interviewer requires. However, a close examination of their answers reveals that the interviewee does not always conform to this norm. When he finds himself facing a rather tough question, or when he thinks the question is inappropriately raised, he may exploit substitutive DEs to cope with these difficulties. Substitutive DE refers to the DE which deviates from the evaluation requested by the interviewer's question. Two subtypes are further identified, viz. evasive DE and negotiative DE.

4.3.1 Evasive DE

The evaluation which is deliberately deployed by the interviewee to evade the question raised by the interviewer is called evasive DE. Heritage (2002) contends that the interviewer's question sets agendas for the interviewee's answer by identifying a specific topical domain as the appropriate or relevant domain of response, an action that should be performed by the interviewee in relation to the topical domain, and the range of the interviewee's response. The data at hand evidences that evasive DE is most often used by the interviewee to shift the action domain. The following example illustrates how the DE is intentionally utilized to evade the question by moving beyond the action agenda set by the question.

Example(15)

Situation: The interviewee is a professor from the University of National Defense. Xu Sanduo is the protagonist in the hot TV series entitled 'Soldiers, Charge'. In the story, Xu Sanduo grows out of an ugly stupid clumsy rural boy into a No.1 soldier through his persistence.

主持人: ^喜不喜欢 ' 许三多这个人, 作为一个 .. ^军人?

嘉　宾: .. (TSK) (H) 嗯, 怎么说呢? 因为毕竟是连续剧, <u>他 ^不是一个真人, 他是一个很多军队, 很多士兵或者说很多生活的一个集合, ^应该说是 = 反映了部队的一定的真实, 但是也可能和部队的实际还有 ^很大的差别。</u>

主持人: 你 <RH> 喜不喜欢 </RH> 许三多这个人?

《防务新观察: 未来士兵拿什么突击》

In example(15), the interviewer asks the interviewee whether he likes Xu Sanduo, the protagonist in a hot TV series entitled 'Soldiers, Charge'. The interviewee begins his turn with a hesitator marker 'zenme shuo ne' (how to say), which betrays that he has realized the question raised by the interviewer. However, he does not respond in accordance with the action agenda that the question calls for — a yes/no response on whether he likes Xu Sanduo. Instead, he works around the issue in terms of evaluating Xu SanduoHu, a person mentioned in the previous turn. An answer like this certainly cannot meet the interviewer's expectation. The deliberateness of the evaluation is reflected by its semantic irrelevance to the interviewer's question. The employment of this DE tactically shifts the focus of the question and makes his answer seem co-operating although his strategy is discovered by the interviewer, who renews the question in a most pointed way.

4.3.2 Negotiative DE

As mentioned in Chapter 1, the interviewee, as an expert in military field, has the qualifications to negotiate with the host of the interview who has less expertise-based power. That is to say, when the interviewer asks a question, the interviewee may quite often ponder whether the question is raised appropriately or whether it is right to the point. If not, then the interviewee would try to adjust the question. Negotiative DE is one of the strategies that the interviewee employs to adjust the question and veer the answer toward the direction which he thinks can better achieve his communicative goals. The ensuing example instantiates a situation in which negotiative DE is utilized:

Example(16)

Situation: Soldiers in the Chinese People's Liberation Army (PLA) take part in a military exercise code-named

'Warrior 2008' in the Inner Mongolia Autonomous Region on September 25, 2008. The exercise is held at Zhu Rihe tactical training base where 5 211 officers and soldiers from Beijing and Jinan Military Commands as well as the Air Force of the PLA conducted counterwork without designated plans.

主持人：让我问杜研究员一个更直接的问题。目前我们的这种训练方法 ^ 能保证我们打赢未来的战争吗？

嘉　宾：通过刚才司令，部长，还有红蓝双方的介绍呢，我感到有一个转变 ^ 非常令我欣慰。就是现在的训练观念确实变了。因为从以前看，输赢胜负好像是一个核心指标，但是现在不一样了，现在输赢胜负这个结果已经 ^ 不能够把整个演习的结果来进行诠释了。现在的状况是怎么样呢，刚刚通过两位的介绍，我总结了两句话，现在是少讲成绩多讲问题，少讲结论多讲过程。为什么呀？他是想在这个过程中让参训者去 <MRC> 暴露问题，去发现问题，去解决问题 </MRC>。这是一个良性的循环。在这个良性的循环中，我们的战斗力就会 ^ 全方位地提高。

《防务新观察：走进励兵 2008》

The military exercise 'Warrior 2008' is a live ammunition exercise which showcases how China's mechanized troops enhance their combating capacity under simulated conditions of information and electronic warfare. What is worth mentioning here is that this military exercise has a fundamental difference with the afore held ones in that there is neither rehearsal nor prepared plan this time and both the red army and the blue army are allowed to freely deploy their defense and offence according to the ongoing situation. This is what the interviewer's 'zhezhong xunlian fangfa' (this training method) refer to in her question. The current question posed by the interviewer, which queries whether the training method adopted in this exercise would ensure the success of the future war, is perceived by the interviewee as inappropriate. The interviewee's intention to negotiate with the interviewer is revealed by the italicized utterances, which says that 'defeat or victory now is not the kernel to interpreting the result of the overall military exercise'. The ensuing utterances focus on the evaluation of the new concept of military training. The negotiative DE that the new concept of military training is a virtuous circle which will improve the combat effectiveness adjusts the evaluation requested by the interviewer and guides the audience to see the new method of military training from a right perspective.

4.4 Digressive DE

Digressive DEs are those evaluations which interrupt the ongoing conversation on topic t_1, and turn to appraise t_2, after having finished appraising t_2, the evaluator returns to the original topic t_1. The topic of a digressive evaluation t_2 may figure in the previous utterance, but is remote from its main purport. Hence, even though deviating from the current topic, there is nevertheless some kind of content relation between the mainstream utterance and the digressive DE. A close look at the data at hand reveals three subcategories of this type of DEs, viz. background-providing DE, supportive DE, and highlighting DE, each of which will be demonstrated in the following sub-sections.

4.4.1 Background-providing DE

Background-providing DE is one type of DE by which the interviewee proffers the contextual information related to what is under discussion so as to facilitate the audience's inferential process or to avoid further questioning. In other words, the DEs of this type digress to pave the way for the addressees' comprehension of the overall discourse given by the interviewee. The deliberateness of these DEs is signaled by their topical irrelevance, sequential disruption, and semantic redundancy. As is known to us all, discussions in military interviews are concerned with international issues, modern technologies of weapons, combat strategies etc., the understanding of which requires specific knowledge in these fields. Therefore, the interviewee must make correct assumptions about the audience's cognitive state and the contextual information that they would be likely to use in the comprehension process. example (17) is a case in point.

Example(17)
Situation: It is said that one tenth of the lecommunication in the world is monitored by America. One of the ssential ways to intercept message is to make use of deep-sea cables.

主持人:“吉米卡特号”究竟是^怎么来实现它的窃听的?
嘉　宾:“吉米卡特号”在水下的窃听呢,(TSK)因为现在美国人对整个艇的设计,特别对多重任务舱的行动方式或者使用方法守口如瓶。(TSK)我们从现在拿到的资料可以=这样进行推测。第一步首先国安局和海军要确定到底哪一条光缆有可能有'重要情报传输。
主持人:确定了之后呢?
嘉　宾:按美国人的说法,他会把海缆吸入小艇,在小艇的空间后排水,排水以后他有一种特殊的手段把光缆切开。<u>这个切开的技术含量是很高的,既不能影响你的通讯信号,还要把信号拿出来。</u>然后通过电缆再传到母艇上，<A> 因为母艇的多型任务舱有一个巨型计算机 </A>，通过计算机来进行分析，研究它所需要的情报，这样就完成了整个一个窃听过程。

《防务新观察：深海谍影——越洋光缆话安全》

In this interaction, the interviewer poses a question on how Jimmy Carter, an advanced American offensive submarine of Seawolf class, does wire tapping. The interviewee copes with the interviewer and offers a rather brief guess about the whole procedure of the wire tapping. During his description of Jimmy Carter's work on message inception, he digresses from the current speech to assess the technology of the opening of cables. This assessment is optional in the ongoing communication, for the reason that the interviewee could have quite well finished his institutional task without offering the assessment. However, by providing the background knowledge about the technology involved in opening cables, the interviewee helps the audience in understanding why America can retrieve complete messages when the cables have to be opened and thus avoid being further questioned on the topic.

4.4.2 Supportive DE

DEs of this type are evaluations which digress from the mainstream of the topic to offer support to the interviewee's requested position as he answers the interviewer's question. Extract (18) below is such an example:

Example(18)

Situation: Iran's continuing evasion of the international supervision of its nuclear activities raises the suspicion that its ulterior motive is to build a nuclear weapon. Barack Obama, the current American president, is the first African American to hold the office. He lived in Indonesia, a country with the greatest population of Muslims, for several years when he was a child. Therefore, people are curious about his attitude toward the Iran nuclear issue.

主持人: ' 但是我们也 ^ 确实注意到奥巴马在担任总统以后向伊朗抛出了橄榄枝 .. 那他到底是什么目的呢? 他准备怎么解决伊朗核问题?

嘉　宾: 伊朗核问题有两种解决办法, <A> 政治解决, 军事解决 </A>。<TSK> 实际上奥巴马并没有说他排除军事解决的 = 方式, 但是政治解决总要在先 .. 而且你看最近希拉里的一些讲话, 我觉得希拉里作为国务卿, 作为一个 (TSK) 比奥巴马资历 ^ 更老一些的人, 她呢说话呢, (TSK) 听她的话恐怕分量 ^ 更重一些。希拉里说得很清楚, 在一定的时间框架内 .. 实施政治解决。如果这个政治解决从现在开始, 持续一年还没解决完的话, 这个奥巴马的 (TSK) 政策是不可能实行下去的。

《今日关注: 伊朗试射导弹威胁了谁?》

The Iran nuclear issue has always been an intractable international issue and the six countries, including the United States, Russia, China, France, Britain and Germany have held consultations on the issue for several times. In this extract, the interviewer mentions that the Obama administration implements a ‘reach-out-hand’ diplomacy with Iran and she asks how Obama would resolve the Iran nuclear issue. The interviewee, a researcher from China Academy of Social Science, holds the position that the political resolution has the priority over military approach, though military approach cannot be excluded. This position is the result of the interviewee's analysis of Hillary's attitude toward the issue, that is, to implement political resolution within a certain period of time. In order to support his point of view, the interviewee intentionally digresses to evaluate Hillary as a more experienced politician whose words outweigh those of Obama. This digressive evaluation implicates that Hillary is a pivot person who may greatly influence the doctrines of the Obama administration. Hence, the employment of the DE endows the interviewee's viewpoint with greater credibility and gratifies his communicative needs of enhancing the persuasiveness of his stance toward what Obama would do to resolve the Iran nuclear issue.

4.4.3 Highlighting DE

Digressive DEs which are classified as highlighting DEs bear no obvious relation both to the interviewee's ongoing utterances and to the topic of the preceding turn. They neither pick up an object of evaluation from the hitherto utterances, nor offer support for the ensuing position. Nor do they contribute to the interviewer's question. They digress from the current speech to highlight a particular evaluative stance, which helps to achieve the speaker's communicative goal. The following is an example:

Example(19)
Situation: On November 17, 2006, the Chinese Marine and the American Marine Corps held a joint military exercise. The interviewee is a Rear Admiral.

主持人: 我们前面的这个短片记录了两军比赛的全过程, (TSK) 好像从画面上没有看出来两军的比赛和陆军有什么不同?
嘉　宾: 还是有点区别的。(TSK) 当时那枪轻武器我们的 5.8 枪族，他们美军来体验一下我们的 5.8 枪族到底怎么样。因为他的口径是 5.56 的，陆战队配的制式的冲锋枪。(TSK) 打的结果呢据说是很满意，因为我们这枪呢精度高，而且当时质量是非常好的，在世界整个 (TSK) 小口径枪里头是比较杰出的一种。另外一些比赛是越障比赛，有些是陆军所不具备的，一个是抬橡皮舟，集体运橡皮舟。运橡皮舟有多种方法，有沙滩运行，有山路运行,还有林涧小路运行。这次选择的是沙滩运行方法，就是大家并排，手垂直，共同抬舟，还有推举的，这个就在丛林中，把这个树要把它让开。这种运橡皮舟是一种很经常的比赛，^ 需要体力，又 ^ 需要协调。

主持人：您谈到的是运橡皮舟比赛这是陆军所不具备的，还有其他的吗？

《防务新观察：两栖神兵》

In this example, the interviewer asks whether there is difference between the competition held by the Marine Corps and that held by the army. The interviewee, Rear Admiral Yin, begins his turn with a confirmation, but then drops the current topic to evaluate the Chinese light weapon, which is unrelated to the question raised by the interviewer. After the evaluation, he resumes the original topic. It is obvious that the evaluation in operation here is 'digressive DE'. In addition, the topic of the DE — the Chinese 5.8mm rifle, is irrelevant to both the topic raised by the interviewer and the overall topic of the current speech. The use of DE saliently flouts the maxim of relevance of conversation principle. The intention of the interviewee is to highlight his positive evaluative stance toward the Chinese 5.8mm semi-automatic rifle. By adopting the 'highlighting DE' to assess the Chinese rifle as high in accuracy, good in quality, the interviewee wants to impress the audience with the rapid development of technology in Chinese military field so as to satisfy his communicative need of constructing a positive group image.

4.5 Interruptive DE

Interruptive DEs are evaluations which are deliberately used by the interviewee to intervene into the ongoing speech of another speaker. The DEs subsumed under this type saliently break away from the turn-allocation system in military interviews. Two kinds of interruptive DEs are evidenced in the data, namely aligning interruptive DE and disaligning interruptive DE.

4.5.1 Aligning interruptive DE

Aligning interruptive DE begins in the middle of the first speaker's ongoing turn without the intention of threatening her/his face. Instead, it works to support the position hitherto expressed by the first speaker, and jointly construct a topic. The simplest expressions of the DEs of this type are non-lexical, e.g. eng,wu (uh, mm), or lexical, e.g. dui (right), shi(yeh)with a falling intonation pattern. When they are uttered at a lower volume level than that of the ongoing turn, the second speaker does not intent to bid for the floor, but shows his alignment with the ongoing speaker's point of view. Here is an example:

Example(20)

Situation: The participants are talking about Japan's massive bombing on Chongqing on June 5, 1941, which created the appalling Tunnel Massacre.

主持人: 这次我到重庆去, 听到 = 当时亲历的一些人, (TSK) 亲自经历过“六·五大轰炸”的一些人的介绍，当时轰炸时特别惨，像隧道大惨案就是它那个隧道两端是通气的，把这端炸了，炸了以后又把那端封上了，中间两千多人躲避空袭全都窒息死亡了。

嘉宾 1：这也就跟日本当时的那个军队有关。日军这个当时采取的轰炸方法实际上就是一种 ^ 野蛮的轰炸方 [法，

嘉宾 2：[对

嘉宾 1：哪人多往哪 [打

嘉宾 2：[对

嘉宾 1：轰炸平民，没有把军用目标和民用 [目标分开

嘉宾 2：[<MRC> 对，对，对 </MRC>，没有。二战空袭有几个指导思想，一个是打工用基础，军 [工厂，

嘉宾 1：[对

嘉宾 2：生产飞机啊，潜艇那些 = 地方；另外就是打平民，打平民的目的就是要消耗你的抵抗意识，很明确。

《防务新观察：来自太空的威胁》

During World War II, Japan's mass bombing on Chongqing lasted five years, causing a casualty of over ten thousand. In the extract, the interviewer mentions the Tunnel Massacre which happened on June 5, 1941. The first interviewee then evaluates the bombing as brutal which did not distinguish the military targets and the civil targets. During the first interviewee's evaluation, the second interviewee intervenes into the ongoing talk three times. The first two occurrences are simple responses of 'dui' (right) with a clear falling intonation contour of agreement, which lend support to the first interviewee's evaluative stance. However, the rate of simple response 'dui' (right) increases in the third time, and the volume level rises which signals the ensuing taking over of the floor. We can see from the interaction that the two interviewees are supporting each other, using the simple response DE 'dui' (right) to participate in the joint topic construction. By converging to each other's stancetaking, the speakers move the interview forward. Instead of being perceived as face threatening by the first speaker, these DEs are welcomed by the current speaker and help to increase the solidarity between the two speakers.

Apart from simple responses showing agreement, aligning interruptive DE may also provide justifications with agreement tokens. When making DE of this type, the interviewee claims a floor to show his alignment with the current speaker. The following extract illustrates such a case.

Example(21)
Situation: In April and September 2008, France succeeded in rescuing the hostages twice from the Somalia pirates by means of trapping.

主持人: 张教授觉得这种 ^ 诱杀的方法怎么样?
嘉 宾 1: 这是很错误 [的。
嘉 宾 2: [嗯 @@]
嘉 宾 1: 第一个他是直接违反国际法。(GLOTTAL) 国际法 ^ 明确规定严禁 <RH> 商船, 民用飞机装武器 </RH>, 或者是伪装成别的东西。所谓伪装呢就包括比方说把一个军舰伪装成一个 = 商船 .. 这个呢首先从法律上来讲呢军舰它是飘扬一个国家的国旗和军旗, 这样丧失了政府的地位, 商船它是公司所有的 .. 这是一个。再一个呢 (TSK) 就是说你军舰就是军舰, 军舰是合法的作战的单位, 商船和民船, 平民是被保护的目标, 你不具备打别人的能力, 所以说如果把军舰伪装成商船, 这是 ^ 完全违反国际法的, 这是不行的, 这是一个。第

二 [个呢,

主持人: [但现在这个索马里海盗的问题恐怕有点特殊啊, [有没有一个 ...

嘉宾 2: [对, ^ 双方都在遵守交战规则的情况下, 这个是适用的, <A> 你讲合法不合法 </A>, 他索马里海盗他有什么法啊, (H) 他都 ^ 无法了。

《防务新观察: 海盗猖獗, 打不打, 怎么打? 》

In this excerpt, the interviewer asks one of the interviewees about his opinion on the method adopted by France in fighting the Somalia pirates. The first interviewee negatively evaluates the method as totally wrong and goes on to justify his position. However, the interviewer deliberately uses a tone unit boundary in the first interviewee's turn and intervenes to show her opposition to his position. The interviewer's utterances are then interrupted by the second interviewee, who, by adopting a DE of a supportive token 'dui' (right) with justification, align with the interviewer's point of view. In doing so, the second interviewee counters the first interviewee's position concerning France's method in fighting the pirates quite vehemently and joins the interviewer in forming a joint opposing stance to the first interviewee. In this case, the DE adopted by the second interviewee is an effort to cooperate with the interviewer and therefore enhances the interviewer's positive face, while threatening both the positive and the negative face of the first interviewee.

4.5.2 Disaligning interruptive DE

Disaligning interruptive DE can be defined as the evaluation intentionally proffered by a second speaker which intrudes upon a current speaker's turn at talk, with the intention of contradicting with the point of view put forth by the ongoing speaker. Such DEs imply that the interviewee considers that whatever he proceeds to say in some sense has priority over what the ongoing speaker has been saying. It is thus a denial of the first speaker's stances and also an assertion of dominance over the interrupted speaker. Hence, it is a strong evidence of the exercise of power. In military interviews, due to the authority of the interviewee, such behavior quite often results in an abrupt stop of the interviewer's turn.

Example(22)

Situation: The participants are talking about how to fight the Somalia pirates. The interviewee is a Rear Admiral who had served in navy for many years and now a professor and doctor supervisor in the University of National Defense.

主持人: 您说“打谈结合”, (TSK) 但问题是“谈”是一个漫长的过程啊, (TSK) 现在这个局势这么紧张的情况下...

嘉　宾: ^不是漫长,<A> 你首先跟政府谈好了, 政府授权, 授权以后我国际维和部队进去 </A>。他的海盗他不能一天到晚在海上漂着, 他得回来呀。比方说咱们军事上讲防空, 我打飞机是一种很好的选择, 满天的飞机我就防空, 这是对的。飞机它得落地呀, 我有打飞机那功夫, 我打机场不更好吗? 你打海盗是一种选择, 但是你上哪儿打去呀? 他得回港啊! 你把港口给摧毁了, 把他老巢给他摧毁了, 不就完了吗? ^这是一个 ' 治本的。

《防务新观察: 海盗猖獗, 打不打, 怎么打?》

In this interaction, the interviewer casts doubt on the interviewee's idea on how to fight the Somalia pirates, viz.

fighting and negotiation. She justifies her doubt with the reason that negotiation is a rather long process, while the situation now on the sea off the Somalia coast is in tension. However, the interviewer's ongoing turn is interrupted by the interviewee's negative assessment. At the point when the interviewee intervenes into the interviewer's ongoing turn by the employment of DE, the interviewer has clearly not yet finished her turn at talk, for the reason that there is no conscious turning down of the volume, no obvious of slowing down of the tempo of delivery. That is to say, the DE does not occur at a ratified transition relevance place. The interviewee's assessment, which denies the interviewer's position on negotiation, cuts into the continuity of interviewer's speech and causes her to close the turn abruptly. This action no doubt threatens the interviewer's positive face, as well as her negative face. Moreover, though in most cases, negative assessments are said to be delivered with all sorts of devices serving to minimize potential conflict, risk of offense or loss of face (Pomerantz, 1984), the interviewee's negative assessment in the present interaction is proffered nakedly without any of these devices, which evidences the interviewee's exercise of power over the interviewer.

4.6 Competitive DE

Competitive DE is another type of DE which signals the interviewee's departure from the Q-A system in military interviews. These DEs are given at the end of a Q-A sequence by the unaddressed interviewee when the present turn is completed, competing for an opportunity to speak and pre-empting the return of the floor to the interviewer. Three further types of competitive DE are in evidence in the data, namely complementary DE, contrastive DE and empathic DE.

4.6.1 Complementary DE

One salient type of competitive DE is complementary DE by which the second interviewee employs to render a previous evaluation made by the first interviewee more complete so as to jointly construct a topic under discussion. A complementary DE is topically relevant to the interviewer's question. It helps to create an active atmosphere and is welcomed by the host of the interview. Most of the complementary DEs are prefaced by discourse markers such as 'buchong yidian' (to add one more point), 'lingyige/lingyi fangmian' (there is another aspect), etc. example (24) presents such a case.

Example(23)

Situation: In November 2008, 10 Pakistan-based gunmen rampaged through hotels and the train station in the financial hub of Mumbai, capital of India, for 60 hours, killing 166 people.

主持人：除了两位刚才说的体现在硬件方面的警力不行之外，还有什么地方体现了印度的反恐的能力 ..^非常差？

嘉　宾：这个呢我们不去评论他的反恐能力好或是差，我们想把这个从火车站第一声枪响到最后这个内卫部队到达孟买案发现场的过程呢，我们先按照印度媒体自己报道的情况我们给他说一下。……

主持人：所以 (H) 您说的这个实际上体现一种 ^ 机制的问题？

嘉 宾 1：按说呢，按照这些专家的分析，<RH> 反恐活动黄金时间是 30 分钟 </RH>。就是在 30 分钟内你反恐部队 ^ 必须到位，这样才能控制这些恐怖分子，占领 ^ 有利的位置。我们想，9 个小时和 30 分钟之间的差距实在是太远了。

嘉 宾 2: 另外一个呢，刚才杜老师说的是他的军方。(GLOTTAL) 另外我觉得印度的整个的民众，用我们的话说是民防体系，由于他不重视这个反恐教育，^ 即便反恐部队没有到达，你民间的这些比如警察、社区，这样的话迅速能起到像，比如说像地震啊这样的灾难来的时候，就是考验一个国家的 ^ 民众的这样一个反应能力，我觉得在这方面呢它确实也比较 ^ 乱，孟买这样的一个金融都市。相反呢，(TSK) 你看有一些发展中国家遇到一些灾难的时候，他的民众反应能力也是很快的，<A> 迅速组织，疏散伤员啊这些东西 </A>。

《防务新观察：印度——恐怖袭击重灾区》

In this extract, the interviewer invites one of the interviewees to evaluate the anti-terrorist capability of India. Though the first interviewee claims he would not assess Indian anti-terrorist capability as good or bad, his position 'jiuge xiaoshi he sanshi fenzhong zhijian de juli shizai shi taiyuan le' (there is great difference between nine hours and thirty minutes) clearly has an evaluative orientation, which implicates that the working efficiency of the India military system is too low. When the first interviewee ends his turn, the second interviewee seizes the opportunity of the floor space and takes over the floor without being assigned the right by the interviewer. The second interviewee's evaluation focuses on the Indian civil defense system, which complements the first interviewee's evaluation on the Indian military system to jointly construct the topic of the anti-terrorist capability of India. It can be clearly seen that complementary DE is used in this extract.

4.6.2 Contrastive DE

Besides complementary DE, the second interviewee who unofficially seizes the floor may also provide DEs which contrast with what the first interviewee says. Contrasting the object of evaluation is one of the features of the DEs of this type. In addition, antonyms are used to form the contrast, as well as the employment of negation, the positive and negative use of the same predicate, the use of a pair of synonyms with positive and negative values, etc. The utilization of contrastive DE has the effect of emphasizing the difference between the entity being evaluated in the current turn and the one evaluated in the preceding turn, in addition to pointing out some similarities between them, for instance, how two persons deal with an emergency differently. In this way, the second interviewee highlights the object of evaluation in his turn so as to achieve certain communicative goal in a specific context. The following excerpt, in which a military expert and a political commissar of a certain air unit are being interviewed, demonstrates the employment of a DE of this category:

Example(24)

Situation: In a night flight practice, the engines of two fighters caught fire. The first interviewee is a military expert, and the second one is a political commissar of a certain air unit.

主持人: 通常情况下飞行员就跳伞了?

嘉宾 1: 反正 ^ 外国飞行员遇到这种情况 ' 都跳伞了。

嘉宾 2: ^ 我们的飞行员在这种情况下, 首先想到的是 ' 挽救国家的巨额财产, 把 ' 心爱的战机飞回来。他们这次只用了<MRC> ^3 分 40 秒 </MRC> 就安全把这个着火的战机在夜间 .. 安全降落。

《防务新观察: 走进中国歼击机部队(上)》

For the engines to catch fire is an extremely dangerous

situation in flight. The interviewer queries whether the pilots opt for parachuting in such a situation. The first interviewee, who is a military expert but has never experienced real flight practice, confirms that the foreign pilots chose to bail out when being caught in such an emergency. As soon as he finishes the turn, the second interviewee pre-empts the return of the floor back to interviewer, deliberately offering an evaluation on Chinese pilots. This DE contrasts with the object of evaluation in the preceding turn in that the preceding evaluation comments on foreign pilots, while in the current turn, the interviewee assesses the domestic pilots. In addition, the contrast focuses on how foreign pilots and the Chinese pilots handle the same emergent situation differently. Antonyms are used to fill the opposition construction—'fei huilai'(fly back) and 'anquan jiangluo' (safely landing) are employed to contrast with 'tiaosan(parachuting)' in the previous turn. By adopting the contrastive DE in the current context, the interviewee highlights Chinese pilots and establishes a positive image of the air unit to which he belongs.

4.6.3 Empathic DE

Communication involves the understanding of others' perceptual, affective, cognitive, social and judgmental perspectives, and it can be enhanced by empathy (Li, 2008). Empathic DEs are the evaluations which are expressed by the second speaker to show his awareness or consideration of the first speaker's affective state. These evaluations are most needed by the first speaker but can not be formulated by himself for diversified reasons. They are semantically irrelevant to what the interviewer questions. Even though pragmatic empathy is quite often linguistically revealed by the unusual employment of indexicals or other deictic expressions that are reflective of the speaker's consideration for others (冉永平, 2007), the empathy of the DE in the data at hand can only be inferred from the specific context in which the DE is utilized. The following is an example in which an empathic DE is proffered by the second interviewee to maintain the first interviewee's face.

Example(25)

Situation: The first interviewee, Huang Song, is the chief technical officer of the military off-road vehicle 'mengshi'. The second speaker is a military expert from the University of National Defense.

主持人: (TSK) 刚才说的这个事故是出现在实验阶段?

嘉 宾1: 是,很初期。

嘉 宾2: 这个是^ 很正常的,车在实验阶段经常出事。这个是^ 很正常的,发现问题以后才能不断地改进。

《防务新观察:猛士出击》

The military off-road vehicle 'mengshi' is independently developed by China, and is dubbed the 'Chinese Hummer'. It has a lot of advantages over other military off-road vehicles, such as high speed, good waterproof effect, etc. However, it is not perfect. One sample vehicle burns automatically on a snowy day. In this extract, the interviewer asks a quite adversary question whether the accident happened in the experimental period. Huang Song, the chief technical officer, admits that there had been accidents. This is rather face-damaging, for it either implies that he has to take the responsibility for the accident, or implies that he is not an eligible chief technical officer. The extra information 'hen chuqi' (at the very beginning) in the turn reveals his embarrassment and his intention to reduce the degree of the damage to his face. In this context, the second interviewee, who senses the affective state of the first interviewee, deliberately assesses the accident as quite normal, competing for the turn without being allocated by the interviewer, The DE is given with justifications that 'it is quiet usual for vehicles to have accidents during the experimental period', and 'only after we discover problems can we make improvement'. The employment of the empathic DE prevents the audience from considering accidents as negative, and helps to maintain the first interviewee's face.

4.7 Summary

This chapter has presented a taxonomy of the DEs utilized by the interviewees to meet their communicative needs in military interviews. The deliberateness of DE used by the interviewees in military interviews is mainly manifested in two ways: ① deliberate deviation from the interviewer's question; ② deliberate deviation from the turn-allocation system in military interviews. Based on different forms of deviation, the DEs are generalized into five groups, viz. additive DEs, substitutive DEs, digressive DEs, interruptive DEs and competitive DEs. The additive Deliberate Evaluations is split into reparative DE, elaborative DE, comparative DE and conclusive DE. The types of DE subsumed under substitutive DE are evasive DE and negotiative DE. The type of DEs concluded under the heading of digressive DE is categorized into three groups, namely background-providing DE, supportive DE, and highlighting DE. As for the interruptive DEs, two groups of sub-types are unearthed, viz. aligning interruptive DE and disaligning interruptive DE. Lastly, the competitive DEs are subdivided into complementary DE, contrastive DE and empathic DE. The taxonomy of DE will turn out to be the essential foundation for the discussion of contextual factors which influence the interviewee's choice of DE and the main pragmatic functions that the employment of DE achieves in military interviews, which will be analyzed in Chapter 5 and Chapter 6 respectively. The classification of DE in military interviews is schematized in the ensuing figure:

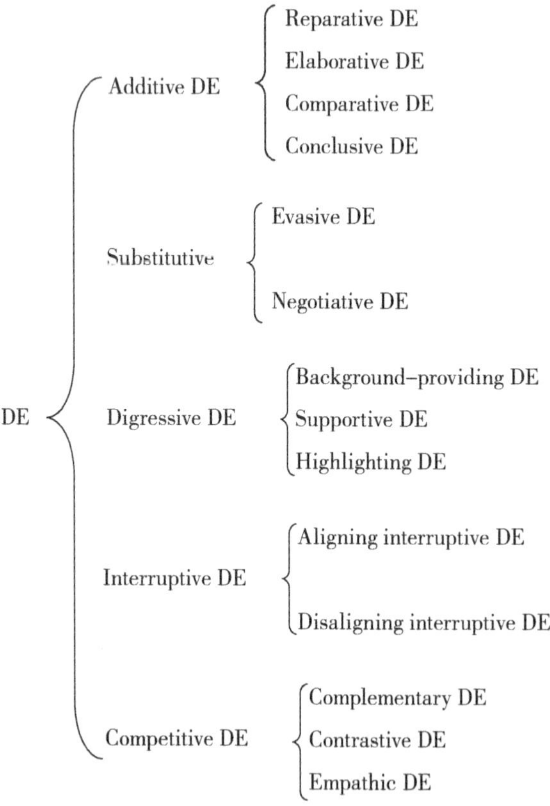

Figure 4-1 Classification of DE in military interviews

Chapter 5
Adaptability of Deliberate Evaluation

5.1 Introduction

Language use is always anchored in a rather complicated context with which it is related in a variety of ways (Verschueren, 1999). This chapter is devoted to adaptability, which is an auspicious concept to account for what people do when using language. In other words, we will deal with the various contextual correlates of adaptability that affect and are affected by the choice of DE. As has been illustrated in Chapter 4, there are diversified ways to realize DE. In the process of verbal interaction, the interviewee must make choice in which type of DE to use so as to approach his communicative needs. This process is a dynamic one in which the choice of DE interadapts with contextual correlates along the physical, social, and mental dimensions. Language utterer and language interpreter are always the central points of communication. And given the specific communicative setting of military interviews, the contextual factors related to the group which the speaker identifies with also greatly influence his choice of DE. Therefore, we distinguish three types of contextual correlates, namely self-oriented, other-oriented and group-oriented. This chapter starts with aspects concerning with the speaker, goes on to those related to the addressee, and ends up in illustrating the group-oriented adaptation.

5.2 Self-oriented adaptation

'Self' here refers to the interviewee who proffers evaluations. The contextual variables start to play a role in the production of DE when they get activated by the self's cognitive process,and this makes them part of language use as elements with which the making of choices is interadaptable. Based on the data at hand, three variables which are associated with self-oriented adaptation are revealed, namely, self-face, identity, and power.

5.2.1 Adaptation to self-face

The most popular definition of face is put forth by Goffman (1967), who states that:

> *The term face may be defined as the positive social value a person effectively claim for himself by the line others assume he has taken during a particular contact. Face is an image of self delineated in terms of approved social attributes — albeit an image that others may share, as when a person makes a good showing for his profession or religion by making a good showing for himself.*[19]

This definition is adopted by Spencer-Oatey in her theory of rapport management (2008). According to this definition, face involves some degree of active self-representation, and is a conglomerate of the self-image the speaker wants to present to the outside world and the image that is bestowed on a speaker by others present. What's more, face is closely associated with particular social attributes. The claim for face is concerned with positive social values. People have a fundamental desire for

[19]Goffman, E. Interaction ritual: Essays on face-to-face Behavior. New York: Pantheon Books. 1967. p.5.

others to evaluate them positively, so they typically want others to acknowledge their positive qualities and not to acknowledge their negative ones(ibid:14). This is typically the case in military interviews. The interviewees in military interviews are professors in military universities, generals or commanders from various army divisions, or chief editors of well-known military journals. That is to say, they generally enjoy a high social status. For them, to present a positive self in the interview is really important. Therefore, they do not claim face for what they think are negative values. For example, they normally would like to show that they are patriotic or peace-loving instead of presenting themselves as fawning on foreign powers or belligerent. When any of their remarks would have triggered a negative value on them and threatened their face, the interviewee would resort to communicative strategies to prevent his public image from being damaged. DE is one of such strategies. To illustrate this, let's consider example (26):

Example(26)

Situation: In 2008, a great financial crisis broke out in America. RAND Corporation, which is entitled as the think tank of America, suggests that American government should recover economy by launching a war.

主持人: 如果^打的话会是什么时候打, 是等到真的是我在经济手段穷尽了以后没有办法解决的时候发动战争, 还是从现在开始战争随时就可以成为一种选择?

嘉　宾: 我觉得^如果选择战争的话可能就是一种突然性, 也可能他采取对伊拉克一样。((省略)) 所以我们看出来, 从^战略的角度来看这个问题的话, ^如果一旦美国的社会出现深刻的金融危机, 经济危机和社会危机的时候，^ 战争会成为 ^ 唯一的选择。当然，<L> 我不是在叫嚣战争，也不是在为美国的战争开脱，实际上，我们 ^ 预测战争就是为了 ^ 防止战争。</L>

《防务新观察：发动战争果真是救市良方吗？》

In this excerpt, the interviewee is invited to foresee when America would launch a war if a war is unavoidable. In his response to the question, the interviewee begins his turn by converging to the norm of question-answer adjacency pair (cf. Sacks et al., 1974). He explicitly formulates his remark as an answer to the interviewer's question by repeating part of the question 'wo juede ruguo xuanze zhanzhen de hua' (I think if choosing to launch a war). However, after expressing his stance to the question, he turns to evaluate his own opinion. An 'additive DE' is adopted here to meet the interviewee's communicative needs. This DE is irrelevant with the interviewer's question, and is semantically inconsistent with the speaker's ongoing utterances. It can be seen that the use of this DE is an obvious deviation from the overarching norm of the news interview and is strategically used. In the interaction, the interviewee, as an expert in media communication, forecasts that launching a war is the only option once there occurs either a deep financial crisis, an economic depression or a social crisis in America. The expression of such a stance may lead the addressees to attribute a pro-war sentiment to him, regarding him as one who will go to war if there are economic problems in a country and viewing him as justifying any possible wars to be launched by America. Belligerency is no doubt a negative quality in today's society. Therefore, in order to avoid presenting a negative self-image, the interviewee deliberately adds an evaluation to emphasize that the purpose of forecasting war is to prevent war. That is to say, he adopts the strategy of 'reparative

DE', a sub-type of 'additive DE', under the impact of the need of 'self-face'.

The above example illustrates how the contextual variable self-face prompts the interviewee's production of DE as a strategy to cope with the problems arising in the interaction. In addition to self-face, identity is another self-related contextual factor that affects the interviewee's choice of DE in military interviews.

5.2.2 Adaptation to identity

The choice of DE can't be immune to the influence of the interviewee's identity. Identity can be defined as the social positioning of self and other.[20] It is a cognitive, socialized, phenomenological or psychic phenomenon that governs human interaction. In line with Bucholtz and Hall, we contend that identity emerges in local discourse contexts of interaction rather than as a static structure positioned in fixed social categories. A speaker may manage his identities from moment to moment in the ongoing interaction and present himself differently in different contexts. In addition, a speaker can categorize himself in a multitude of ways. However, not all of these categorizations emerge at the same time in a face-to-face interaction to exert an impact on the language choice made by the speaker. The speaker may foreground one of his identities to meet his communicative needs, while keeping the others dormant.

The aforementioned ideas about identity in communication can be adapted to the context of military interviews to help us better understand the dynamic interadaptation between identity and the interviewee's choices of DE. In this specific setting, the

---

[20] Bucholtz, M. & Hall, K. Identity and interaction: A sociocultural linguistic approach. *Discourse Studies*, 7 (4-5). 2005. pp. 585-614.

interviewee has different identities: ①the institutional identity as an interviewee or co-interviewee; ②the national identity as a Chinese; ③the personal identity which encompasses gender, age, etc.; ④the professional identity as a serviceman, an editor, a diplomatic officer, etc. During the process of interaction, these various identities are constantly subject to foregrounding and backgrounding. It is the foregrounded identity that enters into the line of vision of the interviewee and becomes a contextual factor that interadapts with the employment of DE in military interviews. The interviewee's professional identity plays an essential role in his selection of DE. Here is an example.

Example(27)
Situation: The interviewees are asked to decide which military equipment poses the greatest threat to the region of Asia and the Pacific. The options are the American Ohio Nuclear-powered Submarine, the Japanese New Tank, and Stealth Fighter. One of the interviewees, who is serving in navy, has chosen the first option as his answer.

主持人：我们来听听宋老师的意见。宋老师会选什么?
嘉　宾：那 ^ 肯定是隐形战机。[因为隐形战机
主持人：　　　　　　　[因为您是空军吗？]@@@
嘉　宾对对对从我们空军的看法就是 <RH> 来得最快最灵活，而且可以使对方的整个防空系统丧失作战能力的，就是这种隐形飞机。</RH> 而且现在的问题是，除了美国有 F-22,<RH> 日本也在搞,韩国也在搞,印度也在搞，俄罗斯也在搞。</RH> 那么这个隐形飞机对我们的影响就是一个 ^ 全方位的。

《防务新观察：利剑丛生话安全》

When being asked whether he regards Stealth Fighter as the military equipment which poses the greatest threat to the region of Asia and the Pacific just because he is an airman, the interviewee, who is an air force expert, answers affirmatively. He then continues to deliberately evaluate Stealth Fighters as the fastest and the most flexible military equipment which may bring omni-directional impact on China. This evaluation is a deliberate use of language for it is optional in that there is no such institutional task imposed on the interviewee to express his appreciation toward Stealth Fighters in the ongoing interaction. Moreover, the evaluation is topically irrelevant with the interviewer's question, and it is a further elaboration on the weapon chosen by the interviewee. Therefore, an 'elaborative DE' is utilized in this extract, which is adopted as a result of adaptation to his identity as an airman. There are three interviewees in the interview, one is from the navy, one serves in the army, and Song is from the air force. Of the three options offered by the interviewer, the American Ohio Nuclear-powered Submarine stands for the power of the navy, the Japanese New Tank represents the strength of the army, and the Stealth Fighter signals the advantage of the air force. One of the interviewees, General Zhang, who is a member of navy, has selected the American Ohio Nuclear-powered Submarine as the most powerful equipment. Zhang's selection no doubt poses threat to the professional identity of the other two interviewees. In this situation, Song chooses to adopt an intensified positive elaborative DE toward Stealth Fighter so as to contest with Zhang's professional identity. In other words, the interviewee's linguistic choice of DE in this context is adapted to the speaker's identity to satisfy his communicative need.

The foregoing example shows how the interviewee's professional identity affects his language choice. In other cases, the interviewee's national identity plays a role in his choice of DE in military interviews.

Example(24)

Situation: March 21, 2000, in a night flight practice, a Soviet-27 double-seated fighter suddenly caught fire. The interviewer and the interviewees are talking about this perilous accident. The first interviewee, Jiao Guoli, is an editor of a military journal; the other one is the commissar of an aviation division.

主持人: 通常情况下飞行员就跳伞了?
嘉 宾 1: 反正 ^ 外国飞行员遇到这种情况都跳伞了。
嘉 宾 2: ^ 我们的飞行员在这种情况下, 首先想到的是 ' 挽救国家的巨额财产, 把 ' 心爱的战机飞回来。他们这次只用了 <MRC> ^3 分 40 秒 </MRC> 就安全地把这个着火的战机在夜间 .. 安全降落。

《防务新观察: 走进中国歼击机部队》

In this example, the interviewer asks one of the interviewees whether it is normal for the pilots to opt for bailing out when the fighter catches fire. The first interviewee, who is the chief editor of the journal of Chinese Air Force, answers that any foreign pilot would have such an option when being involved in such accident. Then, the second interviewee, the commissar of the aviation division, breaks the turn-allocation system to intentionally evaluate Chinese pilots. The type of DE he adopts here is a 'contrastive DE', which is one of the sub-categories of 'competitive DE'. To be more specific, the evaluation on how the Chinese pilots deal with emergencies contrast with the evaluation on the behaviors of foreign pilots in the same situation. This choice of DE is an adaptation to the interviewee's national identity as a Chinese, which is evidenced by his use of the person deixis 'women' (we). As is known to us all, Chinese people always consider it a virtue to take the collective interest over that of the individual and those who only care about their own interest are deprecated for their selfishness. The first interviewee's answer reveals that foreign pilots treasure their own life more than the enormous property of the country, which offers a chance for the second interviewee to show the heroism of the Chinese pilots. In this context, Commissar Li, who surely feels proud of the Chinese pilots who even take the interest of the country as the first priority, adapts to his national identity as a Chinese and deliberately uses DE to create a positive image of the Chinese pilots.

When evaluating, Commissar Li does not choose any explicit evaluative terms, but states that the pilots in our country did not choose to bail out. What first occurs to them is to save the fighter and fly it back. This may invoke a positive evaluation of prowess. In addition, the use of 'only three minutes and forty seconds' in this context invokes the addressees' evaluation that the Chinese fighter pilots are highly skilled and well-trained. What's more, the DE contrasts with what the first interviewee says and highlights the positive attributes of the Chinese pilots.

In (24) and (27), the type of DE is chosen to adapt to the interviewee's foregrounded identity to meet his communicative needs in military interviews. Apart from identity, power is another contextual factor that exerts impact on the interviewee's choice of DE.

5.2.3 Adaptation to power

A wide range of empirical studies have showed that there are close association between language use and power (e.g. Locher,

2004, 2008; Spencer-Oatey, 1996, 2008; Brown Levinson, 1987). However, only a few scholars define the term explicitly in their study (e.g. Brown & Gileman, 1972; Brown & Levinson, 1987; Cansler and Stiles, 1981). In the present study, we adopt Brown and Gileman's definition on power, 'one person may be said to have power over another in the degree that he is able to control the behavior of the other. Power is a relationship between at least two persons, and it is nonreciprocal in the sense that both cannot have power in the same area of behavior.' [21]

Institutional talk is embedded in power relations, and in order to understand what is really at stake, these relations must be made explicit (Magalhães, 2009:385).[22] As mentioned in chapter 1, in the specific setting of military interviews, both the interviewer and the interviewee are powerful. While the interviewer has the institutional power in managing the process of an interview primarily by way of questioning (Thornborrow, 2002), the interviewee's power is mainly evidenced in the use of jargon, the length of the speaking floor, the amount of contribution and the manner of speaking. What's more, power is a quantifiable thing. Some people have more of it than others (Thornborrow, 2002), and this can be reflected in the use of language. It is revealed by the data that the interviewee who enjoys more power speaks at longer lengths, and in a more assertive manner than those with less of it. There are many bases of power, for example, physical strength, wealth, age, institutional roles, etc. (Brown and Gilman, 1972), and the main bases of power that affect the interviewee's production of

---

[21] Magalhães, I. Institutional talk. In Mey, J. (Eds.). *Concise Encyclopedia of pragmatics*. Oxford: Elsevier Ltd. 2000. p.385.

[22] The term 'participation framework' originates from Goffman's work (1981). It refers to the instantaneous view of any social gathering relative to the act of speaking at any one moment. (O'Keefe, 2006: 18).

DE in military interviews are expertise and experience.

A. Daptation to expertise-based power

According to Spencer-Oatey (2000, 2008), if a person, A, has some special knowledge or expertise that another person, B, wants or needs, A can be said to have expertise power over B. In institutional interactions, expertise-based power is articulated partly through the use of specialized lexicon (Draw & Heritage, 1992). In addition, it is an implicit rule in verbal interaction that expertise entitles a speaker a longer turn, while the lack of it deprives one the right of keeping a floor (Li, 2008). In military interviews, the professional knowledge that the interviewee possesses renders him more authoritative and powerful, and influences whether or not he will adopt a DE and how to realize it. The following is an instance of the production of DE as an adaptation to the interviewee's expertise-based power.

Example(28)

Situation: The interviewee, Pang Zhihao, is a researcher from China Research Institute of Space Technology. He is also the vice-editor of the journal of International Space.

主持人: 所谓定向能是指的照毁?

嘉　宾: 属于 <RH> 激光束, 粒子束, 微波束 </RH>。美国有一种刚刚邵教授所说的机载激光器, 这是属于定向的, 它一般是使 = 目前这种工艺还不能使卫星烧毁, 而是使卫星 <MRC> 致盲, 损坏, 失掉它的功能 </MRC>, 一般都是 ^ 软杀伤比较多, ^ 硬杀伤现在还达不到。现在动能最好的是 ^ 硬杀伤, ^ 破坏你的结构。

《防务新观察: 一箭击星, 得失几何》

In this excerpt, the interviewer asks whether directed-energy, a technical term in space technology, refers to destruction by light. This question reveals that either the interviewer or the audience may probably lack the specialized knowledge in this aspect, for the interviewer can raise questions on behalf of herself, as well as on behalf of the audience. In his reply to the question, the interviewee first corrects the interviewer's understanding of directed-energy, and then adds further comments on it. The type of DE he uses here is 'additive DE'. The employment of this DE is triggered by the contextual factor of 'expertise-based power'. It can be inferred from the question that the interviewee, who is an expert in space technology, is considered to have expertise power on the topic under discussion. What's more, there are a bundle of field-specific concepts and terms embedded in his response to the question, such as laser beam, particle beam, micro-wave beam, soft kill, hard kill, etc., which displays his professional knowledge of space technology and distinguishes him from novice or non-expert. A person who is not an expert on the topic would not use such terms, and he may even have difficulties in understanding them. That is why the interviewee keeps on adding explanations on those technical terms that appear in his turn. Therefore, it is the interviewee's expertise power that drives him to use DE. In a word, expertise power is what the interviewee adapts to when he employs additive DE in this interaction.

In addition to expertise, experience also endows the interviewee with power which warrants his employment of DE.

B.Adaptation to experience-based power

Experience provides a person with power in that what the speaker has experienced makes what the speaker says on the related topic more convincing. Take the following extract as an example.

Example(29)

Situation: In the annual national civil service examination in 2009, there appear several 'strange questions' which test the examinees' elementary knowledge of weapons and national defense.

主持人: 这些军事^装备知识一定要在国家公务员考试中出现吗?

嘉　宾: (TSK) 这个是有问题, 军事知识^绝不就是装备。军事里头有很多了。(TSK) 比方说,中国三大战役知道吧, 这种重大的战役, 革命传统应该知道吧。我有一次到一个餐馆吃饭, 那个小姑娘是个领班, 她看见我穿着军装她不认识, 海军军装新换了之后 .. 和国际接轨了, 她看了半天, 她不知道。她分不出来, 我说这个不知道那就算了。我说姑娘, 你给我说说能分得清红军, 八路军, 新四军, 解放军, 这个能分清吗? (TSK) 完了, 这个把她难住了, 她分不清。但是她能分清什么菜, 歌星, 影星, 这个她能说得出来, 这么^简单的事情她^搞不出来。<RH> 她根本根本不知道 </RH>。<u>这些问题, 我感觉我们平时的国防教育 = 这个工作做得还是不太扎实。</u>((点头))

《防务新观察: 偏题还是正题》

In this extract, after offering the expected answer to the question, the interviewee does not give up the floor at hand but adds his evaluative stance toward the national defense education, which is not at all within the topic agenda set by the interviewer. The DE employed in this example is an 'elaborative DE', which is incurred by the interviewee's narration of his experience. The contextual factor that interadapts with the utilization of the DE is 'experience-based power'.

The interviewee narrates his experience of meeting a girl in a restaurant who could not recognize the uniform of the navy. Worse still, she could not tell the difference between the Eight Route Army, the New Fourth Army and the People's Liberation Army. This narration clearly reflects the interviewee's point of view. 'Zheme jiandan de wenti ta gao bu chulai' (She cannot figure out such simple questions) is an external evaluation[23] which manipulates the story material to make a point. 'Jiandan de' (simple) is a lexicon loaded with inherent evaluative meaning. The utterance 'ta genben genben bu zhidao' (she doesn't know at all) is rendered evaluative by the use of high pitch. It is a universal function of intonation to express emotion and attitude. Earlier studies on intonation and evaluation show that utterances or items with evaluative meaning tend to stand out by way of being emphasized by intonation (Wennerstrom, 2001). 'Zhexie wenti'(these problems) refers to the interviewee's generalization that citizens are deficient in national defense knowledge. Triggered by his experience, the interviewee deliberately tacks the negative evaluative statement that the work on national defense education is not solid enough.

What the above discussion is concerned about are the interviewee-related contextual correlates that exercise impact on the interviewee's choice of DE as a pragmatic strategy to cater for his self-oriented communicative needs. Apart from these contextual factors, the other-related ones are also crucial in accounting for the

[23]External evaluation refers to separate clauses from the actual story line in which the teller indicates his stance toward the event in progress (Labov, 1972).

utilization of DE in military interviews. Thus in the next section, another type of adaptation, namely, the other-oriented adaptation is to be discussed.

5.3 Other-oriented adaptation

According to Spencer-Oatey (2008), one key factor that influences people's strategy use is their rapport orientation. Two fundamental orientations are firstly distinguished, namely support of one's own face needs, sociality rights and interactional goals, and support of the other person's. Other-oriented adaptation refers to the process of adapting forms of expression to interpreter(s). Since different types of speech events require different kinds of presences (Verschueren, 1999), interpreter(s) varies as speech events change. In her investigation of media discourse, O'Keeffe (2006: 66) proposes four participation frameworks[24] in media interaction: ①the presenter addresses the audience; ②the presenter and the audience interact; ④ the studio interviewee, the presenter and the non-studio interviewee interact; ④the interviewee addresses the audience. Modifying this to the context of military interviews, we can map three possible participation frameworks which involve the interviewee: ① the interviewee and the interviewer interact; ② the interviewee addresses his co-interviewee(s); ③ the interviewee addresses the audience. These can be visualized in the following figure.

It can be seen from these participation frameworks that in military interviews, 'other' does not only refer to the interviewer, whose questions the interviewee is responding to, but also to the co-interviewee(s), and the audience who are watching the program

[24]The term 'participation framework' originates from Goffman's work (1981). It refers to the instantaneous view of any social gathering relative to the act of speaking at any one moment. (O'Keefe, 2006: 18).

in that social context. In the following section, three other-related contextual factors that interadapt with the interviewee's choice of DE will be analyzed, viz. other-face, cognitive needs, and emotions.

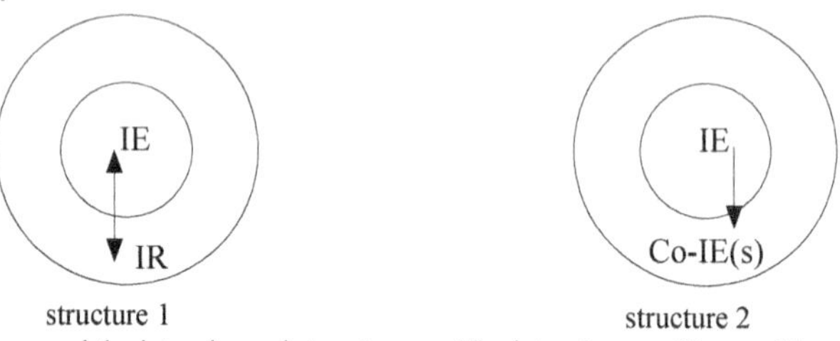

structure 1
The interviewee and the interviewer interact

structure 2
The interviewee addresses his co-IE(s)

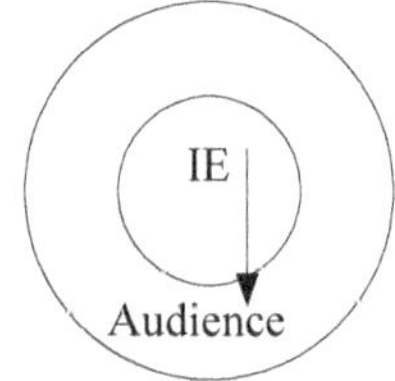

structure 3
The interviewee addresses the audience

Figure 5-1 Participation frameworks in military interviews involving the interviewee,where IE represents the interviewee, IR represents the interviewer

5.3.1 Adaptation to other-face

As mentioned in 5.2.1, in verbal communication, face is meaningful to people in that everyone wants to make his positive attributes known to others. Therefore, supporting other person's face will surely benefit the interpersonal relationship. In military interviews, when the interviewee realizes that his opinion would threaten another person's face, he will turn to DE to explicitly show his concern about the face of others. The following example represents such a situation.

Example(30)

Situation: Soldiers in the Chinese People's Liberation Army (PLA) take part in the 'Warrior 2008' military exercise in the Inner Mongolia Autonomous Region on Thursday, September 25, 2008. The exercise is held at Zhu Rihe tactical training base in north China's Inner Mongolia where officers and soldiers from Beijing and Jinan Military Commands as well as the Air Force of the PLA conducted counterwork without designated plans. Now, the commander and the commissar of the red army, as well as the colonel of the blue army, are at present in the interview.

主持人：你们除了正常的训练外，还有什么特殊的训练吗？

嘉　宾：到这地方我们就是 ^ 针对性的 ^ 主要是战法训练，主要是指挥控制训练，主要是复杂电磁环境下 ^ 打赢现代化战争的能力的训练，给自己 <A> 设难局，设险局，设危局 </A>，也训练自己的部队。同时呢我们也要跟老大哥的红军部队要进行学习。这次我们跟老大哥红军部队学到 ^ 不少东西。这支部队作风 ^ 非常顽强，要求 ^ 非常严格，战法也 ^ 很灵活。

《防务新观察：走进励兵 2008(下)》

In military exercises, the blue army is said to be the sharpening stone of the red army. They improve themselves so as to enhance the combating capacity of the red army, but traditionally, the red army is considered to be stronger. In the interview, the hostess asks the interviewee, a Colonel from the blue army, whether they have special methods of training other than the traditional training subjects. The interviewee first supplies an answer as the interviewer expected. However, he then moves on to add an intensified positive evaluation on the red army. The added evaluation obviously moves beyond the topic agenda set by the interviewer, and is illogically related to the ongoing speech. The topic of the DE is strategically elicited by the interviewee's use of a transitional sentence, viz. 'tongshi ne, women gen laodage hongjun xuedao bushao dongxi'(This time we learned a lot from our elder brother the red army). Hence, the type of DE operating in the interaction is an 'elaborative DE', which is one subtype of 'additive DE' . The employment of this DE is the result of adapting to the contextual factor of 'other-face'. When asked the question, the interviewee answers that they have mainly trained their combating capability under complex electromagnetic environment and that they always design harsh situations to train their soldiers. This is obviously a self-enhancement verbal style which puts emphasis on accomplishments and abilities of the blue army, to which the interviewee belongs. As we all know, the blue army and the red army are always competitors in military exercise. To boast about the self in a mass media would pose threat to the face of the other army. In this case, the interviewee resorts to an 'elaborative DE' and turn to compliment the red army as extremely pertinacious in style, very strict in self-discipline, and especially flexible in tactics. Three content-oriented boosters[25] are used to strengthen the illocutionary force of the DE so as to show the speaker's intention to enhance the co-interviewee's face. In a word, other-face in this interaction is a major contextual factor that prompts the interviewee's utilization of DE.

Other-face is by no means the only contextual correlate that is

[25]According to Holms (1984), content-oriented boosters strengthen the illocutionary force of a speech act by commenting impersonally on the validity of the proposition asserted, or by boosting a focal element within the proposition.

other-oriented. The ensuing section discusses how the addressees' cognitive needs influence the interviewee's choice of DE.

5.3.2 Adaptation to cognitive needs

Cognitive need is an individual or group's desire to obtain information that is necessary for him/her/them to fully understand a topic under discussion. Military interview is an information-oriented institutional interaction. That is to say, it is a type of media news program which aims at gathering or conveying opinions or information. As we all know, the topics in military interviews are related to the specific field of military, the discussion of which inevitably includes professional knowledge. Hence, it is hard for the mass audience who lack the knowledge of this field to catch the full meaning of the opinions given by the experts being interviewed. In other words, the mass audience usually has needs in obtaining the military-related information to fill their cognitive vacancy when watching the program. Being aware of this, the interviewees in military interviews would quite often actively offer the information or opinions they think the audience might need to know even without being asked to do so. Consider the following Example:

Example(31)

Situation: On April 21, 2010, just the day before Iran's mass military exercise on sea in the Persian Gulf and the Strait of Hormuz, an Iran maritime patrol aircraft flew over an American aircraft carrier named 'Eisenhower' which is in service in the Oman Gulf.

主持人：说到这个问题，美国人^真的这么弱吗？还是故意地放进来，然后想用这种东西来打政治牌？

嘉　宾：不是这样，老虎也有打盹的时候。就是这么理解。比方说我还研究过这么一个案例。1987 年，当时两伊战争，伊朗和伊拉克打仗。(TSK) 美国大约是凌晨两三点钟的时候，美国有一艘新服役的护卫舰叫"斯塔克"号在波斯湾里头巡逻。舰长就对他的作战军官说呢，你们俩值班，我去一下厕所。他在厕所就听有人在甲板上喊，不好啦，导弹来了，<@ 于是就赶紧往作战室跑 @>，还没跑到作战室，导弹就把这个舰右舷炸了一个大洞，三十七个水兵 ^ 当即死亡。一看雷达，马上 ^ 又有一颗来了，马上组织拦截，根本没来得及，第二枚导弹又打过来了。最后调查这个事，这个谁打的。开始就怀疑伊朗，伊朗说我没干这事。后来伊拉克说是我干的。<A> 当时美国和萨达姆的关系很好 </A>。他说是我干的。伊拉克以为他击毁了伊朗的一艘舰艇，他很高兴，说是我干的，我们飞行员怎么样？幻影 F1 发射的两枚飞鱼。美国说把我的舰给炸了。<@ 萨达姆说有这事 @>？一查，果然是的。<MRC> 当时美国和伊拉克关系很好 </MRC>。最后美国就要求伊拉克道个歉就行了，没赔偿，啥事也没干。这个"斯塔克"号是 ^ 非常知名的一艘舰，给航母护航的一艘护卫舰，当时世界上 ^ 最先进的一艘护卫舰，' 刚服役没几个月，你说它 ' 多先进啊。这个值班也有打盹的时候，困了，或者一会儿走神了，(TSK) 就这个时候突然来了，来不及拦截。

《防务新观察：伊朗，美国不得不面对的痛》

It is really a piece of incredible news that America, the most powerful country in the world, had its safety threatened by Iran. In this interaction, a polar alternative question is raised. In his reply to the question, the interviewee denies both positions embedded in the question put forward by the interviewer, and presents an alternative one, which is instantiated by a similar case which occurred in 1987. During his narration of the past case which happened between America and Iraq, the interviewee digresses twice from the ongoing narration to offer assessments on the international relationship between the two countries. These two assessments are illogically related to the previous move and are optional in the current turn. However, they provide the necessary background knowledge that the audience need to understand what the interviewee is saying. That is to say, he is employing a 'background-providing DE', which is subsumed under 'digressive DE'. The employment of this type of DE is triggered by the contextual factor of the audience's 'cognitive needs'. Without the background knowledge that America and Iraq were in good relation then, the audience, who acknowledge about the Iraq war launched by America, would feel strange about the friendly conversation between the two countries, and would find it hard to understand the way in which America dealt with the accident — only required an apology from Iraq who had created a death doll of 37 American servicemen and caused great damage to the American destroyer. Anticipating that the audience might lack the relevant information needed for fully interpreting his narration, the interviewee resort to 'background-providing DE' to overcome the problems likely to arise in the interaction. In a word, the employment of DE in this Example is the result of the adaptation to the addressee's cognitive needs.

Apart from other-face and cognitive needs, emotion is another other-oriented contextual correlate that exercise influence in the interviewee's employment of DE. The upcoming section deals with this factor.

5.3.3 Adaptation to emotions

Emotions are among the least tangible aspects of human experience, yet they exert powerful influences upon our thoughts and actions since we, human beings, are emotional creatures. In verbal communication, emotions are very important factors which exert influences on how language choices are made for the speaker's intended communicative purposes. The typical emotions that characterize military interviews are negative emotions such as indignation, sorrow and positive emotions such as patriotic sentiment, national pride, joy, love, etc. These emotions are essential in the production of evaluations and they are crucial contextual correlates that interadapt with the choice of DE. In the following Example, the emotion that prompts the interviewee's use of DE is indignation, i.e., anger arising from some offence or injustice.

Example(32)

Situation: On September 3, 2007, the US claims that it is the Chinese People's Liberation Army who hacked into the Pentagon network. Soon after that some reports say that Chinese hackers launched attacks against the government computer networks of Germany, France, and the UK.

主持人: 不仅是美国，还有德国、法国，包括这次实际上是英国媒体披露出来的，好像都格外地开始关注中国的黑客，为什么?

嘉　宾: 我觉得这个呀，我自己也是有很大的一个疑问。(GLOTTAL) 因为你看，他说中国，他还说以色列，还包括怀疑朝鲜。我觉得朝鲜这样一个国家，他认为黑客高手云集，我 [觉得这里面很大一个 ...

主持人: [<@ 有很多类似的报道 @>]

嘉　宾：对，所以这个都很可笑。而且从整个目前这个情况来看呢，我觉得就像我们刚刚所讨论的，美国他实际上目前是属于垄断全球信息技术的这么一个国家，只有ˆ它最有能力对全球进行' 谍报监控，而且今年我觉得一个很有力的一个事情就是在今年6月 ((省略))

《防务新观察：谁触动了五角大楼的网络神经》

When asked why there are so many countries starting to care about the hackers in China, the interviewee does not offer an answer as requested, but chooses to give comments on America. The type of DE exploited by the interviewee here is 'substitutive DE'. It is a strategic use of language for the reason that the utilization of it obviously departs from the interviewee's institutional task so as to meet his communicative needs. The substitutive DE in this extract is used in adaptation to the contextual factor of 'emotion'. On September 3, 2007, the American government openly accused the Chinese People's Liberation Army of hacking into the Pentagon network. In fact, the spokespersons in China have expressed our willingness to further strengthen international cooperation with other countries to counter cyber crimes. However, up till the time of this interview, the Chinese police have not received any request for investigation assistance from countries such as America, France or Germany. Obviously, the accusation is groundless, irresponsible and out of ulterior motives. It is this fact that stirs up the emotion of indignation in every Chinese. The interviewer's indignation is clearly shown in her interruption into the interviewee's ongoing speech about America's frequent unauthenticated accusation against other countries. And the interviewee immediately converges to her emotion which is linguistically expressed by 'dui, suoyi zhege dou hen kexiao' (right, so this is really ridiculous). Adapting to this emotion, he counter-attacks America as the most capable country in intelligence surveillance, which implicates that America is a country that has a dominant power over other countries. In addition, the strong version of anger impels the interviewee to offer her negative evaluation with evidence, which intensifies its illocutionary force and makes it more convincing and objective.

The preceding Example illustrates the occasion on which the negative emotion of indignation acts as the contextual factor that results in the utilization of DE. The following excerpt, however, is an instance in which positive emotion triggers the production of DE in the military interview talk.

Example(36)

Situation: The trade route through the Gulf of Aden has long been suffering from the pirate plague. China begins to send destroyers and supply ship to the Gulf of Aden off Somalia at the end of 2008, offering protection to Chinese civilian vessels and crews, including those from Hong Kong, Macao and Taiwan, and to foreign vessels on request as well. The first interviewee, Senior Captain Chen, who is the general manager of the department of Security and Surveillance in China Ocean Shipping Company, has the experience of fighting the Somalia pirates. The second interviewee, General Zhang is an expert in military equipment.

主持人：陈船长，这次^中远公司听到我们军队派出军舰去亚丁湾，是^什么样的一种感受呢？

嘉宾 1：<MRC> 这次我们听到我们海军要出去，在这个水域为我们商船队护航的这个信息以后呢 </MRC>，^我本来也是一个'船员，所以我从心底里感觉得到船员的一种感觉，就是 ^ 最简单的一个，就是 ' 高兴、' 放心，心里就 ^ 定了。

嘉宾 2：<A> 我是 1998 年离开海军到国防大学工作的 </A>。十年以后，那么我是前不久又到了南海舰队，到了南海舰队登上了舰艇以后，我是感慨万千呀。好多老华侨离开祖国四五十年了，一看，呀，中国的舰艇 ^ 那么大啊，还有 ^ 那么大的舰艇。我是刚离开 ^ 十年啊，我是 ^ 一直研究武器装备的，我回去以后都特别吃惊啊。我就这么告诉你，我不说多强 .. 这次出去的舰艇，比美国的驱逐舰 ^ 一点点都 ' 不落后，在很多方面比美国都要 ^ 强。如果说和俄罗斯的舰艇相比，比俄罗斯舰艇要先进 ^ 十年以上。

（观众热烈掌声）

《防务新观察：抗击海盗真实全过程》

In this Example, without being assigned the turn to speak, the second interviewee, General Zhang, competes to give evaluation, which infringes the Q-A turn allocation system in military interviews. While the first interviewee, Capital Chen expresses his affect from the perspective of a seaman, General Zhang deliberately takes the standpoint of an experienced military weaponeer. It can be seen that he exploits the strategy of 'complementary DE', a subcategory of 'competitive DE'. This DE is used by way of an adaptation to the contextual factor of 'emotion'. In his answer, Senior Captain Chen expresses his positive feelings of happiness and relief. As we know, this first time for China to send navy to carry out escorting missions outside Chinese waters displays the combat capability of Chinese military far out at sea. Every Chinese finds pride in this big event. However, Chen's words do not mention anything about this feeling, which fails to induce the positive emotion of national pride of the audience. On this occasion, General Zhang seizes the floor to express his great pride in the technical advancement of Chinese vessels. The adaptation to positive emotion of the production of this DE is indicated by the expressions such as interjection 'ya', affect indicators 'gankai wanqian' (thousands of mixed emotions), 'tebie chijing' (feel especially surprised), and also by his emphasized intonation. The illocutionary force of Zhang's evaluation is strategically boosted by the use comparison and intensifiers. The employment of complementary DE triumphantly evokes the national pride among the audience, which is evidenced by their enthusiastic applause. In a word, the complementary DE used by Zhang is the result of the adaptation to emotion so as to gratify his communicative needs in this specific context.

After the discussion about the self-oriented and the other-oriented contextual correlates that inter-adapt with the interviewee's choice of DE, we are now moving to concentrate on another kind of adaptation: the group-oriented adaptation.

5.4 Group-oriented Adaptation

Military interviews are components of the contemporary public sphere, and the interviewee comes to the program not only as an individual person, but more importantly represents the social group to which he belongs. Following Nwoye (1992), we take the concept of 'group' to be a social unit larger than an individual. In the specific setting of military interviews, it may be constituted by a company, a division, a certain branch of military force, or the government, etc. As a result, the interviewee takes part in the interview not only with self-related communicative needs, but also with group-oriented communicative needs, the satisfaction of which will bring great honor or benefit to the group. Consequently, there must be contextual factors that are associated with the group, which would interadapt with the interviewee's linguistic choice of DE. This type of adaptation is dubbed group-oriented adaptation in the present dissertation. Four major contextual correlates are uncovered according to our data at hand, namely group face, group interests, international relationship and public understanding, each of which will be illustrated below.

5.4.1 Adaptation to group face

The faces we have discussed in 5.2.1 and 5.3.1 are concerned with individuals. However, the attributes that people are face-sensitive can also apply to the group or community that people belong to or are identified with (Spencer-Oatey, 2008). While individual face relates to the self-centered desire of the individual to have his/her behavior, attributes, wants and desires approved by others, group face addresses a person's need to act in a way which can bring honor or benefit to the group (Nwoye, 1992). It is created by the sum of faces constituted through interactional dyads and is often dependent upon previous, socially cooperative interactions with like-minds, and like-faced people (Bousfield, 2008). In military interviews, quite often, the interviewee has a strong feeling of belonging to a group, whose image is to be guarded and defended. That is to say, he usually places the wants and needs of the group he identifies with above those of his own. Whenever the group face is threatened, or he feels there is need to protect, maintain or enhance the group face in verbal interaction, he will utilize communicative strategies. DE is one of such strategies. The following Example demonstrates this point.

Example(33)

Situation: The interviewee is the commissar of a destroyer detachment of South China Sea Fleet. Destroyer 166 visited America in 1997. It was the most advanced guided missile destroyer before Destroyer 167 joined the fleet.

主持人: 我们第一次出访美国是在1997年,当时好像是 =166舰, (GLOTTAL) 其实就是我后面的这艘, 是吧? 从这个视觉上看 (TSK) 非常小, 这艘舰艇, 跑了那么长时间跑到美洲, 还跑了美洲四国, (TSK) 一共跑了多长时间?

嘉　宾: 当时航线呢98天, (TSK) 2万多海里。(TSK) 你刚才说呢看起来很小, 实际上在当时应该说在我们国产驱逐舰当中它并不小, 但是现在显得是 (TSK) 小了, 但是它的续航能力 ^ 应该说是可以的。也应该说那次出访也是对我们国产驱逐舰的一种检验和考验, 我们这条舰呢应该说 ^ 经受住了这种检验和考验, 圆满地完成了 = 出访任务。

《防务新观察: 走进中国南海舰队》

A prefaced question is brought forward by the interviewer in this excerpt. In the preface, the interviewer assesses the destroyer as being small. Such an assessment is perceived by the interviewee, who is the Commissar of the destroyer detachment of South China Sea Fleet, as negative. Therefore, after finishing answering the question advanced by the interviewer, he shifts the focus of the topic in the current interaction, and turns to evaluate the Destroyer, with the intention to rectify the interviewer's view on the guided missile destroyer 166. The content of the DE is semantically inconsistent with the interviewee's initial utterance. The type of DE intentionally adopted here is 'reparative DE', the employment of which is the result of adaptation to group face. As we know, nowadays, the advanced guided missile destroyers tend to be large in volume. The interviewer's prefatory statement which describes Destroyer 166 as being small certainly poses threat to the face of South China Sea Fleet. If the Commissar does not take up the strategy of reparative DE in this situation, the audience may perceive the fleet to be technologically backward, which is obviously a negative evaluation on the group which the interviewee identifies with. Out of this consideration, the interviewee deliberately evaluates Destroyer 166 as not being small among the domestic-made guided missile destroyers in the 1990s, and then he changes his evaluative disposition from appreciating the shape of the Destroyer to judging its capacity, viz. its good durable seaworthiness which makes it possible for the Destroyer to perfectly accomplish its mission of visiting the foreign countries. This DE shows the interviewee's disagreement with the interviewer's assessment. And the repeated use of the evidential marker 'yinggai shuo' (It should be said that) indicates that he is basing his viewpoint on certain evidence, which lends power to his self-defense. In a word, the use of the reparative DE by the interviewee is an adaptation to group face so as to satisfy his communicative need of bringing honor to South China Sea Fleet, the group which he belongs to.

5.4.2 Adaptation to group interest

Interest is a rather elusive term. The difficulty with this notion lies in the actual spelling out of what it involves in the interaction (Locher, 2004). In the present study, group interest is narrowed down to the core interest of the country, viz. national sovereignty, national security, and sustainable development. The ensuing excerpt, in which a professor from the Research Institute of International Strategy is interviewed, demonstrates the use of DE resulting from an adaptation to the contextual factor of group interest.

Example(34)

Situation: The 'Peace Mission' series of joint military exercises between China and Russia began in 2005, and are held in every two years.

主持人：从“和平使命——2005”开始到现在，可以说“和平使命”已经形成了一个系列的联合军事演习了，有的评论说，这已经成了一个机制化的联合军演，机制化本身意味着什么?

嘉　宾：机制化是^很重要的，因为训练是要持续进行的，^威胁..也没有消失，又有上合组织的框架，还有中俄这种政治关系，所以机制化是非常必要的。机制化意味着你能够持续地对某个问题进行关注，进行演练，持续提高你的战备水平和你的准备^程度，有的时候演练也可以直接转化为^作战行动，所以对整个^捍卫国家安全，^打击三股恶势力是^非常重要的。

《今日关注：中俄军演，剑指“三股势力”》

In this interaction, the interviewer asks what mechanization of joint military exercises means. The interviewee deliberately adds an evaluation on mechanization, a topic which is mentioned in the previous turn but not the focus of it. The type of DE that the interviewee utilizes here is an 'additive DE', which can be further identified as an 'elaborative DE'. The employment of the DE is out of the consideration for the contextual factor of 'group interest', which is revealed by the interviewee's justification that 'weixie meiyou xiaoshi' (threats do not vanish) and 'hanwei guojia anquan' (safeguard national security). The joint military exercise between China and Russia, which is codenamed 'Peace Mission', is mechanized in 2005, three years after the establishment of Shanghai Cooperation Organization. The purpose of the series of joint military exercises is to respond to the new challenges and threats facing the regional security, especially threats from the three forces, namely international terrorist, extremist and splittist. Such cooperation enhances the mutual trust between China and Russia in the military and security fields. Without doubt, the Peace Mission military exercises are conducive to the peace and stability of the region. It is these group interests that trigger the interviewee's employment of DE in the interaction. By evaluating the mechanization as 'hen zhongyao'(very important)and 'feichang biyao' (extremely necessary), the interviewee clearly shows his supportive stance to mechanization and guides the audience to realize the importance of the mechanization of the joint military exercises.

5.4.3 Adaptation to international relationship

As the discussion in military interviews is frequently related to international issues, the interviewee must bear the international relationship in mind when talking about such issues. Generally speaking, the interviewee will show friendliness to other countries in the discussion if the talk is not concerned with international disputes between the two countries. In such a way, the interviewee can create a positive image of the group he belongs to in the public arena he is involved in. When the interviewer's question touches upon any topic that may bring impairment to the international relationship, the interviewee usually resort to DE to avoid aggravating the international relationship. The following Example is adduced to offer an illustration of this point.

Example(35)

Situation: On Nov. 28, 2007, Destroyer 167, which is named 'Shenzhen', visited Tokyo. This is the first time in 35 years for a Chinese fleet to visit Japan.

主持人：刚才^下边的那位战士(TSK)提到了=就是出访的时候会有一些突发事件，这一般突发事件都会是哪些方面的呢？

嘉　宾：突发事件呢=(TSK)<L>主要还是(TSK)防止恐怖袭击和一些敌对势力制造一些事端</L>。

主持人：你们遇到过吗？

嘉　宾：我们遇到(TSK)像去年我们去日本=就遇到他的右翼分子。<u>应该说，我们去日本大多数日本人民还是对我们很友好的，是持欢迎态度，包括他的官方军方(TSK)都是很热情，</u>但是右翼分子(TSK)是截然相反。我们到东京晴海码头，还没有..靠码头之前，右翼分子就组织人员在码头上喊话，喊了半天没人应他，理他，他也就灰溜溜地<@撤掉了@>。

《防务新观察：走进中国南海舰队》

In this extract, the interviewee adopts a 'highlighting DE' when he responses to the interviewer's Yes/No question. When giving his comments, the interviewee intentionally drops the original topic of right-wringer to assess the Japanese people and the Japanese government. After the assessment on the second topic, the interviewee resumes his narration. The propositional content of the DE is semantically inconsistent with the rest of the utterances in the turn, and the DE is used to accentuate the interviewee's stance toward the Japanese people and government. The employment of this type of DE, a subcategory of 'digressive DE', is the result of the adaptation to the contextual factor of international relationship. As is known to all, the Sino-Japanese relation has been a sensitive topic. Though the relationship between the two countries has been normalized since 1972, the communication in the field of national defense has always been a 'sensitive region of landmine'. The visit to Japan under discussion is reputed to be a successful 'ice-breaking journey' which lays a benign foundation for mutual trust in the field of politics and military between the two countries. In this context, if the interviewee only evaluates negatively on the Japanese right-wingers, the audience might infer that the Chinese army still assumes a negative attitude toward Japan. This will definitely cause damage to the international relationship between the two countries. Taking the international relationship into considerations, the interviewee digresses from the narration about the deed done by the Japanese right-wringers to intentionally foreground the friendliness and hospitality of both the Japanese people and the Japanese government.

5.4.4 Adaptation to public understanding

A government must gain public understanding on its military actions, military expenditure, or policies. They should explain to the public the real situations of controversial issues. Otherwise, the harmonious domestic surroundings and the peaceful international environment will be impeded. Military interviews are public forums for the government to communicate with the mass audience so as to remove misunderstandings. DE is a communicative strategy which is frequently used by the interviewees to reach this communicative goal when misunderstanding may arise. The ensuing Example, in which the vice-director of the foreign affair office of the Ministry of National Defense of China is being interviewed, typifies such a situation.

Example(36)

Situation: The interviewee, Qian Lihua, is the vice-director of the foreign affair office of the Ministry of National Defense of China. With China rising economically and politically over recent years, some in the United States have feverishly preached a 'China threat' theory. One of the main focuses of the theory is the rapid development of Chinese military power.

主持人: 曾经有过所谓的中国军事威胁论，内容是什么?

嘉　宾: 从就是 90 年代开始，有些国家不时地传出中国威胁论，他有时候平静那么一两年，过一两年，或两三年以后，中国威胁论再次翻起，这 = 不足为怪。一个发展中国家，处在一个发展和崛起阶段，^ 必然会引起其他国家的不解和猜疑，甚至产生一些 ^ 敌视的想法，我想这是任何一个大国发展崛起当中所面临的同样的一个问题。这几年，中国威胁论，一个是集中在中国军事威胁，有些国家的媒体和学术界人士觉得中国的军力发展已经超出了国防建设的需要，还有一些传媒界人士认为将会对某些国家在某些地区的利益构成威胁，这是军事威胁。中国威胁论包括方方面面。中国发展解决了 ^ 十三亿人的吃住行的问题，使整个世界的 ^ 六分之一的人口处在一个稳定的状态，这对整个世界的和平与稳定它都是一种 ^ 贡献，<u>所以说中国发展对其他国家构成威胁，他是 <MRC>^ 没有任何道理的 </MRC>。</u>

《新闻会客厅: 国防部官员解码中美军演内幕》

In response to the interviewer's question, the interviewee offers more information than what is required. He does not only provide an explanation for the so-called 'China military threat' theory, an act prompted by the interviewer, but further shifts the focus of the current topic to evaluate those countries which spread such a theory. This surplus evaluation intends to rectify the possible misunderstanding engendered by the widespread China military threat theory. Therefore, one subtype of 'additive DE', viz. a 'reparative DE' is exploited here. This type of DE is chosen to adapt to the contextual correlate of 'public understanding'. As we know, with the rapid development of China's economy and military strength, China has gradually gone from the periphery of the international community to the center of the world stage. Some countries, such as the US and Japan begin to disseminate the 'China threat' theory which would mislead people to form negative evaluations on China. As the question brought forward by the interviewer touches upon this topic, it offers the interviewee a good chance to refute the theory.

When giving the evaluation, the interviewee construes his position as uncontentious by the use of a bare evaluation. [26] While the head act of the DE is monologically asserted, it is nonetheless supported by the justification which is italicized in the Example, thereby signaling his awareness of the existing opposing positions on the issue under discussion and also increases the persuasiveness of the DE. The strategic use of DE assists the interviewee in dispelling misunderstandings so as to achieve a better international

[26]Bare evaluations refer to the evaluations without explicit linguistic markers for modifying illocutionary force. They have been treated as intersubjectively neutral and objective (Lyons, 1977). It opts for material which is considered as factual or established knowledge in a given communicative setting, and makes pragmatic sense to treat such material as unproblematic and uncontentious (Martin, 2008).

environment for the future development of the nation.

The above Example illustrates how DE is utilized as a result of adaptation to public understanding of international issues. In other cases, DE may be used to adapt to public understanding of domestic issues.

Example(37)

Situation: On July 5, 2009, a seriously violent incident erupted in Urumqi, capital of Xinjiang Uygur Autonomous Region. The violence was masterminded by terrorist, separatist and extremist forces both inside and outside China. Rebiya Kadeer, the so-called mastermind behind the July 5 riots in Urumqi, had given a speech in Voice of America stating that the Chinese government is making use of the antiterrorist action to suppress the religious belief of the Uygurs, and that the minorities in Xinjiang do not have freedom in religious beliefs. The interviewee, Mr. Ah, is a Uygur scholar.

主持人：还有包机吗?

嘉　宾：今年可能租37 架包机，(GLOTTAL) 有工作人员、有翻译。工作安排得^ 井井有条，因为集体组织以后，受到沙特政府的^ 表扬，我本人也是多次受到沙特政府的^ 接见，对我们中国的组织工作表示^ 嘉奖。

主持人：就是说，在新疆各少数民族享有^ 充分的宗教信仰的自由，同时还可以有组织的、非常安全的到麦加朝觐。除了宗教信仰自由之外，我们注意到信仰是有47 个民族聚居在一起，(TSK) 而且各民族都有自己独特的文化，各民族的文化也得到了很好的保护，相关情况一起来了解一下。

《今日关注：热比娅的谎言》

In this excerpt, after offering the required answer, the interviewee moves beyond the topical agenda set by the interviewer by means of appreciating the organizational work done by the Chinese government. The evaluation is intentionally added with the purpose to redress the audience's possible negative evaluation on the government. Hence, a 'reparative DE' is in play in this interaction. The option for the employment of this DE is a result of the adaptation to the contextual factor of 'public understanding'. The background introduction in the program has provided us with the lies Rebiya Kadeer has spread. These malicious lies are intended to distort the fact and to mislead the public to misunderstand the central government, with the ulterior motive to split China. When the interviewer catches the interviewee's line that the government even organizes the Muslims in Xinjiang to make pilgrimages to Mecca, he wants to further discover the truth. The interviewee, Mr. Ah, a Uygur who has experienced the pilgrimage to Mecca and quite well understands the interviewer's communicative intention, flouts the conversational maxim of quantity to deliberately take up a reparative DE to evaluate the organizational work as well-done.

What is noteworthy here is that in this example the interviewer opts for a narrative mode[27] to present his particular value orientation. Instead of directly denying the possible negative evaluation on the government polices toward minorities, the interviewee chooses to narrate that he himself has been warmly received by the Saudi Arabia government who highly praised the China government in organizing the pilgrimages. This choice

[27]Narrative is an indirect way of realizing evaluation for the reason that it is closely connected with the speaker's attitude. Labov, the scholar who is famous for his narrative model, explicates that narratives invoke meta-discursive practices which enable interactants to present their evaluation toward the past event (Labov & Waletzky 1972).

enables the interviewee to advance his evaluative stance as arising naturally and inevitably from the fact of his own personal experiences. As a consequence, the interviewee construes his evaluative stance as self-evidently right, just and uncontroversial.

It can be clearly seen that the DE shows the reality of the government's policies on minority religions belief and that the Uygur in Xinjiang are in fact fully enjoying their freedom of religions belief. In a word, the use of a reparative DE and its specific linguistic choice made by the interviewee in this example interadapts with the contextual correlates of 'public understanding' so as to satisfy his communicative needs of driving off public misunderstandings and to maintain the stability of the nation.

5.5 Summary

In this chapter, we focus our attention on the adaptability of DE in military interviews. The contextual factors that interadapt with the utilization of DE are analyzed, which are categorized into three groups, viz. self-oriented, other-oriented, and group-oriented. The self-oriented type associates the adaptation with the contextual correlates such as self-face, identity, and power. The other-oriented type involves the adaptation to other-face, cognitive needs, and emotions. And the group-oriented contextual correlates involves group face, group interests, international relationship, and public understanding. The contextual correlates which are analyzed result from our close examination of the data collected so far. Though possibly being unexhausted, they have exhibited that DE in military interviews is a communicative strategy chosen by the interviewee as the result of dynamic adaptation to various contextual correlates so as to satisfy his communicative needs.

The contextual correlates are summarized and presented in the ensuing figure.

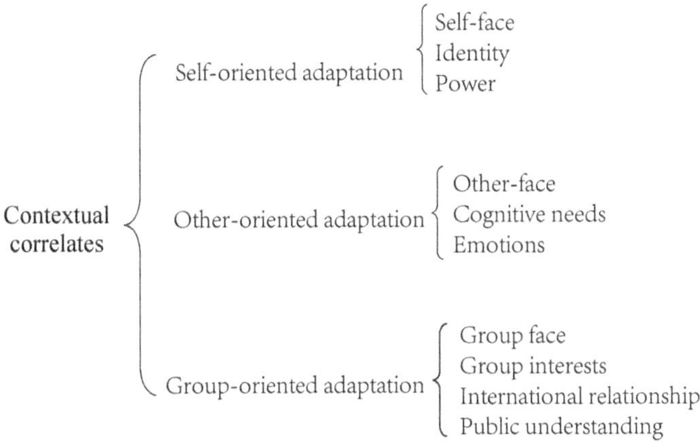

Figure 5-2 Contextual correlates related to DE in military interviews

Chapter 6
Functions of Deliberate Evaluation

6.1 Introduction

The use of language in a given context is capable of leading to the satisfaction of the speaker's communicative needs. The Linguistic Adaptation Theory, which holds a perspective view of pragmatics, considers it a task for pragmaticians to explore the functions of a language phenomenon in actual context of language use (Verschueren, 1987,1999). In Chapter 4 and Chapter 5, we have described various types of DE and revealed the multifarious contextual factors that may influence the adaptation process, which has provided us with the basic tools needed to describe the aspect of the meaningful functioning of DE in terms of extralinguistic and linguistic co-ordinates. Therefore, in order to exhibit a comparatively comprehensive and sufficient picture of DE, this chapter is dedicated to a display of the functions contributed by it to the global dynamics of the communication event. As mentioned in Chapter 3, during the process of realizing various functions, the interviewee manipulates different rapport orientations so as to construct his identity as positive. Hence, this chapter will also intend to explore the links between DE, rapport management and identity construction for the sake of unearthing the pragmatic mechanism hidden behind the employment of DE.

6.2 DE, rapport management and identity construction

As discussed in Chapter 5, the choice of various types of DE occurs in a dynamic adaptation process to various contextual correlates in different communicative contexts. DE can then be seen as having an aspect of managing social relations in interaction. The process of managing social relations in interaction is called 'rapport management' in Spencer-Oatey's theory (2008). This term is meant to underscore the fact that interlocutors invest 'rapport' into their ways of communicating by adapting their language to different contextual correlates so as to reach different communicative goals that they might be pursuing. In addition, the term addresses the relational aspect of communication in that it highlights the social relations the interlocutors have with each other. It is crucial to stress that the term 'rapport management' does not only refer to the harmonious pole of linguistic behavior, but also covers the entire spectrum of interpersonal linguistic behavior. As mentioned in Chapter 3, rapport management includes four orientations, namely rapport enhancement orientation, rapport maintenance orientation, rapport neglect orientation and rapport challenge orientation. In addition, the concept of face, which is central in the traditional politeness theory, is still essential in the theory of rapport management. However, it is defined slightly different. According to the definition of face in the theory of rapport management, face is not a fixed construct. Rather, it is a product which emerges at the actual moment in interaction. What's more, it is crucial that face is only loaned to an individual from society. In other words, it depends on the acceptance of others and can be considered as a collaborative achievement, accomplished through face-to-face interaction with others.

The construction of identity through language means has aroused great interest in numerous fields. Among these studies, Bucholtz and Hall's (2005) theory is said to have provided the best contemporary instruction for the study of identity construction. According to the theory, identity is the social positioning of self and other. It is an emergent product rather than pre-existing source of language. In addition, it is relational. That is to say, it is the active negotiation of an individual's relationship with larger social constructs. This notion of identity can be connected to the notion of face since both are linked to an interactant's understanding of a particular self that he/she wishes to propose in a specific communicative context. Therefore, the notion of identity can be nicely tied up with the notion of rapport management: rapport management refers to the ways in which the construction of identity is achieved in interaction, while identity refers to the product of these linguistic and non-linguistic processes (Locher 2008).

In military interviews, the interviewee expresses, communicates, and ultimately negotiates his identity through many different channels, for instance, the way he comports himself, the way he uses language. According to the theory of identity in interaction, evaluation is one important way of indexing identity. Therefore, the employment of DE, which is an intentional use of evaluation, is one of the languages used to construct identity. We can also claim that the way in which we use DE plays a crucial role when we are maintaining, enhancing, neglecting or even challenging relationships in interpersonal communication. Just as Martin and White (2005:2) propose that evaluations are of interest not only because they reveal the speaker's/writer's feelings and values, but also because their expressions can be related to the speaker's/writer's status as construed by the text, and because they operate rhetorically to construct relations of alignment and rapport between the speaker/writer and the actual or potential respondents. It can then be inferred that DE, as the interviewee's deliberate employment of evaluation in verbal interaction, is concerned with the construction of his identity and also related to rapport management.

6.3 Communicative functions of DE in military interviews

Researching into the communicative functions of DE directly refers to its problem-solving nature. When there occurs a communicative problem during the course of an interview — such as the need for self-protection — the interviewee would choose a DE strategy whose function is to deal with the problem in question. As a result of the adaptation to various contextual correlates in a specific communicative context, DEs perform functions which may not be reached by other ways of language use. In this sense, we can say that the advantage of the employment of DE is its contribution to the realization of communicative functions.

The communicative functions of an institutional talk consist of its social functions and its transactional functions. When performing social functions, the talk is more interpersonally oriented, and is aimed at fostering collegial relationships; when performing transactional functions, it is more task-oriented, and is directed at furthering the objectives of the organization (Drew & Heritage, 1992; Holmes, 2007). This is also true with DE, a communicative strategy frequently adopted by the interviewee in the institutional setting of military interviews. As presented in Chapter 3, DE can be used by the interviewee to maintain or enhance interpersonal relationships so as to meet the other-oriented communicative needs. It can also be employed to approach the institution-specific goals of military interviews, and thus satisfies the group-oriented communicative needs. Apart from these, DE can be utilized to gratify the self-directed communicative needs as well. Therefore, we distinguish three types of function of DE in military interviews, namely interpersonal-oriented functions, self-oriented functions, and group-oriented functions. These functions can be seen as forming a continuum, with the interpersonal-oriented functions representing the social end, the group-oriented functions representing the transactional end, and the self-oriented functions standing in between. The details of each type of function will be given below.

6.3.1 Interpersonal-oriented functions

Interpersonal-oriented functions refer to the functions that exert impact on the negotiation of social relations between the speaker and the addressees. They are concerned with the effects that are induced by the employment of DE on the attitude that the participants hold to each other. The data at hand evidences three interpersonal-oriented functions, namely maintaining interpersonal relationship, altruistic functions, and decreasing psychological distance.

6.3.1.1 Maintaining interpersonal relationship

Evaluations can realize the function of constructing or maintaining relations between the speaker or writer and the hearer or reader (Thompson & Hunston, 2000). When DEs are used to diminish the negative impact on interpersonal communication, they are considered to be realizing the function of maintaining interpersonal relationship. This function of DE prevents the interpersonal relationship between the participants from getting worse, and thus has a rapport maintenance orientation.

A. Mitigating the force of disagreement

Disagreement is defined by Rees-Miller (2000:1088) as a speaker (S) disagrees when she/he considers untrue some proposition (P) uttered or presumed to be espoused by an addressee (A), and reacts with a verbal or paralinguistic response, the propositional content or implication of which is not P.[28] Due to its negatively affective nature, disagreement falls into the category of illocutionary acts which have the potential to damage another person's face. Consequently, in a military interview which is a context of mutual vulnerability of face, the interviewee will normally employ certain strategies to mitigate the force of disagreement so as to minimize its negative impact on interpersonal relationship.

Example(38)

Situation: Barack Obama, an African American, was inaugurated as the 44th American president on January 20, 2009. This interview is about his future doctrines.

主持人：那么关于第一点，就是说奥巴马在国内政坛的根基比较浅，这一点你怎么说？

嘉　宾：(TSK) 我觉得 ... 当然，奥巴马是一个很年轻的总统，他从政的时间，就是在国家层次从政的时间并不是很长，但是我觉得也很难说他是一个根基很浅的总统。因为他背后是 = 整个的民主党，是 = 投他票的大多数

[28]Rees-Miller, J. Power, severity and context in disagreement. *Journal of Pragmatics*, 32, 2000. p1088.

选民，是 = 在过去八年布什执政期间积累的很多的人才，很多的精英。他们都要通过奥巴马的这个政府来表达自己的声音，来表达自己的意愿，来把他们的想法贯彻到政策上。所以我觉得 ^ 很难说他是个根基很浅的总统。

《防务新观察：奥巴马全球战略之猜想》

Noticing that the interviewee evaded part of her question, the interviewer renews the evaded part in this excerpt and asks what the interviewee thinks of the view that Obama has a rather shallow root in domestic political arena. The interviewee first intends to disagree with the embedded view, which is revealed by the stance marker 'wo juede' (I think), but then he abandons it and digresses to assess Obama, which neither provides support to his ensuing stance, nor provides useful background knowledge to facilitate the audience's interpretation, but hopes to highlight his stance. It is obviously that he utilizes a 'highlighting DE' here, which is subsumed under 'digressive DE'. This DE operates as an adaptation to the contextual factor of other-face. To negate the initial assessment on Obama embedded in the interviewer question poses threat to the face of other military experts or commentators who hold it and a bare disagreement will certainly do no good to the social relations. When disagreement on evaluation emerges in communication, the speaker would often find strategies to reach some form of agreement (Linde, 1997). In this interaction, the interviewee resorts to DE before he explicitly expresses his disagreement. The delay between 'wo juede' (I think) and 'dangran' (of course) signals his intention to mitigate the upcoming disagreement (cf. Pomerants, 1984). The DE is a negative one since 'hen nianqing' (very young) and 'congzheng shijian bing bushi henchang' (without a rather long history of being in the saddle in the senior political arena) connote that Obama is a president lacking in political experience. It shows the interviewee's negotiation with the negative assessment in the previous turn, and can thus be considered as a hedged opinion (cf. Linde, 1997; Walkinshaw, 2009). It can then be inferred that the DE employed in the excerpt attenuates the opposition of the different stances and mitigates the illocutionary force of the speaker's disagreement.

Due to the function of mitigation, the use of DE helps in lowering the degree of face threat brought by the disagreement, and is thus propitious to realizing the harmonious relationship between the interviewee and other experts. As the product of the process of rapport management, the interviewee's identity is constructed as a thoughtful and less aggressive young scholar.

B. Mitigating interpersonal conflict

In verbal communication, interpersonal conflict occurs when the interlocutors hold different views, opinions, stances or perspectives toward the same topic they are talking about. This is reflected by the speech acts such as argument, opposing, rebutment, etc. (冉永平, 2010). These speech acts are negative ones which threat the face of the other interlocutors and will do harm to the interpersonal relationship. In military interviews, when there emerge different points of view among the interlocutors, the interviewee may resort to DE so as to mitigate interpersonal conflict and to maintain a harmonious interpersonal relationship.

Example(39)

Situation: The first interviewee is a female, while the second interviewee is a male.

主持人：所以您的意思是这也体现了^我们男女平等的这种意识的进步？

嘉宾 1：哎，这是一种社会意义，文明程度的一种 [体现。

嘉宾 2： [其实我们也可以反问一句，<RH> 为什么女性就不能开战斗机呢 </RH>？

主持人：因为女人在 = 可能有人会说，因为女人在体能上明显弱于男性。同时还要面临着结婚生子这样一些压力。

嘉宾 2：<TSK> 同样男人的压力不会比女人小。男人可以开，女人照样可以开呀。当然这是我们反问。<u>但是从我 .. 作为一个 = 男士，我来观察，我觉得我们^中国的女人^不比美国女人差，甚至比美国女人说要强</u>。美国女人驾驶 F-15 战斗机，我们经常谈到这个 F-15，应该是力量，要求都^非常强的一种机型，美国的妇女可以驾驶 ...

《防务新观察：巾帼挑战超音速战机》

Two opposing stances emerge in this interaction. One of the interviewees, Liu Xiaolian, a female major general of Chinese air force, holds the view that the appearance of female combat aeroplane pilots signals the raised awareness of the equal right between males and females, and training the female soldiers to fly fighter is the embodiment of the development of social civilization. This point of view is challenged by the other interviewee, expert Jiao, who is a male. However, Jiao's stance is in turn opposed by the interviewer, who is a female. When formulating her turn, the interviewer attributes her point of view to an identified external source with the purpose to distance herself from the remarks and thus try to maintain a neutralistic posture. Nevertheless, her biased stance is betrayed by her initial unattributed remarks—'yinwei nüren' (because women). The interviewer's position which is intensified by giving reason is once again countered by expert Jiao. Therefore, there forms a typical structure of a conflict episode which comprises the following moves: statement à counterstatement to A à counterstatement to B (Gruber, 2001). Then, we can say interpersonal conflict occurs in the interaction.

In the ensuing turn, expert Jiao still opposes the view held by the two females in the interview. However, in order to mitigate the interpersonal conflict, Jiao shifts the current argument to evaluate Chinese women to be no weaker or even more powerful than American women. The strategy employed here is 'comparative DE', a subcategory of 'additive DE'. The employment of this DE is the result of adaptation to the addressee's face. In his DE, Jiao uses the rhetoric of comparison. By comparing the Chinese women with American women, the interviewee highlights the value of the evaluated and thus upgrades the illocutionary force of the evaluation. As we all know, the American female pilots are very famous around the world and the first generation of American female combat aeroplane pilots came into existence as early as 1993. By saying that Chinese female pilots are not worse, or even better than American female pilots, the speaker boosts the force of his positive evaluation. Positive evaluations of the addressee can serve to mitigate or soften face-threatening acts (Holmes, 1986; Blackwell, 2010). In this interaction, the interviewee's repeated opposition to the other two participants' stances certainly threatens their face and leads to interpersonal conflict. DE is therefore employed to mitigate the conflict, and even avoid the possible accusation from the female audience who are watching the program. In this way, the interviewee maintains a harmonious interpersonal relationship with the host, General Liu, and the female audience of the program.

During the process of the rapport management, the interviewee foregrounds his gender identity of male and his national identity of Chinese. His gender identity is indexed by the overt mention of identity category— 'zuowei yige nanshi' (as a male), and his national identity is revealed by the deixis 'wo men' (we). This 'we' here is a pragmatic empathic deixis which can be used to narrow down the psychological distance between the interlocutors (Ran, 2007). In this way, Mr. Jiao succeeds in presenting a positive identity of a less aggressive co-interviewee.

6.3.1.2 Altruistic functions

Altruistic functions refer to the functions realized by the employment of DE when the speaker is more concerned with the interests of others, rather than those of the self. Two sub-functions are evidenced in the data, namely implementing compliment, and balancing information asymmetry.

A. Implementing compliment

Compliments are typically social lubricants which enhance rapport. They are speech acts which explicitly or implicitly attribute credit to someone other than the speaker, usually the person addressed, for some 'good' (possession, characteristic, skill, etc.) which is positively valued by the speaker and the hearer (Holmes, 1986). In military interviews, DE is quite often used by the interviewee to implement compliment. By expressing admiration, approval, ect. to the addressees, the interviewee intends to enhance a harmonious relationship and also to construct a positive self identity.

Example(40)

Situation: Three generations of test pilots are being interviewed. The interviewee, Li Zhonghua, is the youngest of them.

主持人：中华呢，对前辈很熟悉吗？

嘉　宾：^非常熟悉，应该说我是踏着我们前辈的路走过来的。我在 = 读大学的时候，(TSK) 1980 年我就知道王昂是当时的试飞英雄，是我们的 ^ 偶像；到了 1989 年进入试飞员学校的时候，王昂部长当时参加了我们的开学典礼，而当时黄炳新团长就是我进入试飞团当时的团长，黄炳新团长的很多飞行过程中的 ^ 壮举也激励着很多试飞员。他们都是我 ^ 特别尊重，^ 特别敬仰的英雄。

《新闻会客厅：三代人话战斗机试飞传奇》

In the interaction, an 'elaborative DE' is adopted by the interviewee. After offering a confirmation to the interviewer's yes/no question, the interviewee precedes to express his great respect and ardent adoration to the two predecessors. This choice of DE is motivated by the contextual factor of 'other-face'. In addition, the illocutionary force of this positive affective evaluation on the other interviewees is increased by the repeated use of the content-oriented booster 'tebie' (especially). Since boosting the force of a positively affective speech act can be understood to be an expression of friendliness or 'camaraderie' (Lakoff, 1975), the intensified compliment constructs a positive image of the other two interviewees, decreases the social distance between the evaluator and the two evaluated test pilots, and helps to enhance the rapport between them.

During the process of rapport management, the interviewee, who has been awarded the title of 'ace test pilot' and 'heroic pilot' by the Central Military Commission, foregrounds his identity as a younger and less experienced pilot than the two other interviewees. This can be evidenced by his appellation of 'qianbei' (predecessor) to the other two pilots present at the interview. In a word, by setting a positive image of the others by the use of DE, Li constructs his identity as a modest, unpretentious and polite young pilot.

B. Balancing information asymmetry

As we mentioned in Chapter 5, the mass audience of military interviews may lack military knowledge related to a certain topic under discussion in the interview. That is to say, there exists an information asymmetry between the interviewee and the audience. If the interviewee does not try to fill the information gap, the audience would have difficulties in catching the full meaning of what the interviewee intends to say or they would not enjoy the program fully. In this case, DE is a linguistic tool that can fulfill the function of balancing the information asymmetry. In other words, it can be employed by the interviewee to intentionally assess an object for the sake of gratifying the audience's desire for certain information. Balancing information asymmetry is an altruistic action which can benefit the less erudite audience, as well as exert positive effect on the social relations between the interviewee and the audience. The following is an example:

Example(41)

Situation: USA-193, an American military espionage satellite, malfunctioned shortly after it was launched in December 2006. It was then destroyed on February 21, 2008, by a modified

SM-3 missile. The event highlighted the growing distrust between the US and China, and was viewed by some to be part of a wider 'space race' involving the US, China, and Russia.

主持人：现在可能很多人关心空间碎片的问题。这次撞毁究竟产生了多少碎片？

嘉　宾：据报道有 500 多片。但是体积很小，没有大过橄榄球的。(TSK) 虽然没有大过橄榄球，这已经算 ^ 大碎片了。空间碎片分 3 类，10 厘米以上的算 ^ 大碎片，1 到 10 厘米算 ^ 小碎片，1 厘米以下算 ^ 微小碎片。

主持人：以这样 ^ 大的碎片真的会对其他的在轨卫星或飞行器有影响吗？ <A> 因为美国 </A>，我们 ^ 清晰地记得，美国曾经指责其它的国家这样做可能会对其他的在轨卫星有影响。

嘉　宾：他如果不再入大气层是有影响的。因为目前主要是跟踪 10 厘米以上的，10 厘米以上的目前太空中有 1 万个，1 到 10 厘米有 10 万个，如果是大于 10 厘米，又有 500 多片，估计目前他跟踪的主要是这个，如果不再入大气层会对航天器有影响。

《防务新观察：一箭击星，得失几何》

In this excerpt, after providing the number of the debris as requested, the interviewee moves on to deliberately elaborate on the volume of them. The strategy employed here is 'elaborative DE', a subtype of 'additive DE'. The DE here is composed of a head speech act and a justification. The interviewee evaluates the debris as large ones even though they are no larger than rugby. This evaluation is justified by the interviewee by means of explicating the criteria for qualifying large, small, and tiny space debris. The utilization of DE here is adapted to the contextual correlate of the audience's 'cognitive needs'. If the interviewee does not further provide the DE, the audience may not fully understand the possible consequence that may be brought by the collision, for they lack the specialized knowledge about space debris. Being aware of the existence of this information vacancy in the audience, the interviewee intentionally uses DE to fill it. By doing this, he balances the information asymmetry, and facilitates the audience's interpretation of the ensuing discussion on the topic of space debris.

The use of the DE in this extract is propelled by the interviewee's craving for enhancing the rapport relation between himself and the audience. When the interviewee uses the DE, he foregrounds his identity as an expert in space science. This can be inferred from his specialized knowledge in evaluating and defining the volume of the debris, since earlier studies on institutional discourses revealed that the use of specific technical vocabularies is a means of constructing expert system (Giddens, 1991; Drew & Heritage, 1992). What's more, the head act of DE here is supported by the use of justification, which helps to build the interviewee as rational. Therefore, the process of rapport management constructs the interviewee as a considerate and rational space science expert.

6.3.1.3 Decreasing psychological distance

In military interviews, the interviewee may attend to and anticipate the psychological state of the audience, and then selects from a range of pragmatic strategies to converge to the emotions of the audience. DE is one of such strategies.

Example(42)

Situation: In covering the Beijing Olympic Torch Relay in San Francisco, CNNs commentator Jack Cafferty attacked China, saying that imported Chinese products are 'junk', Chinese people are 'basically the same bunch of goons and thugs they've been for the last 50 years'. This attack on Chinese people ignited the fire of indignation in every Chinese.

主持人：这个卡夫蒂对中国的攻击，当时是在一个什么样的上下文中 = 说的，针对什么事？

嘉　宾：(TSK) 嗯，　就是当时咱们奥运的圣火在美国的旧金山传递的过程之中美国CNN推出了一档新闻评论节目。卡夫蒂作为CNN ^资深的评论员他以这样的面貌出现，应该说是 <MRC> ^非常的不礼貌，^非常傲慢，充满了偏见的 </MRC> 这样一些评论。在前后文里边呢，他实际上是表达了一种情绪，这种情绪里边有什么呢？比如说，他点到了美国对伊拉克的战争，点到了贸易逆差的问题，还点到了一些其他方面的问题，[然后呢 ...

主持人：[美国对伊拉克的战争和中国有什么相干吗？

《防务新观察：国家安全不能忽视媒体》

In this example, the interviewer queries about the event that triggers Cafferty's vicious attack on China. The interviewee starts to answer the question. However, when he mentions the news commenting program of CNN, he deliberately turns to evaluate Cafferty, who is a senior commentator of the program. After the evaluation, he resumes to offer the information sought by the interviewer. Apparently, a 'digressive DE' is used by the interviewee in the interaction. In addition, this digressive DE is irrelevant to the interviewer's question, and servers to highlight the speaker's negative stance to Cafferty. Therefore, it can be further identified as a 'highlighting DE'. This strategy is selected by taking the contextual correlate of 'emotion' into consideration.

As we know, before the 25th Olympic Games were held in Beijing, the Olympic torch was relayed around the world according to the Olympic routines. When covering the Torch Relay in San Francisco, the American CNN commentator Jack Cafferty viciously attacked China, which deeply hurt the feelings of the Chinese, and thousands of Chinese Americans gathered in San Francisco protesting against this commentator, demanding CNN to fire him and to make a sincere apology to ethnic Chinese people all over the world. The Chinese government also condemned Cafferty and requested CNN to apologize to Chinese people. It can be inferred from this background that the Chinese audience must be furious about Cafferty. Converging to the audience's negative emotion, the interviewee intentionally evaluates Cafferty negatively as extremely impolite, extremely arrogant and totally biased in giving his comments. Conveying negative stances towards an absent third party makes the relationship between the participants in an encounter closer and helps to build rapport (Goodwin & Goodwin, 1992; Boxer, 1993; Ruusuvuor & Lindfors, 2009). The employment of DE in this interaction can easily gain the audience's affiliation with the speaker, and can thus play the role of decreasing the psychological distance between the interviewee and the potential audience. In this regard, it orients to enhancing the rapport of the social relationship. The negative evaluation on Cafferty also helps in constructing the interviewee as a patriotic Chinese media expert.

The foregoing example illustrates how DE as a result of adaptation to negative emotion functions in decreasing the psychological distance. The following is an example which demonstrates the interviewee's adaptation to positive emotion so as to achieve the same function.

Example(43)

Situation: The first interviewee, vice division commander Wang, is talking about the difficulties in flying through the desolate area. The third interviewee, Jiao Guoli is a colonel and the editor of the magazine Chinese Air Force.

主持人：这个无人区为飞行带来哪些难度呢？

嘉宾 1：地面没有任何的地面情报支持和指挥给你

主持人：意味着你穿过这个无人区的时候听不到任何声音？

嘉宾 1：没有任何地面指挥。基于无人区那条航线的特点，起飞以后，大概飞了五六百公里以后，就进入了没有人指挥你的无人区。那个地方 ^ 一旦出现了险情和特殊情况，这样无助的境界， <A> 有位飞行员说，你如果那里飞机出了问题，你下去先把自己崩了拉倒了</A>，就没有人能给你提供 ^ 任何的救援

嘉宾 2：@@ 没人来救你了

嘉宾 3：这是一种 ^ 大无畏的英雄气概。我觉得应该给掌声。

《防务新观察：走进中国歼击机部队》

In this extract, the strategy of 'competitive DE', which can be further categorized into 'empathic DE', is employed by one of the interviewees who deliberately takes his evaluative stance toward the aviators without being allocated the floor by the interviewer. The utilization of this DE results from the adaptation to the contextual factor of 'emotion'.

When asked whether he cannot receive any signals when flying through the desolate area, Wang replies that he cannot receive the commands from the command post, and when encountered with any emergency, there is nothing he can do but commit suicide. These utterances imply the aviators' selfless dedication to their career. The high pattern of the interviewee's intonation contour betrays his pride and self-sacrificial spirit. However, he does not proffer any explicit evaluation on himself or other aviators. This may be due to his modesty, which is influenced by the traditional Chinese culture. Taking Wang's affective state into consideration, another interviewee, Mr. Jiao, breaks the Q-A system in the military interview, and deliberately assesses that the aviators are courageous and heroic. This evaluation is 'unofficial' because it is not requested and is self-initiated. Apart from that, the evaluation is not in any way a response to the question raised by the interviewer. Instead,by taking the turn, the interviewee is inviting the audience to give a warm applause to show respect to the Chinese aviators. This is an act of organizing the interview and should have been carried out by the interviewer. Thc noticeable breaking away from the principles of military interviews shows the speaker's empathy with Wang, and converges to the psychological state of both the co-interviewee and the aviators who are present at the interview.

During the process of language use, the user of the empathic DE manipulates the rapport enhance orientation by taking the other person's psychological state into consideration. A positive identity of the speaker is therefore presented by the DE as cooperative and diplomatic.

The functions of DE discussed above are concerned with other-directed communicative needs. In the following section, we will demonstrate the functions orienting to benefiting the user of the DEs in military interviews.

6.3.2 Self-oriented functions

The self-oriented functions of DE in military interviews gratify the interviewee's self-directed communicative needs. When the interviewee adopts a DE to realize self-oriented functions, he has little concern for the quality of the relationship between others and himself. Therefore, DEs which perform such functions have a rapport neglect orientation.

6.3.2.1 Protecting the self

When being interviewed, the interviewee must watch every word he utters or every stance he holds, for whatever he says will be immediately spread throughout the whole society. This is especially the case in military interviews, for the reason that the discussion on certain topic would quite often involve national pride and country image. When the interviewee's point of view cannot meet the social expectations, he is more likely to construct a negative self-image and incur criticisms from the audience. Under such circumstances, the interviewee may adopt DE as a communicative strategy to maintain a positive self-image and thus to protect himself from being criticized. The following example, in which Senior Colonel Li Jie is being interviewed on the joint exercise held by the Chinese Marine and the American Marine corps, is a case of DE employed for the purpose of self-protection.

Example(44)

Situation: On November 17, 2006, the Chinese Marine and the American Marine Corps held a joint military exercise. The results show that the Chinese Marine Corps achieved higher score.

主持人: 那还能从哪里看呢?

嘉　宾: 这里头也有一个 = 情况, 因为他毕竟是在朱诺号的这几百人当中选出的 20 人, 你这个, 咱们这个海军陆战队从人比较多选拔的这个情况以外，还有一个就是天时地利人和这个情况，因为训练场都在你们，就是^咱们自己国家，所以这种情况下比起来呢，当然有很多的偶然性。

主持人：所以您觉得这个结果不能 [完全说明实力？

嘉　宾：[那没这个意思。<u>但是我们在这个方面^应该来说个人素质和战斗技术能力还是^相当强的。</u>

《防务新观察：两栖神兵》

When the interviewer says that the Chinese Marine Corps achieved higher scores in the joint military exercise, the interviewee, General Li, replies that when taking other factors into consideration, we should say that it is just accidental for Chinese Marine Corps to win out in the exercise. These remarks may imply that the Chinese Marine Corps are less powerful than the American counterpart. Such a position would surely hurt the national pride of the audience and threaten the country image. What's more, in his evaluation, the interviewee uses 'ni' (you) and 'nimen' (you) to refer to the Chinese Marine Corps and 'China', which betrays his empathy with America and depathy with Chinese Marine Corps. Both his implied position and his uses of deictic expressions may constitute his public image as fawning on foreign powers, or even worse, an image of not loving one's own country. In this context, the interviewee intentionally adopted the strategy of 'reparative DE', which can be subcategorized into the heading of 'additive DE'. This strategy is motivated by the need to adapt to the contextual factor of 'self-face'. When being further asked whether he thinks that the result of the joint military exercise can reveal the real competence of the Marine Corps, the interviewee, being aware of the possible damage of his public image incurred by his previous words and the likely criticism from the audience, deliberately adds an assessment that the Chinese Marine Corps have rather good personal quality and combating technology. According to Fisher and Adams (1994), a strategy that attempts to avoid the problems likely to be incurred by one's comments, such as misunderstanding, misinterpretation or embarrassment, functions to manage impression and protect the identities of the speaker. In this excerpt, by the utilization of the DE, the interviewee repairs the interviewer's and the audience's ill conception on him and avoid constructing a possibly negative self image. Therefore, it helps the interviewee to realize his goal of protecting himself from being criticized.

The analysis above shows that the reparative DE is used in a context in which the interviewee is more concerned about his own face than that of others. Hence, it has a rapport neglect orientation. In managing a rapport neglect orientation, the interviewee intentionally adds a positive DE after his requested answer. What's more, the use of 'wo men' (we) is intended to highlight his national identity as a Chinese. The evidential marker 'yinggai shuo' (It should be said that) implies that his evaluation is based on evidence, though not explicitly pointed out. In addition, the booster 'xiangdang' (very) functions to increase the illocutionary force of the positive DE. All these contribute to presenting the interviewee as a patriotic and objective Chinese military expert.

6.3.2.2 Reinforcing persuasiveness

Military interviews are platforms for the interviewee to convey his attitudes and opinions toward various topics concerning military issues. However, he is not just offering opinions, more important, he wants his opinions to be accepted by the mass audience. That is to say, he wants to influence the audience cognitively. From this perspective, most of the communication in military interviews can be said to be persuasive communication. Persuasion is the coproduction of meaning that results when an individual or a group of individuals uses language strategies and/or visual images to make audiences identify with that individual or group (Burke, 1969). In military interviews, when the interviewee wants to persuade the audience to align with his point of view, he would employ DE as a strategy to reinforce the persuasiveness of his assertion. Let's take the ensuing excerpt as an example:

Example(45)

Situation: A British and a French submarine, both of which nuclear-powered and carrying nuclear weapons, collided in the Atlantic Ocean on February 16, 2009.

主持人：很多人说这个核潜艇相撞的几率几乎是零，(TSK) 那么这次相撞，您刚才也谈到了，可能会暴露出很多问题。^究竟暴露了哪些问题？

嘉　宾：我觉得 = 主要暴露出了，当然如果从他们内部来说，你像英国的简氏战舰年鉴，<u>这是^非常有名的工具书，全世界^最有名的工具书</u>，他的一个编辑说，他说这个^不是技术问题，是程序问题。那么什么是程序问题，说白了就是两个人出去要做一件事，谁也不告诉谁，两人就进入了一个茫茫的黑黑的通道里去了。

《防务新观察：核艇相撞，北大西洋起波澜》

When asked what problems are revealed by the collision of the nuclear subs, the interviewee begins to launch his assertion, but then drops and attributes his point of view being expressed to a third party, the editor of Jane's Fighting Ships. In other words, the interviewee digresses to present his opinion as being grounded in the subjectivity of an external source. As a well-known military commentator and chief editor of the military magazine Navel and Merchant ships, the interviewee would not just borrow an idea from an ordinary person and thus destroys his public image. Adapting to his professional identity, the interviewee adopts a 'supportive DE", which is subsumed under the strategy of 'digressive DE'.

According to Martin and White (2005), when attributing a point of view to an external source, the authority of this source is of great importance for the reason that high credibility can be implied via the use of sources which/who have high status in the field. Therefore, the interviewee intentionally proffers the evaluation that Jane's Fighting Ships is a very famous reference book, which provides the audience with the background knowledge of the external source to which the interviewee attributes the opinion. In addition, the repetition in the evaluation 'feichang youmingde gongjushu' (a very famous reference book'), 'zui youmingde gongjushu' (the most famous reference book) boosts the illocutionary force of the speech act and the degree of authority of the evaluation is enhanced accordingly. Thus, in this case, although it is the editor of the journal of Jane's Fighting Ships who is presented as advancing the view, the interviewee is clearly implicated in the value position. As a result, the intentional employment of the supportive DE in this example helps to align the audience with the assertion put forth by the interviewee and thus succeeds in realizing the interactional function of reinforcing persuasiveness.

As has been analyzed above, the DE is used to increase the credibility of the speaker's pointed of view. Therefore, it is self-oriented and is rapport neglect. This management of rapport orientation succeeds in constructing the interviewee as a credible and authoritative military expert.

6.3.3 Group-oriented functions

The group-oriented functions performed by DE in military interviews are divided into four sub-functions, namely constructing a positive group image, implementing refutation, clarifying the truth, and manipulating the audience. Each will be detailed in the following sub-sections.

6.3.3.1 Constructing a positive group image

Group image refers to how a group is perceived by the public. It is partially deliberate and partially accidental, partially self-created and partially exogenous. Military image is a general impression or evaluation formed by the public about the external characteristics, internal spirits, and the behavior of a military group (文琦、磨玉峰, 2007). Nowadays, many countries actively work to create and communicate a positive military image to the public. A country that ignores its military images is more prone to encounter an array of problems. Some of the warning signs that an army might have problem in its image building involves frequent riots, being distrusted by the citizens, vicious attack from foreign press, and a poor relationship with other countries, etc. It is thus vital for the leaders of a military group to realize the importance of creating, maintaining and enhancing a good image, and every group members should be aware of this. Just as the first Chinese military spokesperson General Hu says (胡昌明, 2009), image is both strength and combating effectiveness, and military image building is an important component of national image building.

Several factors have contributed to the increasing importance of military image construction in recent years. First, due to the lack of military communications with other countries, people abroad, being misled by the unfair and biased reports of some foreign media, have a negative impression on Chinese army. The wide spreading of the so-called China threat theory, the disruptive activities which happened abroad during the Beijing Olympic torch relay, the accusation of the insufficient military transparency etc. witness the foreign people's misunderstandings of Chinese army. Second, the society's growing expectation that the Chinese army should be powerful, helpful and socially responsible is another vital dimension. Being misunderstood by people at home may result in serious riot which would bring devastating damage to the harmonious development of the society. Finally, the rapid development of the media technology and the internet makes it more convenient and efficient for an army to convey its positive side to its various audiences.

Group image which is related to the cognitive representation of a group is formed and shaped through actions (Richards, 2006). Verbal interaction is an important means to build and negotiate the image of a group since what we say and how we say it reveal something of ourselves and who we take ourselves to be. It is in concrete social activities and within specific instances of discourse that group images become the object of resistance, alternative formulations and renegotiation (De Fina, 2006). When we produce utterances in conversation, we do much more than impart information corresponding either to the propositional content of our talk or propositional inferences that can be drawn from what is explicitly uttered. We also say some important things about ourselves as communicating members of the socio-

community to which we belong(Heisler et al.,2003:1618).[29] In military interviews, the interviewee is quite aware that what he says in the program has the potential to reflect positively or negatively on his self image as well as on the image of the social group to which he belongs. For that reason, his utterances always provide metaphorical information about the group image he wants to present. Moreover, he is also competent in the use of different strategies that contribute towards positive group presentation in verbal interaction. DE is such a strategy used by the interviewee to create a positive group image.

Military interviews operate under the government's guidance. Therefore, when the interviewee intends to construct a positive group image, he would consciously orients to the six values of national image building which are pointed out by the government, namely modernization, openness, peace-loving, political stability and economical development, striving, and nomocracy. In addition, as military interviews are public arenas which target at the audience both at home and abroad, the users of DE in the program with the purpose to build a positive group image should also consider the values that are treasured by various groups of audience across diversified cultures. The social psychologist, Shalom Schwartz (2001) has developed a universal framework of value constructs that has been empirically validated in over 63 different cultural groups. He found 10 different value constructs emerged in the vast majority of countries/cultures, which can be applied both to individuals and to groups. These values are power, achievement, hedonism, stimulation, self-direction, universalism, benevolence,

[29]Heisler, T. Vincent, D. & Bergeron, A. Evaluative metadiscursive comments and face-work in conversational discourse. *Journal of Pragmatics,* 35(10-11). 2003. p.1618.

tradition, conformity, and security.

Media offers substantive chances to publicize a military group's achievement, capability, and other positive values. It is a powerful and efficient instrument for a military group to convey its image. Therefore, in military interviews, the interviewee will catch every opportunity to present the positive side of the group he belongs to or identifies with. Based on the two categorizations of values listed above, and also a thorough examination of the data at hand, we discover four major values that are involved in the interviewee's employment of DE with the purpose to construct a positive military image. These values are listed as follows:

- Being technologically advanced
- Being peace-loving
- Self-sacrificing generosity
- Being capable

During the process of a military interview, the interviewee would resort to the communicative strategy of DE to present the positive side of the military group he identifies with according to these four values so as to achieve the following functions.

A. Constructing a group image of being technologically advanced

This function is related to 'modernization' listed in the value of national image building. It is also concerned with 'achievement' in Schwartz's value constructs. In his address at the opening of the NPC Sessions in 2007, Premier Wen Jiabao said building a solid national defense system and a powerful people's army was a strategic task in socialist modernization. The advancement of military technology is a signal of a powerful national defense system of a country. And constructing a military image of being technologically advanced is an effective measure of deterrence to prevent hostile actions from other countries. It is directly related to a country's international status in the field of military. At the same time, it can trigger national pride in the audience. From this perspective, it can be said to have a rapport enhancement orientation. Here is an example:

Example(19)

Situation: On November 17, 2006, the Chinese Marine and the American Marine Corps held a joint military exercise.

主持人：我们前面的这个短片记录了两军比赛的全过程，(TSK)好像从画面上没有看出来两军的比赛和陆军有什么不同?

嘉　宾：还是有点区别的。(TSK) 当时那枪轻武器我们的 5.8 枪族，他们美军来体验一下我们的 5.8 枪族到底怎么样。因为他的口径是 5.56 的，陆战队配的制式的冲锋枪。(TSK) 打的结果呢据说是很满意，因为我们这枪呢精度高，而且当时质量是非常好的，在世界整个 (TSK) 小口径枪里头是比较杰出的一种。另外一些比赛是路障比赛，有些是陆军所不具备的，一个抬橡皮舟，集体运橡皮舟。运橡皮舟有多种方法，有沙滩运行和山路运行和林间小路运行。这次选择的是沙滩运行方法，就是大家并排，手垂直，共同抬舟，还有推举的，这个就在丛林中，把这个树要把它让开。这种运橡皮舟是一种很经常的比赛，^需要体力，又^需要协调。

主持人：您谈到的是运橡皮舟比赛这是陆军所不具备的，还有别的吗?

《防务新观察：两栖神兵》

In this example, the interviewer queries whether there is difference between competitions held by the Marine Corps and those held by the army. The interviewee offers a confirmation in the early stage of his turn, but then abandons the ongoing topic to evaluate the Chinese light weapon, which is irrelevant to the question raised by the interviewer. After the evaluation, he continues the original topic. That is to say, a strategy of 'digressive DE' is adopted by the interviewee. The utilization of the DE does not provide background information for the current speech, nor does it give support to the interviewee's overall position. Rather, it is used to highlight the interviewee's evaluative stance. Hence, it can be sub-categorized into the strategy of 'highlighting DE'. The employment of this strategy is motivated by the contextual correlate of 'group face'. In military interviews, face need is more important a collective concern than a personal one. In this interaction, the interviewee digresses to assess the Chinese 5.8mm rifle as high in accuracy and good in quality so as to impress the audience with the rapid development of technology in Chinese military field. In a word, the digressive DE in this example functions to construct a positive Chinese military image of being technologically advanced.

When using the DE, the interviewee holds a rapport enhancement orientation. The assessment is put against the background of the small bore rifles in the whole world, which intensifies the illocutionary force of the speech act and triggers the audience's emotion of national pride. In addition, the DE is attributed to an external source by the use of evidential marker — 'jushuo' (it is said that), which makes the assessment more objective. As a result, the interviewee establishes a self identify of an objective Chinese general who is proud of the development of the Chinese modern technology of weapons.

B. Constructing a group image of being peace-loving

Constructing an image of being peace-loving is one of the aims of national image building of China. It reflects the speaker's desire for safety, harmony and stability of the world. Hence, it is also related to the value construct of security in Schwartz's value constructs. A military group which is peace-loving will be perceived by other countries to be less aggressive, and will avoid being criticized as threatening the peace of the region, or even the peace of the world. The following is an example that shows how DE is employed to construct a group image of being peace-loving.

Example(46)

Situation: The interviewee, Qian Lihua, is the director of foreign affair office of the Ministry of National Defense of PRC.

主持人：中国讲究兵不厌诈，现在我们^尽量寻求军队军事方面的开放，会不会使我们处在劣势呢？

嘉　宾：其实 = 随着中国国家实力的不断 = 发展壮大，(TSK)军队的建设也在不断发展。但是我们与外宾交往的目的还是为了增进了解，加强互信，促进友谊，发展合作，我们不去威胁任何人，我们也不会 = 向海外扩张，即便中国强大了，我们军事实力增强了，我们也不会去威胁任何人，我们也不去威慑任何人，这与我们国家的社会制度，与我们的军事战略，与我们传统的军事文化是密不可分的。

《新闻会客厅：国防部官员解码中美军演内幕》

In this excerpt, the interviewer questions whether seeking

military openness will put China in a disadvantageous position since Chinese consider that nothing is too deceitful in war. This question is no doubt inappropriate in military interviews for the reason that China has always been criticized to be not transparent in military, and the government is adopting various means to add transparency in this respect. In this context, General Qian Lihua opts for the strategy of 'substitutive DE' in his reply by providing an evaluation on Chinese military policy, which deviates from the requested evaluation. This type of DE is adopted by taking the contextual factor of 'international relationship' into consideration.

For years, the U.S. has considered China as a country that lacks military transparency and deserves high vigilance. An American Quadrennial Defense Review says that 'lack of transparency and the nature of China's military development and decision-making processes raise legitimate questions about its future conduct and intentions within Asia and beyond.' It can be seen that China's persistent military buildup, though justified and normal, has lead to the deterioration of Sino-US relations. To maintain a harmonious international relationship, there is a need for China to show its stance on military policy on public occasions. Keeping this in mind, General Qian Lihua deliberately shows his evaluative stance on Chinese military communication and military buildup. He assesses military communication as 'increasing understanding, enhancing mutual trust, facilitating friendliness and developing cooperation', and evaluates military buildup as 'not threatening any other country'. These DEs realize the pragmatic function of building a military image of being peace-loving.

By building a military image of being peace-loving, the interviewee converges to the audience's point of view and thus has a rapport enhancement orientation. In addition, it can be observed that a bare evaluation is opted for by the interviewee. This linguistic choice makes the evaluation more objective and makes pragmatic sense to consider the evaluation as unproblematic and uncontentious. Therefore, as a product of the rapport management, an identity of objective and authoritative officer in charge of military foreign affaires can be constructed.

C.Constructing a group image of self-sacrificing generosity

Never being afraid of sacrificing the self for the good of others is part of the vow of Chinese People's Liberation Army. In public arenas such as media interviews, a serviceman would try to show this attribute to the audience so as to construct a positive group image. Self-sacrificing generosity is concerned with the value construct of universalism in Schwartz's value list, which refers to the tolerance and protection for the welfare of all people, and is therefore validated across different culture groups. Let's consider the following excerpt:

Example(47)

Situation: The interviewee is a vice chief of staff of a certain branch of paratroops.

主持人: 有一个说法说，对于空降兵来讲，如果打败了就是全军覆没，即便打胜了也是九死一生。这是一种文学化的表达呢，还是说现实确实如此?

嘉　宾: (TSK) 有点文学化的表达吧，空降兵面临的作战环境^确实有这方面的因素，说九死一生，在特定的环境下，特定的条件下，确实是这样的。<u>但是空降兵是这样的，</u>

就是 <MRC> 空降兵绝不以自身的和局部的成败论英雄 </MRC>, 空降兵历来是以正面部队的胜利为自己的胜利, 以历来战役全局的胜利为自己的胜利, '必要的时候就 ^ 牺牲自己, 保全大局, 这是空降兵部队, 空降兵官兵的责任, 也是我们的荣誉, 我想也是空降兵官兵所 ^ 必须要承载的历史使命。

《新闻会客厅: 空降兵背 10 公斤降落伞展英姿》

There is a saying that for paratroops, no one would survive if being defeated, and even if they win, the victory is achieved by a slight majority. This saying stirs up the interviewer's curiosity about its authenticity and leads to her question as to whether the saying is just an expression of literature or is a reflection of the reality. The interviewee first answers the question as requested, but then shifts the focus of the original topic of the question to deliberately give a positive evaluation on paratroops. The evaluation adopted here is 'elaborative DE'. It is the speaker's identity that motivates the utilization of this DE.

Being a vice chief of staff of a paratroop, the interviewee would try to impress the audience with a positive group image. The DE here is employed to achieve this goal. By intentionally saying that it is an honor for members of paratroops to scarify the self so as to guarantee the overall success in war, the interviewee successfully constructs a group image of self-sacrificing generosity, which will trigger the audience's admiration or respect for the paratroops in China. For this reason, the speaker holds a rapport enhancement orientation in the interaction.

When offering the DE, the interviewee foregrounds his identity as a member of paratroops, which is revealed by his use of 'women' (we). In addition, a high level modality[30] — 'bixu' (must) is used in the evaluation, which helps the interviewee to show his judgement of the DE in relation to obligation. High level modalities indicate the leaders have a high affinity with the proposition they made, and help in constructing the identity of an accountable leader (Ho, 2010). Therefore, the interviewee in this interaction succeeds in building up an identity of an accountable leader of a certain branch of paratroops.

D. Constructing a group image of being capable

An army which has outstanding combat capability is surely considered to be a qualified army which has the ability to protect the lives and properties of the people it is serving for. Generally speaking, there are six requirements for the combat capability of a modernized army, viz. cooperative engagement capability, quick reaction capability and mobile operation capability, counter-electronic capability, logistical support capability, survival capability, and organizational and command capability. The following interaction, in which the vice team leader of the national rescue team is being interviewed to talk about their rescue action after the severe earthquake in Si Chuan, is an instance in which the interviewee uses DE to construct a group image of being capable of quick reaction and manoeuvrability.

Example(48)

Situation: The interviewee, Liu Xiangyang, is the vice team leader of the national rescue team, which participated in the rescue action after the severe earthquake in Sichuan.

[30]Halliday and Matthiessen (2004) identify three 'values' of modality, namely high, median, and low.

主持人：我了解到你们是第一支进入灾区的救援队伍，你们是什么时候接到命令的？

嘉　宾：是的，我们是^第一支到灾区的队伍。我们接到命令的时候是当天下午。

主持人：地震发生之后两个小时？

嘉　宾：两个小时。接到这个全力出动命令，当时我们队伍<MRC>14 分钟 </MRC>就集合完毕。集合完毕以后，我们按上级的要求，^迅速乘了一个车队，^长途奔到南苑机场。

主持人：接到命令之后 14 分钟完成集结，这听上去^不可思议。

嘉　宾：因为我们的队伍长期在战备，这是一支^国家级队伍。

《防务新观察：军魂铸就“国字号”救援队（一）》

In this episode, the interviewer wants the interviewee to confirm whether they received the order to enter the Sichuan earthquake hit area two hours after the disaster broke out. The interviewee, who is one of the members of the rescue team, confirms as required by the interviewer. His institutional task should have been finished with his confirmation. Nevertheless, he continues to intentionally give a more detailed evaluation on the reaction and the maneuverability of the national rescue team. The type of DE he makes use of is ‘elaborative DE’, which is adapted to the contextual factor of ‘group face’.

The elaborative DE employed is not inscribed but invoked (cf. Martin and White, 2005). That is to say, instead of explicitly making his assessment positive or negative, the interviewee provokes the audience’s positive assessment on the reaction and the maneuverability of the national rescue team via counter-expectation. In the excerpt, the expression ‘14 fenzhong jiu’ (only 14 minutes) is an indicator of counter-expectancy which implies that it is impossible for ordinary people to get together in 14 minutes. Therefore, it provokes the assessment that the reaction capability is unexpected and incredible. The evaluation given by the interviewee is not itself positive or negative, but has a potential to provoke in the addressees a positive assessment of the national rescue team. By using the expressions such as '14 fengzhong jiu' (only 14 minutes), 'xunsu' (rapidly), 'changtu' (long distance) in his DE, the interviewee reaches his communicative goal of constructing for the group he belongs to a positive image of being capable, i.e., quick in reaction and flexible in maneuverability. This is further confirmed by the overt positive evaluation given by the interviewer.

By provoking the positive assessment on the rescue team from the addressees, other positive emotions such as admiration, respect may also be triggered, hence, as far as rapport is concerned, the DE has a rapport enhancement orientation. In addition, by way of presenting his assessment on his own group in an implicit manner, the interviewee construes himself as being modest and intelligent.

6.3.3.2 Implementing refutation

With the rapid development of its economy and military power, China is considered as a potential threat to some countries. In order to protect their own interest, these countries would frequently accuse China groundlessly. For example, almost every year, report from the American Pentagon asserts that the fast modernizing of Chinese army could pose a threat to the US and other armed forces in the Asia-Pacific region and beyond. Other accusations are concentrated on issues such as cyber attack, insufficient military transparency, unfair treatment to minorities, etc. These accusations 'grossly interfered in China's internal affairs and sowed discord in relations between China and other countries' (杨洁篪, 2005). In military interviews, when the talk touches upon the unwarranted charges against China's normal national defense construction from some hostile countries, the interviewee would employ DE as a weapon to refute those accusations, so as to maintain the dignity of our country. The following example shows how the interviewee uses DE to refute the so-called 'China threat theory'.

Example(49)
Situation: A spokesman of National Defense of Science and Technology says that China now has the ability to build an aircraft carrier. This stirs up the fierce debate on whether China should have an aircraft carrier. And some other countries once again spread the so called 'China threat theory'.

主持人: ^这么多艘都在世界各地的海洋上服役着，也没听说过什么威胁论啊？
嘉　宾: 是啊。<@其他国家都没有什么@>,^尤其是美国，你看，它有十二艘，它都是九万吨以上的，这么大的家伙在世界各地跑，也没有人说美国有航母威胁论。所以我觉得就是<MRC>有些别有用心的,而且是害怕中国发展的，害怕中国拥有航母的这些人在这炒作</MRC>。

《新闻会客厅：解放军大校驳航母威胁论》

When China releases the news that it has the ability to build an aircraft carrier and is intending to build one, other countries such as Korea, Japan, America, etc. begin to accuse China that its military buildup is not consistent with its stated goal of a peaceful rise and the plan to build an aircraft carrier of its own will pose threat to the peace of the world. However, the truth is that China is far from the first country to build aircraft carriers. Up till 2007, there are 23 aircraft carriers serving on the territorial waters of ten countries, which include America, Korea, Britain, India, Japan, France, Russian, etc. Therefore, the interviewer asks a question why there never was any threat theory since so many aircrafts are now in service in other countries. Senior Colonel Li Jie, a researcher from Chinese Navy's Military Academy, first answers the question, but then moves on to refute the China threat theory with a DE. The type of DE employed here is 'additive DE', which is tacked with the purpose of redressing the existing possible negative evaluation on China. The use of this DE is a result of the adaptation to the emotion of indignation, that is to say, the evaluation is adopted intentionally because of his great anger toward those countries which charge China groundlessly for the sake of their own benefits.

In order to make the evaluation more convincing, the interviewee adds justification to support his evaluation. The fact that no one puts forth America aircraft carrier threat theory even though this powerful country has as many as twelve aircraft carriers of more than ninety thousand tons in service in various regions throughout the world makes the interviewee's assessment more effective. The DE given by the interviewee shows to the audience that a Chinese aircraft carrier is just a valid requirement for the country and the growth of Chinese navy is both expected and warranted. By proffering the DE, the interviewee proves the China threat theory to be erroneous and gives America, a country that is enthusiastic about charging China for various groundless excuses, a counterblow.

The DE used here repays the previous offence from America and some other countries' unfair accusation of Chinese normal military growth. Therefore, it holds a rapport challenge orientation to those who support the so-called China threat theory. When offering the evaluation, the interviewee also provides an argument in support of his assessment. By this, the interviewee presents himself as a patriotic and rational military expert on navy.

6.3.3.3 Clarifying the truth

A harmonious environment is vital for China for it is now putting its effort into modernization construction and is in the process of a peaceful rise. However, the separatist forces have never stopped their sabotages. One of their strategies is to spread scaremongering against the Chinese government to misguide people's belief. These lies may distort the truth of facts and even lead to instability of the country. DE is an effective strategy which the interviewee can turn to for clarifying the truth so as to maintain a harmonious environment for the economy development of the country. The following example, in which the host is interviewing the consultant of the Chinese Association of Islamism, illustrates how DE is used by the interviewee as a strategy to clarify the truth.

Example(50)

Situation: On January 10, 2007, taking the chance of being invited to a discussion on Chinese policy toward the Uygur in Xinjiang by the Voice of America, Rebiya Kadeer said that ever since the year of 2003, the education problem of the Uygur has been neglected by the central government and the Chinese government is now even planning to eradicate the language of this minority.

主持人：阿老师，您长期以来一直在新疆生活，维吾尔族受教育的情况^到底是怎么样的？

嘉　宾：新疆的维吾尔族也好，其他少数民族也好，他们的教育问题..从中央到地方是^非常重视的，也是非常关心。有一些人..说是现在把少数民族学生要汉化，(TSK)要消灭别的民族的语言和文化，这个^完全是谎言。基于学习汉语来说，(TSK)每一个中国人一般来说都要会说国家的语言，我去过很多国家，他们也不是一个民族组成的，都是多民族组成的，但是他们都有一个^共同国语，比如在前苏联各少数民族都会说俄语，像伊朗也有很多少数民族，但是都^会说波斯语，其他国家也是这样的。有些人造谣说，(TSK) <A> 消灭少数民族语言，消灭维吾尔族语言 </A>，这^不符合实际情况。

《今日关注：热比娅的谎言》

Rebiya Kadeer's words about the unfair treatment of the Uygur in China may mislead the innocent people who do not know the truth. Therefore, when asked about the reality of the situation of the Uygur, the interviewee, who has been living in Xinjiang ever since he was born, deliberately adopts the 'reparative DE' to point out that the rumors that the minority students are denied fair treatment and that the language and the culture of minorities will be eradicated are totally lies which do not conform to the reality. The employment of the DE here is adapted to the contextual factor of his experience power. We can see from the prefatory of the interviewer's question that Mr. Ah is an aboriginal Uygur. That is to say, Mr. Ah's identity is highlighted by the interviewer in his question. And the experience of an aboriginal Uygur is a factor that prompts Mr. Ah's first DE. In addition, in order to support his second evaluation, Mr. Ah resorts to his experience in other countries which are composed of more than one nationality. By using the DE with the guarantee of his own experience, Mr. Ah clarifies the truth of the present condition of the education of the Uygur and at the same time makes it more convincing.

In this interaction, bare evaluations are used, which implies that the interviewee treats his evaluative stance as uncontentious. Therefore, in terms of the negotiation of rapport orientation, the interviewee tries to maintain the rapport or affiliation to the addressees who may be misled by the lies spread by Rebiya Kadeer. At the same time, by the utilization of a bare evaluation based on his own life experience, the interviewee constructs himself as an honest and patriotic Uygur.

The following is a similar example.

Example(51)

Situation: China is the host of the 29th Olympic Games held in 2008. However, the Tibetan separatists also call this year 'the year of Tibetan rebellion' and they tried various means to exert pressure on the central government to acknowledge the independence of Tibet. The second interviewee, Dr. Zhaluo is the director-assistant of the Institute of Ethnology and Anthropology of the Chinese Academy of Social Science

主持人：从这些暴力活动来看的话，这些“藏独”分子展现出了一个什么样的特点？

嘉宾 1：第一是有组织。这一次拉萨，还有甘南，还有四川的川西北阿坝地区基本上都是前后同时发生。我看到网上报道，甘南地区搞打砸抢烧的头上都缠一个黑布条，胳膊上也缠着，说明他们是有组织的，而且聚集了那么多人，同时往一个地方搞打砸抢烧，已经有很多的证据证明是境外的达赖集团和境内的分裂势力相互联系、相互配合，从有一些犯罪嫌疑人的供述情况来看也证明了这个问题，达赖集团，特别是“藏青会”，一直在遥控指挥怎么打砸抢烧，完了以后再怎么办，他们都有一系列的计划，^完全是一个 <MRC> 有组织、有预谋的活动 </MRC>。

嘉宾 2：“3·14”事件发生以后，达赖喇嘛有一个《告全球华人的呼吁书》，里面就讲道，这些事件是民众自发的和平请愿，我觉得这种说法是 ^ 站不住脚的，我们看到在国内的 ^ 多个点同时发生这样的暴力事件，在国外很多个使馆也 ^ 同时发生围攻事件，如果是一个自发的互动就不会有形式相同、时间相同的一些政治暴力事件发生，所以我觉得这起事件现在基本可以肯定是一个 <MRC> 有预谋的、有计划的政治事件 </MRC>。

《今日关注：达赖集团破坏奥运意欲何为？》

After the ‘3·14’ event, Dalai publicly defines the series of riots as unprompted peace petitions of the citizens. This definition no doubt covers the truth of the riots. When the interviewer asks about the features of the Tibetan separatists revealed in the process of violence, one of the interviewees, Doctor Zhaluo takes the floor without being assigned the turn to offer his evaluative stance toward the characteristic of the riots. The type of DE which is adopted here is ‘competitive DE’. The opinion conveyed by the DE complements what the first interviewee has said. The employment of the competitive DE is the outcome of adaptation to the contextual factor of ‘public understanding’. In addition, it is based on the solid evidence that several Chinese embassies in foreign countries were besieged at the same time with the same means. He then inferred that the 3.14 event and the other disturbances are premeditated and intentionally planned. This evaluation in turn supports his first DE that what Dalai said is groundless. The employment of DEs in this example performs the function of clarifying the truth of facts and ultimately helps to gain public understanding so as to maintain a peaceful and harmonious environment for the development of the country.

In this example, the interviewee shows his alignment with the first interviewee's point of view. However, his evaluations are framed by the subjectivizer 'wo juede' (I think), and is attenuated by the downtoner 'jibenshang' (basically), which leave space for potential disagreement. Hence, the interviewee maintains rapport with both the first interviewee and the audience who might have doubt about his evaluative stance. Besides, from the above discussion, we can see that as a result of the rapport management, the interviewee presents himself as a rational, persuasive and objective person.

6.3.3.4 Manipulating the audience

Manipulating the audience is one of the functions performed by DE in military interviews to persuade the audience to see things in a particular light, and to behave in the way explicitly or implicitly advocated by the evaluation. This function is said to be the most essential function realized by evaluation (冯平, 1995). Feng finds that when evaluations are used deliberately in media communication, its function of manipulating the mass audience becomes more salient. Here is such an example:

Example(52)

Situation: In the annual national civil service examination in 2009, there appear several 'strange questions' which test the examinees' elementary knowledge of weapons and national defense. This triggers controversy on whether these questions should appear in such examinations. The interviewee is a famous net military commentator.

主持人：忠平你作为是^一个一个网友吧，来判断一下(H)国家的有关部门在设置这样的一个题目的时候，出于什么样的考虑就一定要..加入这样的一种题目？

嘉　宾：就是希望我们以后的国家公务员能够^真正地重视国防教育。在我们老百姓的心目中，不光是国防知识，包括国防意识都^很淡漠。(TSK)这两个题其实说明不了什么问题，它只是给大家敲了一个警钟，但从^真正意义上来讲的话，他是在唤起我们的^公务员，你需要有这方面的知识，要掌握这种国防意识。在我认为的话，意识比知识^更重要。我不在乎我们今天是考什么苏-30啊=或者是其他的一些武器装备的这样一些东西，<A>关键在于大家要重视这个事，这个是很关键的</A>。

《防务新观察：偏题还是正题？》

In his reply to the interviewer's question, Song Zhongping, the interviewee who is a net military commentator, deliberately tacks three evaluations to his requested answer so as to realize his communicative needs. The evaluations that the interviewee adopts here are 'additive DEs', which are the outcome of the speaker's adaptation to the contextual factor of 'group interest'. These DEs combines to elaborate on the importance of the citizens' sense of national defense. As a famous net military commentator, Song surely knows the destructive consequences that may be brought by people's weak national defense awareness. Bearing the long-term national interest in mind, Song deliberately deviates from the topical agenda set by the interviewer to show his stances that people are indifferent to both national defense knowledge and national defense awareness, the two questions concerning national defense knowledge have warning functions, and most essentially, people's awareness of national defense is more important than mastering national defense knowledge. These three evaluations point out the existing problems in China's national defense. According to Thompson and Hunston, 'Expressing something as a problem makes it difficult for the reader not to accept it as such.'[31]In this interaction, the interviewee expresses his negative attitude toward people's lack of national defense awareness. As Feng's (冯平, 1995) investigation on evaluation reveals, the evaluator frequently uses evaluations to show positive or negative attitude toward others' behavior, and thus manipulates or control their actions. By using these evaluations deliberately, the interviewee manipulates the mass audience to realize the necessity to enhance the sense of national defense, and thus reaches his communicative goal.

In this example, the interviewee uses two bare evaluations and an attenuated one with subjectivizer 'wo renwei' (my view is that). What the interviewee cares about is not the interpersonal relationships but the interest of the group. Therefore, the DEs have a rapport neglect orientation. In the interaction, the interviewee foregrounds his identity of a Chinese citizen, which is revealed by the identity marker 'women laobaixing' (we civilians). The utilization of DE results in constructing the interviewee as an objective and patriotic civilian commentator.

---

[31]Thompson, G & Hunston, S. Evaluation: An introduction. In S. Hunston and G. Thompson (Eds.). *Evaluation in text: Authorial stance and the construction of discourse*. Oxford: Oxford University Press. 2000. p.8.

6.4 Summary

In this chapter, we have investigated the communicative functions of DE in military interviews. Three groups of functions are identified, namely the interpersonal-oriented functions, self-oriented functions, and group-oriented functions. The interpersonal-oriented functions include maintaining interpersonal relationship, altruistic functions, and decreasing psychological distance. The self-oriented functions comprise protecting the self and reinforcing persuasiveness. The group-oriented functions consist of constructing positive group images, implementing refutation, clarifying the truth, and enhancing people's awareness of national defense. These functions involve both social and transactional ones, which reflect the typical feature of the functions performed by talks in an institutional context.

Besides the functions, this chapter also explores the hidden mechanism that propels the realization of these functions. It is found out that the identities of the speakers are not predefined, but open to constant flux and negotiation. During the process of interaction, one of the interviewee's identities is foregrounded which combines with the communicative needs to motivate the process of adaptation. When using DE, the interviewee manipulates various rapport orientations and achieves communicative functions. As a result, the communicative needs are satisfied and a positive self identity is constructed.

DE can then be considered as an important means by which the interviewee constructs his identities in military interviews. When serving interpersonal-oriented functions, it contributes to the more social aspects of an individual identity, and constructs the interviewee as thoughtful, less aggressive, cooperative, modest, unpretentious, or polite, etc. When performing self-oriented functions, DE is used to avoid presenting a negative aspect of individual identity, either professional or social. With regard to group-oriented functions, it tends to serve institution-specific purposes, and presents the more professional aspects of the interviewee's identity. For example, it might build the interviewee as a rational and objective expert, an authorative officer, or an accountable group leader, etc. However, sometimes, the dividing line between these varied functions may be fuzzy. For instance, when performing the altruistic function of balancing information asymmetry, DE may simultaneously fulfill the institutional goal of educating the audience and constructing a professional individual identity. Similarly, when serving group-oriented functions, DE may also be doing relational work at the same time. Therefore, the clear-cut demarcation between the three groups of functions is made for convenience of analysis. The fine-grained analysis of the examples reveals how DE realizes a range of communicative functions and how the interviewee constructs a specific identity through his lexical, syntactic and discursive choices when using DE in response to contextual influences.

The functions that are achieved by the utilization of DE are schematized in the following figure.

Figure 6-1 Functions of DE in military interviews

Chapter 7 Conclusion

7.1 Introduction

Military interviews in China, televised or broadcasted, are a series of new program operating under the guidance of the government's determination to enhance the military transparency of China. Just like other interviews, this program revolves round questioning and responding, i.e. the interviewer asks questions to elicit information and opinions from the informed interviewees who have no other choice but respond to those questions. As a consequence, it is a venue for Chinese servicemen and military experts to publicly convey, formulate, and defend their stances toward persons, things, or issues involved in recent military events. Sometimes, opinions are proffered in reply to the interviewer's requests, but other times, opinions are used strategically, i.e. initiated by the interviewees to achieve certain communicative goals. It is the latter case that intrigues us and we dub it 'DE'. Given the topic sensitivity of this genre of interview, DE is pervasive in military interviews. Military interviews in China have not yet, to my knowledge, been delved into before. Neither has the work been conducted on the deliberate use of evaluation. What I hope I have achieved through this dissertation is a tentative investigation of the use of DE and an explanation of this language phenomenon. In this chapter, I will wind up my research by summarizing the major findings, pointing out implications, discussing the limitations, and putting forth suggestions for future research.

7.2 Major findings

Taking the past studies on evaluation as a springboard, the present investigation has attempted to explore various aspects of the interviewee's intentional use of DE in military interviews, encompassing its classification, adaptability process, functions, and mechanism, which has yielded the following findings.

7.2.1 Evaluation as a communicative strategy

Confined by the interview rules, the role of the interviewee is rather passive (Yang, 2007). He is required to say only what the interviewer asks him to say without the right of initiating a topic, making unsolicited comments, etc. However, sometimes the interviewee's communicative needs cannot be satisfied without deviating from these rules. For instance, when the interviewer's positive image is being threatened, or when there emerge opposing stances, the interviewee has to break the interview rules to protect the self or to mitigate conflicts. Most importantly, the interviewee comes to the program not only as an individual, but as a member of a certain military group, who co-works with the interviewer to realize the institution-specific communicative goals, such as enhancing the audience's national defense awareness, building a positive military image, refuting unjustified accusations, fostering patriotism, etc. Nevertheless, there are times when these goals cannot be realized by merely obeying the interview rules. A careful observation of the evaluations in military interviews indicates that besides proffering evaluations as the interviewer requests, the interviewees use evaluations as a device to cope with various problems arising in interaction so as to reach their communicative goals. The use of these evaluations breaches the overarching norm of interaction in military interviews, such as the pre-allocation turn system or the Gricean maxim of relevance. In addition, they are optional and are sensitive to communicative contexts. Therefore, DE is considered as a communicative strategy, which is used deliberately and intentionally. The emergence of DE in interaction can not be explained from the perspectives of syntax or semantics, but has to be considered in terms of its pragmatic motivations. The present study thus has taken a pragmatic approach to this phenomenon.

7.2.2 Categories of DE

As the choice of DE is purposive, this linguistic behavior is performed rather deliberately. The interviewee in military interviews manipulates language in various ways so as to satisfy his communicative needs. As defined in chapter 3, DE is a communicative strategy which deviates from the norm of the interaction. In the specific context of military interviews, the deliberateness of DE is found to be manifested in two ways:①deliberate deviation from the interviewer's question; ②deliberate deviation from the turn-allocation system in military interviews. Based on the forms of deviation, five groups of DE are identified, namely additive DE, substitutive DE, digressive DE, interruptive DE and competitive DE.

Additive DE subsumes reparative DE, elaborative DE, comparative DE and conclusive DE. Reparative DE tries to redress the addressees' existing or possible opinions which would bring damage to the speaker's public image. Elaborative DE shifts the topic or topic focus of the ongoing speech in the turn. Comparative DE is made against the background of another object. Conclusive

DE reiterates the central point of the utterances and signals the finality of the current turn.

Substitutive DE includes evasive DE and negotiative DE. Evasive DE shifts the action agenda or topic agenda set by the interviewer's question. And negotiative DE adjusts the question put forth by the interviewer.

Digressive DE encompasses background-providing DE, supportive DE and highlighting DE. Background-providing DE digresses to offer the addressees the background knowledge necessary for them to interpret the speaker's utterances. Supportive DE digresses from the ongoing turn to sustain the speaker's position. Highlighting DE digresses to foreground the speaker's certain stance on a particular topic.

Interruptive DE covers both aligning interruptive DE and disaligning interruptive DE. Aligning DE intervenes into the ongoing speaker's turn to show support to his stance; while disaligning DE intrudes upon the ongoing speaker's turn to express an alternative position to his on the topic under discussion.

Competitive DE comprises complementary DE, contrastive DE, and empathic DE. Complementary DE semantically complements the first speaker's position so as to jointly construct a topic under discussion. Contrastive DE is semantically contrastive with what the other interviewee says. And empathic DE shows the second interviewee's empathy with the first interviewee.

The various types of DE constitute the linguistic repertoire from which the interviewee chooses an optimal one to cope with the difficulties in verbal communication in military interviews. Which one would be chosen is determined by whether the type of DE can gratify the language user's communicative need in a specific context.

7.2.3 The adaptability of DE in military interviews

The interviewee's linguistic choice of DE in military interviews has been found to be the result of adaptation to related contextual factors. The adaptation process of DE in the present study is divided into self-oriented adaptation, other-oriented adaptation, and group-oriented adaptation.

Self-oriented adaptation gratifies the language utterer's communicative needs. The contextual correlates made salient in this process are self-face, identity, and power. DE adapts to self-face because the speaker fundamentally desires other's positive evaluation. Whenever a negative value on him is triggered and threatens his face, the interviewee would resort to DE to prevent his face from being damaged. DE adapts to the speaker's identity because DE is reflective of the speaker's identity. DE adapts to power because the powerful interviewee has more authority with regard to the topic under discussion, which results in his longer contribution.

Other-oriented adaptation satisfies the addressees' communicative needs, and the related contextual factors are other-face, cognitive needs, and emotions. DE adapts to other-face for the reason that people in social interactions do not only support their own faces, but also the faces of those with whom they interact. DE adapts to the addressee's cognitive needs because there exists information asymmetry between the authorative interviewee and the rather innocent audience in the interviews. By deliberately providing the military-related evaluation, DE can thus fill the audience's cognitive vacancy. DE adapts to the addressee's emotions because the topics discussed in military interviews quite often has the potential to invoke the audience's negative emotions (e.g. indignation, sorrow, etc) or positive emotions (e.g. patriotic sentiment, joy, etc). The need to enhance the sense of national pride, to maintain the dignity of the country motivates the speaker's use of DE.

Lastly, the group-oriented adaptation meets the communicative needs of the group which the interviewee identifies with. The pertinent contextual correlates are group-face, group interests, international relationship, and public understanding. DE adapts to group-face because in military interviews the interviewee has a strong feeling of belonging to the group he identifies with and he has the need to bring honor to the group. DE is a device to protect, maintain or enhance the group face in verbal interaction. DE adapts to group interests for the reason that military interviews are forums to enhance people's national awareness, and the core interests of the country, such as national security, sustainable development, etc., drive the speaker to use DE. DE adapts to international relationship because the discussion in military interviews unavoidably concerns national interests, political stances, etc. A peaceful international relationship requires the interviewee to adopt DE to avoid the possible international conflicts. DE adapts to public understanding because military interviews are public arenas for the government to communicate with the mass audience to remove misunderstanding so as to maintain a peaceful domestic environment. By proffering evaluation deliberately, the interviewee can help the public to see the real situations of controversial issues.

It is the aforementioned contextual factors that impel the interviewee to opt for DE as a communicative strategy in the ongoing interaction. Different contextual factors affect language use in their unique ways and result in different types of DE. Self-face motivates the interviewee to use reparative DE to avoid possible negative evaluation from the public. The interviewee's foregrounded identity incurs his use of supportive

DE and competitive DE. Power entitles the interviewee with more authority and speaking right, and calls for the use of negotiative DE, elaborative DE or interruptive DE. Other-face drives the interviewee to adopt additive DE for the sake of maintaining or enhancing a good interpersonal relationship. The addressee's cognitive needs require the interviewee to digress to use background-providing DE or to add elaborative DE so as to facilitate the audience's comprehension of the ongoing speech. The addressee's emotions propel the interviewee to use empathic DE or highlighting DE so as to decrease psychological distance and enhance interpersonal relationship. The adaptation to group face results in the interviewee's use of contrastive DE and elaborative DE. The factor of group interest is especially relevant to additive DE. International relationship constrains the interviewee to use digressive DE and substitutive DE to avoid international conflicts. The factor of public understanding leads the interviewee to utilize reparative DE to redress the audience's possible misunderstanding of the government.

In a word, DE in military interviews is a product of the dynamic process of inter-adaptation between linguistic choices and context in language use.

7.2.4 Functions of DE in military interviews

The study of function from a pragmatic perspective emphasizes the functional relatedness of a language phenomenon with the other facets of human life. The present study reveals three groups of functions performed by DE in military interviews, viz. interpersonal-oriented functions, self-oriented functions, and group-oriented functions. These three groups of functions can form a continuum, with the interpersonal-oriented functions represent the social end, the group-oriented functions represent the transactional end, and the self-oriented functions stand in between.

When DE is found to be exerting impact on the negotiation of social relations between the speaker and the addressees, it is said to be performing interpersonal-oriented functions. By mitigating the force of disagreement or mitigating interpersonal conflict, DE realizes the function of maintaining interpersonal relationship. The altruistic functions of DE are displayed in two sub-functions, namely implementing compliment, balancing information asymmetry. Decreasing psychological distance is another function that has an interpersonal orientation.

The self-oriented functions gratify the self-related communicative needs. When the interviewee's point of view fails to meet the social expectation and is likely to incur criticism, DE can be used as a self-protection device. When the interviewee wants the addressees to align with his point of view, DE may be resorted to so as to reinforce the persuasiveness of his stance.

A large proportion of the functions performed by DE are related to the group to which the interviewee belongs. They serve the institution-specific purposes and satisfy the group-oriented communicative needs. First of all, DE contributes to the construction of a positive group image. Given the institutional nature of military interviews, DE is mainly applied to construct a group image of being technologically advanced, of being peace-loving, of self-sacrificing generosity, and of being capable. Apart from these, DE can also be employed to realize the group-oriented functions such as implementing refutation, clarifying the truth, and manipulating the audience.

Armed with these various functions, DE may unquestionably be counted as a communicative strategy, which may be exploited to meet the speaker's communicative needs in a specific situation.

7.2.5 Deliberate Evaluation, rapport management and identity construction

Evaluation is inherently related to identity. By expressing one's feelings and values, one construes who he is. In human communication, people tend to show their positive attributes to others instead of negative ones. For example, people want the others to consider them as brave, patriotic, or capable, rather than cowardly, traitorous, or incapable. That is to say, people always want to build a positive identity in the way of using language. It is this that triggers the interviewee's employment of DE in military interviews.

The use of DE involves the interviewee's deliberate breaching of the overarching norms in military interviews. Therefore, it is not surprising that DE exhibits incongruence, such as topical irrelevance, semantic redundancy, sequential disruption, or illogicality. This incongruence can only be explained by the assumption that the language user in this situation is trying to construct a positive identity by the use of DE.

In military interviews, the interviewee's identities are open to constant negotiation in the dynamic process of interaction rather than predefined. The self-work of the interviewee is the management of his institutional identity (e.g. as an interviewee), professional identity (e.g. as a professor, an airman, a soldier, etc.), national identity (e.g. as a Chinese), and personal identity (e.g. as a male or a female) from moment to moment in the ongoing interaction. In order to meet his communicative needs in a specific situation, the interviewee may deliberately foreground a certain identity, and DE is a language device that can index it.

In order to construct a positive self in public, the interviewee manipulates various rapport orientations to show his communicative intention and thereby realize an array of functions of DE. When mitigating interpersonal conflict, the interviewee holds a rapport maintenance orientation; when implementing altruistic functions or decreasing psychological distance with the addressees, the interviewee holds a rapport enhancement orientation; when he is more concerned with himself instead of others, the interviewee is holding a rapport neglect orientation, such as in the process of protecting himself; when DE is performing group-oriented functions, the interviewee may assume different rapport orientations toward different interest groups. For example, when accomplishing the function of implementing refutation by utilizing DE, the interviewee may hold a rapport challenging orientation to those who had created the previous offence, but holds a rapport enhancement orientation to those who support his point of view.

By manipulating various rapport orientations to realize a multitude of functions by using DE, the interviewee succeeds in constructing a positive self identity.

7.2.6 The adaptation model of DE in military interviews

Taking the achievements and limitations of the previous researches as a starting point, the present study has proposed an identity-based adaptation model to approach DE as the interviewee's communicative strategy in military interviews from a functional perspective. This model incorporates Spencer-Oatey's Theory of Rapport Management, and Bucholtz and Hall's Theory of Identity and Interaction into the overarching Linguistic Adaptation Theory put forward by Verschueren, and thus offers a rather comprehensive account for the use of DE in the specific institutional context.

There is a close tie between DE and identity. DE is a pragmatic strategy adopted by the interviewee to satisfy his communicative needs at the expense of infringing the ground rules of interview, as well as the maxims of Grice's co-operative principle. When deliberately evaluating the world around him, the interviewee is quite aware that what he evaluates and how he does it has the potential to reflect positively or negatively on his identity, which is in a constant flux during the course of interaction. It is the interviewee's communicative needs that trigger the foregrounding of one of his identities, and the two combine to impel the interviewee to choose DE as a communicative strategy. This global strategy is realized through various means at a local level. That is to say, after the global strategy has been decided on, a specific type of DE is chosen from a range of possibilities as a result of adaptation to the contextual correlates in a negotiable manner. In this regard, the employment of DE is a result of the interviewee's constant linguistic-choice making with a high degree of consciousness.

The interviewee's choice of DE as a pragmatic strategy and its specific way of realization involve the dynamic linguistic adaptation to various contextual correlates. The adaptation process can be classified into self-adaptation, other-adaptation, and group-adaptation. This process is bidirectional, instead of unidirectional. On the one hand, the speaker's linguistic choices made in accordance with the contextual correlates result in his choice of DE as a communicative strategy, as well as his choice of how to realize it. On the other hand, the employment of DE, which is impelled by a combination of the interviewee's communicative needs and his foregrounded identity, exerts impact on the hearer's cognitive world, gets him to adapt to the interviewee's foregrounded identity and other contextual factors, and thereby realizes an array of functions. Given the specific context of military interviews, the functions of DE reveal both a social trend and a transactional trend. That is to say, DE can be used to maintain or enhance interpersonal relationships, as well as to satisfy or approach the institution-specific goals of military interviews. Apart from these, DE is also used to satisfy the speaker's personal communicative needs. During the process, the interviewee manipulates various rapport orientations and constructs his identity as positive. When performing interpersonal-oriented functions, DE contributes to the construction of the more social aspect of the interviewee's individual identity. When serving self-oriented functions, DE helps in avoiding a negative evaluation from the addressees. When doing group-oriented functions, DE is used to serve institution-specific purposes, and the more professional aspect of the interviewee's identity is presented.

The proposed adaptation model combines identity, rapport management, and adaptation together, and achieves a more comprehensive explanation for the deliberate use of evaluation in military interviews.

7.3 Implications

We can draw several implications from our study.

First, the present study observes the use of evaluation in face-to-face interaction, and focuses our academic interest on the evaluations which are deliberately delivered as a communicative strategy in pursuing the language user's communicative goals. This pragmatic perspective, meaningful though tentative, attempts to explore evaluation from a brand new angle.

Second, this research has yielded some theoretical

contributions. Instead of adopting the appraisal theory, a theory which is frequently used in the study of evaluation, the current study takes the linguistic adaptation theory as our overarching explanatory framework. However, we do not just follow the theory blindly, but amalgamate other two theories, namely the theory of rapport management and the theory of identity and interaction with it to formulate a more convincing model to analyze the process and the dynamic nature of DE. The whole model embraces various means of DE, the contextual factors that may interadapt with the possible choices, the functions that may be realized, and the working mechanism. All these components jointly contribute to a model that best fit with the explanation of the employment of DE. The rather comprehensive and convincing model of the study may shed some light on other pragmatic research on communicative strategies. In this regard, it can be thought to have made some theoretical contributions.

Third, some practical implications are also achieved. As we have mentioned, military interviews are arenas for Chinese servicemen or military experts to articulate, formulate and defend their stances. The current research displays a range of means by which the interviewee takes stances deliberately to approach his communicative purposes and thus can help him to use evaluation more effectively. Additionally, the study assists the interviewee in achieving the institution-specific goals of military interviews. For example, it shows the interviewee how to use DEs to guide the audience's cognition, how to maintain the dignity of our country, and how to enhance the audience's national defense awareness, etc. Moreover, this investigation into the deliberate use of evaluations by the interviewee can smooth the way for the audience to understand the evaluative language in military interviews with less cognitive effort and lend wings to them to catch the genuine intentions conveyed by the speaker.

Last but not least, the study of DE can enlighten our daily communication. DE is the intentional positioning of the speaker's attitude in interaction with the communicative goals in mind. When a person deliberately offers an evaluation, he is not only uttering a sentence, but expresses a thought, an illocutionary force, or a stance. It signals a relation between a subject and an object, and bridges the interpersonal relation, emotions, and cognition between the interlocutors. Therefore, the present study on DE may instruct people to use evaluation appropriately to establish, maintain, or enhance relationships with others in daily communications.

7.4 Limitations of the present study

As a first attempt to examine the deliberate use of evaluations in military interviews from a pragmatic perspective, the present study is not without its limitations.

Essentially, this study suffers from its major weakness of subjectivity. The reasoning process and the generalization of the final findings have been made in a speculative and introspective way, rather than experimental. Although we have made effort in decreasing the degree of the subjectivity of the study by appealing to linguistic evidence and background knowledge of the interaction during the inferential process, controversies may still arise in various aspects. It is inevitable that the analysis is still subjective to some extent.

Next, the present study is restricted by a relatively small number of extracts representing a relatively small number of data sets. Even though we have put great effort in collecting our data by watching the programs and doing the transcription work, there must still be some types of DE escaping from the present classification. This limitation unavoidably makes the findings uneasy to be generalized.

Furthermore, some of the analysis in the present study seems to be superficial. For example, we divide the contextual factors into three large groups, namely self-oriented, other-oriented, and group-oriented. And the same trichotomy is applied to the categorization of functions. However, sometimes a contextual factor cannot be strictly said to be self-oriented or other-oriented, neither can the functions. The adoption of such a categorization has been made merely for ease of elucidation and exploration of the point to be made. In other words, the trichotomy of both the contextual correlates and the functions is considered as a convenient way for us to discuss the deliberate use of evaluations within the particular context of military interviews.

7.5 Suggestions for future study

The limitations identified above help us to see areas in which future research might take place.

To begin, the present study on DE has confined the data to one genre, viz. military interviews. Since this communicative strategy is also found to be adopted by language users in other genres of communication, such as daily conversation, press conferences, TV shows, etc., exploring the deliberate use of evaluation in these different genres will benefit us in broadening, refining and testing the findings achieved here through this dissertation, and will yield more profound and interesting findings than those of the present study.

In addition, cross-cultural study on DE would be an intriguing topic. 'Every act of evaluation expresses a communal value-system, and every act of evaluation goes toward building up that value system'.[32] That is to say, in conveying stances or opinions, evaluation ever and always regenerates cultural norms and values. People from different cultural groups may produce and interpret evaluations differently. Hence, when utilizing DE, the speaker must be aware of the conflicts of values and ideologies in different cultures so as to avoid misunderstanding between interlocutors or failure of communication in cross-cultural contexts. To study DE cross-culturally will no doubt facilitate communication.

Moreover, corpus-based studies on DE will be welcomed. Standard corpus investigation software makes it particularly easy to quantify forms of a language phenomenon, and helps in revealing latent patterning. It can also calculate comparative frequencies of the occurrence of various structures in a given corpus, and thus draw academic attention to the variation between different genres. In this regard, this approach is necessary if the researcher intends to discover more about the resources of DE and wants to carry out a comparative study between various genres on this topic.

Finally, language is not the only channel for conveying DEs, paralinguistic channels such as intonation, prosody, gestures, gaze, etc. are also important in transmitting the speaker's value judgement. To investigate DEs in these fields would be an appealing adventure.

The above suggested areas are what we, in my opinion, need to consider and explore in the future, given our current understanding of DE. New areas will inevitably arise as we further the study.

---

[32]Thompson, G. and Hunston, S. Evaluation: An introduction. In S. Hunston and G. Thompson (Eds.). *Evaluation in text: Authorial stance and the construction of discourse*. Oxford: Oxford University Press. 2000. p.6.

All in all, despite all the endeavors we have made on the study of the deliberate use of evaluations in military interviews from a pragmatic perspective, much remains to be done in the future.

References

[1]Argar M. 1985 Institutional discourse. Text, 5(3): 147-168.

[2]Austin J L. 1962. *How to do things with words.* Oxford: Clarendon Press.

[3]Bamberg M & Damrad-Frye D. 1991. 'On the ability to provide evaluative comments: further explorations of children's narrative competencies'. *Journal of Child Language*, 18: 689-710.

[4]Bednarek M. 2006. *Evaluation in media discourse.* London/ New York: Continuum.

[5]Bednarek M. 2009. Dimension of evaluation: Cognitive and linguistic perspectives. *Pragmatics and Cognition*, 17 (1): 146-175.

[6]Benwell B & Stokoe E. 2006. *Discourse and identity.* Edinburgh: Edinburgh University Press.

[7]Biber D. 1988. *Variation across speech and writing.* Cambridge: Cambridge University Press.

[8]Biber D, Johansson S, Leech G, Conrad S & Finegan E. 1999. *Longman grammar of spoken and written English*. Harlow: Longman.

[9]Blackwell S E. 2010. Evaluation as a pragmatic act in Spanish film *narratives. Journal of Pragmatics,* 42 (11): 2945-2963.

[10]Bousfield D. 2008. *Impoliteness in interaction.* Amsterdam/Philadelphia: John Benjamins Publishing Company.

[11]Boxer D. 1993. Social distance and speech behavior: The case of indirect complaints. *Journal of Pragmatics*, 19 (1): 103-125.

[12]Bratman M E. 1999. *Faces of intention: Selected essays on*

intention and agency. Cambridge: Cambridge University Press.

[13]Brown P & Gilman A. 1972. Pronouns of power and solidarity. In P Giglioli (Eds.) Language and social context (pp. 252-282). Harmondsworth: Penguin Books.

[14]Brown P & S C Levinson. 1987. *Politeness: Some universals in language usage*. Cambridge: Cambridge University Press.

[15]Bucholtz M & Hall K. 2005. Identity and interaction: A sociocultural linguistic approach. Discourse Studies, 7 (4-5): 585-614.

[16]Bybee J L & Fleischman S. 1995. *Modality in grammar and discourse.* Amsterdam/ Philadelphia: John Benjamins Publishing Company.

[17]Burke K. 1969. *A grammar of motives*. Berkeley: University of California Press.

[18]Cansler D C & Stiles W B. 1981. Relative status and interpersonal presumptuousness. *Journal of Experimental Social Psychology*, 17: 459-471.

[19]Carter R & Simpson P. 1982. The sociolinguistic analysis of narrative. *Belfast Working Paper in Linguistics*, 6: 123-152.

[20]Chen X R. 1999. *The pragmatics of interactional overinformativeness*. Unpublished PhD. Dissertation. Guangzhou: Gongdong University of Foreign Studies.

[21]Clayman S & Heritage J. 2002. *The news interview: journalists and public figures on the air*. Cambridge: Cambridge University Press.

[22]Conrad S & Biber D. 2000. Adverbial marking of stance in speech and writing. In S Hunston & G Thompson (Eds.), *Evaluation in text: Authorial stance and the construction of discourse* (pp. 56-73). Oxford: Oxford University Press.

[23]Dascal M. 2003. *Interpretation and understanding.* Amsterdam: John Benjamins Publishing Company.

[24]De Fina A. 2006. Group identity, narrative and self-presentation. In De Fina A, Shiffrin D & Bamberg M. (Eds.), *Discourse and identity.* Cambridge: Cambridge Press.

[25]Dippold D. 2009. Face and self-presentation in spoken L2 discourse: renewing the research agenda in interlanguage pragmatics. *Intercultural Pragmatics*, 6 (1): 1-28.

[26]Draw P & Heritage J. 1992. *Talk at work: Interaction in institutional settings*. Cambridge: Cambridge University Press.

[27]Du Bois J W, Schuetze-Coburn S Cummings S & Paolino D. (1993). Outline of discourse transcription. In J A Edwards & M A Lampert (Eds.), *Talking data: Transcription and coding in discourse research* (pp. 45-89). Hillsdale, NJ: Lawrence Erlbaum Associates.

[28]Du Bois J W. 2002. *Stance and consequence*. Paper presented at the Annual meetings of the American anthropological association.

[29]Du Bois J W. 2004. *Searching for intersubjectivity: 'too' and 'either' in stance alignment.* Paper presented at the 25th conference of the international computer archive of modern and medieval English.

[30]Du Bois J W. 2007. The stance triangle. In R. Englebretson (Eds.), *Stancetaking in discourse: Subjectivity, evaluation, interaction* (pp. 139-182). Amsterdam/ Philadelphia: John Benjamins Publishing Company.

[31]Edwards D. 2006. Discourse, cognition and social practices: the rich surface of language and social interaction. Discourse Analysis, 8(1): 31-40.

[32]Eggins S & Slade D. 1997. *Analysing casual conversation.*

London / New York: Cassell.

[33]Ehlich K. 1993. HIAT: A transcription system for discourse data. In J A Edwards & M A Lampert (Eds.), *Talking data: Transcription and coding in discourse research* (pp.123-148). Hillsdale, NJ: Lawrence Erlbaum Associates.

[34]Englebretson R. 2007. *Stancetaking in discourse: Subjectivity, evaluation, interaction.* Amsterdam/ Philadelphia: John Benjamins Publishing Company.

[35]Fairclough N. 1989. *Language and power.* London: Longman.

[36]Fairclough N. 2003. *Analysing discourse: Textual analysis for social research.* London: Routledge.

[37]Finegan E. 1995. Subjectivity and subjectivisation: an introduction. In D Stein & S Wright (Eds.), *Subjectivity and subjectivisation* (pp. 1-15). Cambridge: Cambridge University Press.

[38]Firth J R. 1930. *Speech*. London: Benn's Sixpenny Library.

[39]Fisher B A & Adams K L. 1994. *Interpersonal communication: Pragmatics of human relationships*(2nd ed.). New York: McGraw-Hill.

[40]Francis G. 1986. *Anaphoric nouns*. Discourse Analysis Monographs No. 11. University of Birmingham: English Language Research.

[41]Francis G. 1994. 'Labelling discourse: An aspect of nominal-group lexical cohesion', in Coulthard (Eds.), *Advance in written discourse analysis* (pp. 83-101). London: Routledge.

[42]Francis G. 1998. *Collins cobuild grammar patterns 2: Nouns and adjectives*. London: HarperCollins.

[43]Fraser B. 2009. Topic orientation markers. *Journal of*

Pragmatics, 41: 892-898.

[44]Geer B D. 2004. 'Don't say it's disgusting!' Comments on socio-moral behavior in Swedish families. *Journal of Pragmatics*, 36(11): 1705-1725.

[45]Geer B D Yulviste T, Mizera L & Tryggvason M T. (2002). Socialization in communication: Pragmatic socialization during dinnertime in Estonian, Finnish and Swedish families. *Journal of Pragmatics*, 34(12): 1757-1786.

[46]Gile H & Powesland P F. 1975. *Speech style and social evaluation.* New York: Academic Press.

[47]Goffman E. 1959. *The presentation of self in everyday life*. Edinburgh: University of Edinburgh.

[48]Goffman E. 1967. *Interaction ritual: Essays on face-to-face Behavior*. New York: Pantheon Books.

[49]Goffman E. 1981. *Forms of talk*. Philadelphia: University of Pennsylvania Press.

[50]Goodwin C & Goodwin M H. 1987. *Concurrent operations on talk: Notes on the interactive organization of assessments.* Paper presented at the IPRA papers in pragmatics.

[51]Goodwin C & Goodwin M H. 1992. Assessments and the construction of context. In A D A C Goodwin (Ed.), *Rethinking context: Language as an interactive phenomenon* (pp. 147-189). Cambridge: Cambridge university press.

[52]Grice H P. 1975. Logic and conversation. In H P Grice (Eds.), *Studies in the way of words.* Cambridge, MA: Harvard University Press.

[53]Gruber H. 2001 Question and strategic orientation in verbal conflict sequences. *Journal of Pragmatics*, 33: 1815-1857.

[54]Gu Y G. 1990. Politeness phenomenon in modern Chinese. *Journal of Pragmatics*, 14: 237-257.

[55]Haddington P. 2004. Stancetaking in news interviews. *SKY Journal of Linguistics*, 17:101-142.

[56]Haddington P. 2006. The organization of gaze and assessments as resources for stance taking. *Text & Talk*, 26(3): 281-328.

[57]Haddington P. 2007. Positioning and alignment as activities of stancetaking in news interviews. (pp. 283-317). In Englebretson (Ed.) *Stancetaking in discourse*. Amsterdam/ Philadelphia: John Benjamins Publishing Company.

[58]Halliday M A K. 1994. *An introduction to functional grammar*, 2nd edn. London: Edward Arnold.

[59]Halliday M A K & Matthiessen C M I M. (2004). *An introduction to functional grammar,* 3rd edn. London: Edward Arnold.

[60]Haugh M. 2008. Intention in pragmatics. *Intercultural Pragmatics*, 5(2): 99-110.

[61]Haverkate H. 1983. Strategies in linguistic action. *Journal of Pragmatics,* 8(7): 637-656.

[62]Hayakawa S I. 1972. *Language in thought and action* (3rd edn). New York: Harcourt Brace Jovanovich.

[63]Heisler T Vincent D & Bergeron A. 2003. Evaluative metadiscursive comments and face-work in conversational discourse. *Journal of Pragmatics*, 35(10-11): 1613-1631.

[64]Heritage J & Greatbatch D. 1991. On the institutional character of institutional talk: The case of news interviews. In D Boden & D Zimmerman (Eds.), *Talk and social structure: Studies in ethnomethodology and conversation analysis* (pp. 93-137). Oxford: Polity press.

[65]Heritage J. 2005. Conversation analysis and institutional talk. In K. F. Fitch and R. E. Sanders (Eds.), *Handbook of language*

and social interaction (pp. 103-148). Mahwah, NJ: Lawrence Ehlbaum.

[66]Hicks D. 1990. Narrative skills and genre knowledge: Ways of telling in the primary school grades. *Applied Psycholinguistics,* 11 (1): 83-104.

[67]Ho V. 2010. Constructing identities through request e-mail discourse. *Journal of Pragmatics*, 42: 2253-2261.

[68]Hoey M. 1983. *On the surface of discourse*. London / Boston: Allen & Unwin.

[69]Hoey M. 2001. *Textual interaction : An introduction to written discourse analysis.* London/ New York: Routledge.

[70]Holmes J. 1984. Modifying illocutionary force. *Journal of Pragmatics*, 8:345-365.

[71]Holmes J. 1986. Compliments and compliment responses in New Zealand English. *Anthropological Linguistics*, 28 (4): 485-508.

[72]Holmes J. 2007. Story-telling at work: A complex discursive resource for integrating personal, professional and social identities. *Discourse Studies*, 7(6): 671-700.

[73]Hunston S & Thompson G. 2000. *Evaluation in text: Authorial stance and the construction of discourse*. Oxford: Oxford University Press.

[74]Hunston S. 2007. Using a corpus to investigate stance quantitatively and qualitatively. In R. Englebretson (Eds.), *Stanctaking in discourse.* Amsterdam/ Philadelphia: John Benjamins Publishing Company.

[75]Hurvitz S & Schlesinger I M. 2009. Studying implicit messages: A different approach. *Journal of Pragmatics, 41*(4): 738-752.

[76]Hyland K. 1998. *Hedging in scientific research articles.*

Amsterdam / Philadelphia: John Benjamins Publishing Company.

[77]Hyland K. 2000. *Disciplinary discourses: Social interactions in academic writing*. Harlow/ New York: Longman.

[78]Hyland K. 2004. *Disciplinary discourses: Social interactions in academic writing*. Ann Arbor: University of Michigan Press.

[79]Hyland K. 2005. Stance and engagement. *Discourse Analysis,* 7(2): 173-192.

[80]Hymes D. 1972. Models of interaction of language and social life. In J J Gumperz and D Hymes (Eds.), *Direction in sociolinguistics: The ethno-graphy of communication* (pp. 35-71). New York: Holt, Rinehart and Winston.

[81]Ide S. 1989. Formal forms and discernment: Two neglected aspects of universals of linguistic politeness. *Multilingua*, 8 (2/3): 223-248.

[82]Keenan E O & Schifflein B B. 1976. Topic as a discourse notion: a study of topic in the conversation of children and adults. In Charles N L. (Eds.). *Subject and topic.* (pp. 335-384). New York: Academic Press.

[83]Keisanen T. 2007. Stancetaking as an interactional activity: challenging the prior speaker. In R. Englebretson (Eds.), Stancetaking in discourse. Amsterdam/ Philadelphia: John Benjamins Publishing Company.

[84]Kernan K T. 1977. Semantic and expressive elaboration in Children's narratives, In S Ervin-Tripp (Eds.), *Child discourse.* (pp. 19-102). New York: Academic Press.

[85]Labov W. 1972. *Language in the inner city: Studies in the black English vernacular.* Philadelphia: University of Pennsylvania Press.

[86]Labov W & Fanshel D. (1977). *Therapeutic discourse :*

Psychotherapy as conversation. New York: Academic Press.

[87]Labov W & Waletzky J. 1967. Narrative analysis. In J. Helm (Eds.), *Essays on the verbal and visual arts* (pp. 12-44). Seattle: University of Washington Press.

[88]Lakoff R. 1975. *Language and woman's place*. New York: Harper.

[89]Lemke J L. 1998. Multiplying meaning: Visual and verbal semiotics. In J R Martin & R Veel (Eds.), *Reading science: Critical and functional perspectives of discourse of science* (pp. 87-111). New York: Routledge.

[90]Levinson S. 2006a. Cognition at the heart of human interaction. Discourse Analysis, 8(1): 85-93.

[91]Levisnon S. 2006b. On the human 'interaction engine'. In N. Enfield & S. Levinson (Eds.), *Roots of human sociality: Culture, cognition and interaction* (pp. 39-69). Oxford: Berg.

[92]Li H H. (2008). *A pragmatic study of mitigation in television interview talks.* Unpublished Ph. D. dissertation. Guangzhou: Guangdong University of Foreign Studies.

[93]Linde C. 1993. *Life stories: The creation of coherence.* New York: Oxford University Press.

[94]Linde C. 1997. Evaluation as linguistic structure and social practice. In B L Gunnarsson, P Linell & B Nordberg (Eds). *The construction of professional discourse* (pp. 151-172). Harlow: Longman.

[95]Locher M A. 2004. *Power and politeness in action: Disagreement in oral communication*. Berlin/New York: Mouton de Gruyter.

[96]Locher M A. 2008. Relational work, politeness, and identity construction. In Antos & Ventola (Eds.), *Handbook of interpersonal communication.* Berlin/New York: Mouton de

Gruyter.

[97]Lombardo L. 2004. That–clause and reporting verbs as evaluation in TV news. In L Haarman, J Morley & A Partington (Eds.). *Corpus and discourse* (pp. 221-238). Bern: Peter Lang.

[98]Lyons J. 1977. *Semantics* (Vol. 2). Cambridge: Cambridge University Press.

[99]Lyons J. 1994. Subjecthood and subjectivity. In M. Yaguello (Ed.), *Subjecthood and subjectivity: Proceedings of the colloquium 'the status of the subject in linguistic theory'* (pp. 9-17). Paris: Ophrys.

[100]Lyons J. 1995. *Linguistic semantics: An introduction.* Cambridge: Cambridge University Press.

[101]Macken-Horarik M & Martin J R. (Eds.). (2003). *Negotiating heteroglossia: Social perspectives on evaluation.* Special issue, Text, 23.

[102]Maclean M. 1988. *Narrative as performance: A Baudelarian experiment.* London: Routledge.

[103]MacWhinney B. 1991. *The CHILDES project.* Hillsdale, NJ: Lawrence Erlbaum Associates.

[104]Magalhães I. 2009. Institutional talk. In Mey J. (Eds.). *Concise Encyclopedia of pragmatics.* (pp. 385-386). Oxford: Elsevier Ltd.

[105]Malinowski B. 1923. The problem of meaning in primitive languages. In C K Ogden & I A Rechards. (Eds.) *The meaning of meaning: A study of the influence of language upon thought and of the science of symbolism* (pp. 296-336). New York: Harcourt, Brace & Company.

[106]Malle B F. 2001. Folk explanations of intentional action. In B F Malle, L J Moses & D A Baldwin (Eds.), *Intentions and intentionality: Foundations of social cognition* (pp. 265-286).

Cambridge, MA: MIT Press.

[107]Mao L R. 1994. Beyond politeness theory: 'Face' revisited and renewed. *Journal of Pragmatics*, 21: 451-486.

[108]Martin J R. 2003. Introduction. *Text*, 23(2): 171-181.

[109]Martin J R & Rose D. 2003. *Working with discourse: Meaning beyond the clause*. London / New York: Continuum.

[110]Martin J R & Rose D. 2007. *Working with discourse: Meaning beyond the clause* (2nd ed.). London/ New York: Continuum.

[111]Martin J R & White P R R. 2005. *The language of evaluation: Appraisal in English*. New York: Palgrave Macmillan.

[112]Matsumoto D. 1988. Re-examination of the universality of face: Politeness phenomenon in Japanese. *Journal of Pragmatics*, 12: 403-426.

[113]Myers-Scotton C & Ury W. 1977. Bilingual strategies: the social function of code-switching. *International Journal of the Sociology of Language*, 13: 5-13.

[114]Nuyts J. 2000. *Epistemic modality, language, and conceptualization.* Amsterdam/ Philadelphia: John Benjamins Publishing Company.

[115]Nwoye O G. 1992. Linguistic politeness and sociocultural variation of the notion of face. *Journal of Pragmatics*, 18: 309-328.

[116]O'Connell D C & Kowal S. 2009. Transcription systems for spoken discourse. In D'hondt, S., östaman, J. & Verschueren (Eds.). *The pragmatics of interaction*. (pp.240-254). Amsterdam/ Philadelphia: John Benjamins Publishing Company.

[117]Peterson C & McCabe A. 1983. *Developmental psycholinguistics : Three ways of looking at a child's narrative.* New York: Plenum Press.

[118]Pomerantz A. 1984. Agreeing and disagreeing with

assessments: some features of preferred/dispreferred turn shapes. In J. Heritage (Eds.), *Structures of social action: Studies in conversation analysis* (pp. 57-101). Cambridge: Cambridge University Press.

[119]Pratt M L. 1977. *Towards a speech act theory of literacy discourse.* Bloomington: Indiana University Press.

[120]Rauniomaa M. 2007. Stance markers in spoken Finnish: *Minun mielesta* and *minusta* in assessments. In R Englebretson (Eds.), *Stancetaking in discourse* (pp. 221-252). Amsterdam/ Philadelphia: John Benjamins Publishing Company.

[121]Richards I A. 1964. The four kinds of meaning. In I. A. Rechards (Eds.) *Practical criticism: A study of literary judgment.* (pp. 179-188). London: Routledge & Kegan Paul.

[122]Richards K. 2006. *Language and professional identity.* New York: Palagrave Macmillan.

[123]Rees-Miller J. 2000. Power, severity and context in disagreement. *Journal of Pragmatics,* 32: 1087-1111.

[124]Ruusuvuor J & Lindfors P. 2009. Complaining about previous treatment in health care settings. *Journal of Pragmatics,* 41: 2415-2434.

[125]Sack H Schegloff E & Jefferson G. 1974. A simple systematics for the organization of turn-taking for conversation. *Language,* 50: 697-735.

[126]Scheibman J. 2007. Subjectivity and intersubjectivity uses of generalizations in English conversation. In R. Englebretson (Eds.), Stancetaking in discourse (pp. 111-138). Amsterdam/ Philadelphia: John Benjamins Publishing Company.

[127]Schiffrin D. 1994. *Approaches to discourse.* Oxford: Blackwell Publishing.

[128]Schwartz S. 2001. Value hierarchies across cultures.

Journal of Cross-cultural Psychology, 32 (3): 268-290.

[129]Searle J R. 1969. *Speech acts: An essay in the philosophy of language.* Cambridge: Cambridge University Press.

[130]Searle J R. 1983. *Intentionality: an essay in the philosophy of the mind.* Cambridge: Cambridge University Press.

[131]Shoaps R. 2007. 'Moral irony': Modal particles, moral persons and indirect stance-taking in Sakapultek discourse. *Pragmatics,* 17(2): 297-335.

[132]Sinclair J M. 1988. Mirror for a text. *Journal of English and Foreign Language*, 1: 15-44.

[133]Specer-Oatey H. 1996 Reconsidering power and distance. *Journal of Pragmatics,* 26: 1-24

[134]Specer-Oatey H. 2000. *Culturally speaking: Managing rapport through talk across cultures.* London: Wellington House.

[135]Specer-Oatey H. 2007. *Theories of identity and the analysis of face. Journal of Pragmatics*, 39: 639- 656.

[136]Spencer-Oatey H. 2008. *Culturally speaking: culture, communication and politeness theory.* Cornwall: MPG Books Ltd.

[137]Sperber D & Wilson D. 1986. *Relevance: Communication and cognition* (1st ed.). Oxford: Blackwell Publishing.

[138]Sperber D & Wilson D. 1995. *Relevance: Communication and cognition* (2nd ed.). Oxford: Blackwell Publishing.

[139]Taylor G. 1986. The development of style in children's fictional narrative, in A. Wilkinson (Eds.). *The writing of writing* (pp. 215-233). Milton Keyness: Open University Press.

[140]Thompson G & Hunston S. 2000. Evaluation: An introduction. In S Hunston & G Thompson (Eds.). *Evaluation in text: Authorial stance and the construction of discourse.* Oxford: Oxford University Press.

[141]Thornborrow J. 2002. *Power talk: Language and*

interaction in institutional discourse. London: Pearson Education.

[142]Tirkkonen-Condit S. 1989. Professional vs. non-professional translation: A think-aloud protocol study. In T C Seguinot (Eds.) *The transition process school of translation* (73-85). York University: H. G. Publications.

[143]Tomasello M. 1999. *The cultural origins of human cognition.* Mass: Harvard University Press.

[144]van Dijk T A. 1988. *News analysis: Case studies of international and national news in the press.* Hillsdale, N J Lawrence Erlbaum Associates .

[145]van Dijk T A. 2008. *Discourse and context: A sociocognitive approach.* Cambridge: Cambridge University Press.

[146]Verschueren J. 1987. *Pragmatics as a theory of adaptation.* Paper presented at the IPrA working document 1, Antwerp.

[147]Verschueren J. 1995a. The pragmatic perspective. In Verschueren J & J O Östman (Eds.), *Handbook of pragmatics.* Amsterdam/Philadelphia: John Benjamins Publishing Company.

[148]Verschueren J. 1995b. The pragmatic return to meaning: notes on the dynamics of communication, degrees of salience, and communicative transparency. *Journal of Linguistic Anthropology,* 5: 127-156.

[149]Verschueren J. 1998. A pragmatic model for the dynamics of communication. In Kasher, A. (Eds.), *Pragmatics: Critical concepts.* Vol. 5. London: Routledge.

[150]Verschueren J. 1999. *Understanding pragmatics.* London: Edward Arnold.

[151]Vološhinov V N. 1973. *Marxism and the philosophy of language*. Cambridge, MA: Harvard University Press.

[152]Walkinshaw I. 2009. *Learning politeness*. Bern: Peter

Lanf AG, International Academic Publishers.

[153]Webber P. 2004. Negation in linguistic papers. In G. Camiciotti & G. Bonelli (Eds.), Academic discourse: New insights into evaluation (pp. 181-202). Berlin: Peter Lang.

[154]Wennerstrom D A. 2001. Intonation and evaluation in oral narratives. Journal of Pragmatics, 33(8): 1183-1206.

[155]White P R R. 1998. Telling media tales: The news story as rhetoric. PhD. Thesis. Sydney: University of Sydney.

[156]Wilkinson J. 1986. Describing children's writing: Text evaluation and teaching strategies. In J Harris & J Wilkson (Eds.), Reading children's writing: A linguistic view (11-31). London: Allen & Unwin.

[157]Wu R J. 2004. Stance in talk: A conversation analysis of mandarin final particles. Amsterdam: John Benjamins Publishing Company.

[158]Yang J. 2006. Evasion: The interviewee's pragmatic strategy in Chinese ecnomic news interview. Unpublished Ph. D. dissertation, Guangzhou: Guangdong University of Foreign Studies.

[159] 冯平（1995）， 评价论。北京：东方出版社。

[160] 胡昌明 (2009), 设立国防部发言人制度是国家和军队形象建设的需要。http://military.people.com.cn/GB/1076/115150/8707046.html

[161] 胡壮麟 (2009), 语篇的评价研究。 外语教学 , 30 (1): 1 – 6。

[162] 李战子 (2004), 评价理论在话语分析中的应用和问题。外语研究 (5): 1 – 6。

[163] 刘戈 (1998), 评价与描述：从语词看评价。 外语研究 (2): 38 – 42。

[164] 刘戈 (1999), 评价行为的语用观。中国俄语教学 (3): 26 – 29。

[165] 刘戈 (2000), 评价行为的话语分析。外语研究 (1): 22 – 24。

[166] 刘世铸、韩金龙 (2004), 新闻话语中的评价系统。 外语电化教学 (3): 17 – 21。

[167] 冉永平 (2007), 指示语选择的语用视点: 语用移情与语用离情。外语教学与研究(5): 331–337。

[168] 冉永平 (2010), 冲突性话语的语用学研究概述。外语教学(1): 1 – 5。

[169] 王振华 (2004), 评价系统及其运作。外国语 (6): 13–20。

[170] 王振华 (2004), "硬新闻"的态度研究。外语教学 (5): 31 – 36。

[171] 王振华、马玉蕾 (2007), 评价理论: 魅力与困惑。 外语教学 (6): 19 – 23。

[172] 文琦、磨玉峰 (2007), 军队形象塑造研究。教育与人 (2): 81–83。

[173] 吴亚欣 (2004), 语用含糊——汉语言交际的策略。太原: 山西人民出版社。

[174] 杨洁篪 (2005), 就美国国防部发表所谓中国军力报告向美方提出严正交涉。http://www.mfa.gov.cn/chn/gxh/tyb/wjbxw/t204294.htm

[175] 张德禄、刘世铸 (2006), 形式与意义的范畴化。 外语教学与研究 (6): 3 – 7。

[176] 周文 (2007), 新军事变革背景下中国军事新闻传播研究。四川大学博士学位论文。四川: 成都。

Acknowledgements

I am indebted to a number of people, whose help has made this dissertation possible.

First and foremost, I owe a deep and special debt of gratitude to my supervisor Prof. Ran Yongping, who has guided me patiently with his erudition and multi-faceted approach to pragmatics all the way through these years. I profit a lot from his professional instructions which show me the way to think, to write, and to do research. His academic spirit, conscientiousness, and generosity have greatly influenced me, and will accompany me through my academic life. Without his valuable guidance, critical comments and enlightening suggestions, this dissertation would not have materialized.

I am very grateful to all the other professors working at the CLAL of Guangdong University of Foreign Studies, whose course I attended and benefited a lot from in the direction of achieving an integrative perspective on the study of language.

Enormous gratitude goes to Dr. Li Haihui at Jinan University, for his invaluable ideas in personal discussion, constant concern, and unfailing support during the writing of this dissertation, as well as his careful proofreading of the draft.

I am also indebted to Geoffrey Raymond from University of California, for sharing with me his view on such issues as evaluation and identity through e-mail.

I would also like to thank my friends in the Ph. D. program of Guangdong University of Foreign Studies. Special thanks go to Cheng Jie, Liu Ping, Lai Xiaoyu and Li Chengtuan, for their comments and supports. Additional thanks are due to Chen Jinshi and Li Liang, for offering me unselfish help when I encountered computer problems.

On a personal level, the writing of this dissertation would not have been possible without the understandings of those closest to me, who have provided endless love and steadfast support. Therefore, I would like to extend my deep gratitude to my parents, my parents-in-law, my sisters, my dear husband and my lovely son, for everything that words cannot tell.

Appendix Transcription Conventions

(Based on Du Bois et al. 1993)

Speech	
Transitional continuity	
Final	◦
Continuing	,
Appeal (seeking a validating response from the listener	?
Speakers	
Speech overlap	[ ]
(numbers inside brackets index overlaps)	[2 two words 2]
Accent and lengthening	
Primary accent	^
(prominent pitch movement carrying intonation meaning)	
Second accent	'
Unaccented	
Lengthening	=
Pause	
Long pause (0.7 seconds or longer)	...(N)
Medium pause (0.3 – 0.6 s)	...
Short pause(brief break in speech rhythm) (0.2 or less)	

..

Latching (0)

Vocal noises

Alveolar click (TSK)

Glottal stop LOTTAL

Inhalation (H)

Laughter (one pulse) @

Laughter during speech (1-5 words) @
(e.g. @two @words)

Quality

Tempo and rhythm

Allegro: rapid speech <A> </A>

Lento: slow speech <L> </L>

Marcato: each word distinct and emphasized
<MRC> </MRC>

Rhythmic: stresses in a beatable rhythm <RH> </RH>

Transcriber's perspective

Researcher's comment (( ))

后　记

2010 年 12 月 10 日，是我博士论文答辩的日子。我八十多岁的父亲和七十多岁的母亲，以及我的两位姐姐都来到了答辩现场，被答辩的教授幽默地称为“强大的亲友团”。顺利答辩后，我的母亲赋诗道：“字字珠玑灯下舞，辩答讲述畅如流。寒窗念载功夫在，今日喜看立俊畴。”看着父母脸上洋溢的笑容和喜悦，我觉得这几年的努力和付出是值得的。

2007 年 9 月，我来到广州白云山下的广东外语外贸大学攻读博士学位。这所大学位于白云山脚下，校内到处是亚热带高大茂盛的树木，一年四季都有鲜花开放，从白云山上淌淌流下的清澈的云溪从校园穿过，真是“白云山青，碧溪水蓝”，自有一派南国美丽的风景。

这里风景如画，让我更为感叹的是这儿质朴的学风。每天清晨，云溪旁便有学生在高声朗诵；傍晚时分，在教学楼、图书馆，学生们已开始了夜晚的学习。我所就读的外国语言学及应用语言学研究中心是国家级的人文社科重点研究基地，拥有二十多名专职研究员。这些学者们潜心钻研、淡泊名利，每人都在自己的领域有所建树。有一次和同学晚上近十二点出来学校散步，看到中心许多办公室还灯火通明，后来才知道许多学者在办公室经常工作至深夜，这大概是这些学者们每年都能取得累累硕果的原因吧。

读博期间，我有幸师从冉永平教授。冉老师睿智而严格，治学严谨，但为人谦和。在他身上我学到的不仅是如何做学问，还有如何做人。犹记第一次老师的讲话，他说农民生产粮食，而学者生产的是知识，在平时要有“问题意识和创新意识”，做学问要“多读、多思、多写、多问”，要“心眼活、功夫死、我为主”，要大方地和他人进行学术交流，集思广益，看准就要坚持，学术研究的最高境界便是“共同快乐”。这些教诲将陪伴我今后的学术生涯，成为一笔宝贵的财富。

博士论文的选题和写作过程是艰辛的。每日于资料室、图书馆埋头苦读，在浩瀚的资料中寻求那个将和我相伴多年的选题。从选题之初的迷茫与彷徨，到逐渐明朗，从第一个问题的提出，到论文框架的形成，从第一个词的落笔到论文的整体完成，经历了日日夜夜的思考和研读，有时半夜披衣而起，只为那脑海中一闪而过的灵感。这样压力巨大的日子，如若孤单离群是绝然无法度过的。幸而广外的博士生们有着自己独特的减压方式——运动。学习一天后，每天下午五点钟左右，朋友们相约或爬山、或打球、或游泳。运动后便是聚餐和讨论。我们珍惜这难得的单纯的读书的日子，并相信不同方向的同学们的讨论会给我们带来思想的火花。一起读博的同学就是这样一路扶持和鼓励，从而培养了深厚的感情。三年多的读博生活，我们同时收获了知识和友谊。

毕业后我回到国防科技大学外语系工作，发现离开三年，系里的变化也是巨大的。每周组织教学科研交流会，频繁邀请国内外知名学者前来讲学，鼓励教员参加国内外各种学术会议。学科建设也在如火如荼地进行，现有硕士点的建设、新的硕士点的申请、博士点也在筹备之中。这一切都给教员们提供了良好的发展机会和宽松的科研环境，也为本书的出版提供了一个契机。

这本书得以顺利完成和出版得到了许多人的帮助，在此我对以下单位和个人表示衷心的感谢。

首先，我要感谢广东外语外贸大学外国语言学及应用语言学研究中心的老师们。他们的精彩授课开拓了我的学术视野，他们的高尚严谨的治学态度为我树立了学习的典范。在预答辩结束后，霍永寿教授连中餐也顾不上吃，耐心回答了我所有的问题，并为论文的修改提供了宝贵的意见。恩师冉永平教授自我入校便对我进行了悉心的指导，在语用学这片学术天地中耐心地领我前行，在教我做学问的同时也教我如何做人。论文的选题、构思、写作和修改过程中，老师都付出了不少心血。此书即将出版时请求老师作序，他欣然同意，字里行间处处流露出对我的殷殷期望，令我感动自心底油然而生。记得以前教师节拜访老师献上薄礼时他总是婉拒，并说：“你们给我的最好的礼物就是你们的学术成就。”因此，对老师的感激除却这声“谢谢”，更重要的是今后为实现学术梦想的不懈努力，以不负他的期望。

其次，我要衷心感谢国防科技大学人文与社科学院的院领导和外语系领导。感谢他们的关心与支持，为我提供了整整三年专心攻读博士学位的时间，在我回到工作岗位后对我的教研工作提供了良好的条件，此书的出版也得到了系里学科建设经费的资助。

感谢暨南大学我的师兄李海辉博士，在我论文写作的过程中给予了我无私的帮助。很多问题就是在美丽的暨南大学校园内，一边喝着红酒，一边和师兄的讨论中得以解决的。

同时，感谢加利福尼亚大学的 Geoffrey Raymond 博士在邮件中详细解答我关于会话中的身份构建方面的问题。

我要深深地感谢我的家人。在我的读博期间，我的公公婆婆和我的丈夫在长沙悉心照顾着我年幼的儿子，让我没有了后顾之忧，得以全心全意攻读博士学位。前往广东外语外贸大学读博时，我的儿子还不到五岁。每次道别他都眼泪汪汪，但嘴里却说：“妈妈，我会好好表现不让你分心的。你认真写论文，早点回来！”正是这稚嫩的话语使我即便是在遇到困难的时候也不会轻言放弃，而是去尽快寻求解决的答案，以期能早日学成归来陪伴他，见证他每一刻的成长时分。在广州，我的父母和两位姐姐则无微不至地关心着我，周末回姐姐家等着我的必是一桌好菜，生活中缺什么立马就会送来学校，到后来因为论文写作没有时间回去，他们便在周末驾车来学校看望。从入校，到预答辩、答辩、毕业典礼，每次他们都不曾缺席，这个“强大的亲友团”陪着我走过我的博士生涯，充满着巨大压力的博士论文写作过程因为有他们的关心和陪伴而不再那么辛苦。感谢上天赐予了我这样一个充满爱的温馨家庭！

在这个初夏的夜晚，和风从窗外轻轻拂过，我的儿子在他的房间甜蜜地酣睡，我的年迈的父母在讨论着如何上网聊天这一新的交流方式，我的丈夫在我的身边看着我结束这一篇后记。这一刻，我心宁静；这一刻，别无所求。

龚双萍

2012 年 5 月 12 日于长沙